Militant Democracy and Its Critics

Militant Democracy and Its Critics

Populism, Parties, Extremism

Edited by
ANTHOULA MALKOPOULOU AND
ALEXANDER S. KIRSHNER

EDINBURGH
University Press

Edinburgh University Press is one of the leading university presses in the UK. We publish academic books and journals in our selected subject areas across the humanities and social sciences, combining cutting-edge scholarship with high editorial and production values to produce academic works of lasting importance. For more information visit our website: edinburghuniversitypress.com

First published in hardback by Edinburgh University Press 2019

Edinburgh University Press Ltd
The Tun – Holyrood Road, 12(2f) Jackson's Entry, Edinburgh EH8 8PJ

Typeset in 10/13 Giovanni by
IDSUK (DataConnection) Ltd

A CIP record for this book is available from the British Library

ISBN 978 1 4744 4560 3 (hardback)
ISBN 978 1 4744 4561 0 (paperback)
ISBN 978 1 4744 4562 7 (webready PDF)
ISBN 978 1 4744 4563 4 (epub)

CONTENTS

LIST OF CONTRIBUTORS

Giovanni Capoccia, University of Oxford, UK

Alexander S. Kirshner, Duke University, USA

Anthoula Malkopoulou, Uppsala University, Sweden

Jan-Werner Müller, Princeton University, USA

Ludvig Norman, Stockholm University, Sweden

Bastiaan Rijpkema, Leiden University, Netherlands

Cristóbal Rovira Kaltwasser, Diego Portales University, Chile

Stefan Rummens, KU Leuven, Belgium

András Sajó, Central European University, Hungary

Peter Stone, Trinity College Dublin, Ireland

Svetlana Tyulkina, University of New South Wales Sydney, Australia

Tore Vincents Olsen, University of Aarhus, Denmark

ACKNOWLEDGEMENTS

We should like to thank three anonymous reviewers, as well as the editors at Edinburgh University Press, particularly Adela Rauchova, Jenny Daly and David Lonergan. Elliot Mamet provided valuable research assistance in compiling the manuscript.

Chapter 5 was previously published as 'Three models of democratic self-defense: militant democracy and its alternatives', *Political Studies* 66 (2): 442–458. The authors gratefully acknowledge permission by SAGE Publications Ltd to republish the article in the present volume.

Militant Democracy and Its Critics

Anthoula Malkopoulou

How should democracies respond to anti-democratic political parties? Right-wing extremism is resurgent in many countries. Far-right parties have achieved electoral breakthroughs in Sweden and Greece. The state of Hungarian and Polish democracy is at best tenuous. Incumbent parties are typically confounded by undemocratic electoral movements. And official responses to the phenomenon inevitably stir political controversy. Militant democracy refers to the idea that elected governments should erect legal barriers to protect democracy from extremist parties. And it is an idea that has gained increasing attention from political theorists, as well as scholars of law and comparative politics (Capoccia 2013).

The term 'militant democracy' was first defined in 1937 by the constitutional lawyer Karl Loewenstein (1937a). A German émigré in the US, Loewenstein's focus was, naturally, the rise of fascist and Nazi parties in Europe. He defended 'anti-extremist legislation', including the prohibition of anti-democratic parties and party militias, restrictions of basic civil rights such as the freedom of assembly and freedom of speech, and the establishment of a political police (Loewenstein 1937b). Understandably, future Hitlers and Mussolinis were the target of this anti-fascist justification of democracy's defence.

Fast-forward eighty years. The debate has changed since Loewenstein made his contribution, shedding his preoccupation with fascism and communism. Religious fundamentalism looms larger now. And states are grappling with illiberal, authoritarian or populist strategies that do not require leaders to disavow the language and institutions of democracy (Müller 2016a: 262). In the midst of these confrontations, a nuanced legal-theoretical debate has emerged between those who support militant measures (Fox and Nolte 1995; Sajó 2004; Tyulkina 2015a), those who are sceptical (i.e. 'neo-militant' democrats) (Niesen 2002; Issacharoff 2007; Rummens and Abts 2010; Kirshner 2014; Müller 2016a) and outright critics (Minkenberg 2006; Rosenblum 2008; Invernizzi Accetti and Zuckerman 2017; Malkopoulou and Norman 2018).

Considering the rise of illiberal forms of politics in the last few years, it is not surprising that a great number of scholars lend their support to militant measures (Sajó 2004; Capoccia 2005; Thiel 2009a). These views are validated in public practice by increased calls to use legal sanctions, such as the 2017 attempt to ban the National Democratic Party of Germany or the EU's decision to initiate the process for sanctioning the Polish and Hungarian governments in 2017 and 2018 respectively. Yet, among contemporary advocates, many are concerned with militant democracy being itself an arguably illiberal and anti-democratic practice. As a result, they have sought to rehabilitate it by identifying liberal grounds for militant policies; in the process they shy away from the most draconian measures suggested by Loewenstein (Issacharoff 2007; Rummens and Abts 2010; Müller 2012b, 2016a; Kirshner 2014). Neo-militant democrats argue, for example, that decisions to exclude should be guided by strict normative criteria, such as protection of core democratic values (Brettschneider 2007), the right to participate (Kirshner 2014) or the ability to revise past decisions (Rijpkema 2015). Critics of this effort have found much to disagree with. Their objections range from concerns about militant theories' narrowly legalistic and asocial understanding of how to respond to extremism (Mudde 2004b; Malkopoulou and Norman 2018) to doubts about the legitimacy and effectiveness of party bans (Bale 2007; Invernizzi Accetti and Zuckerman 2017). Finally, other scholars have drawn attention to the potentially moderating force of political participation (van Spanje and van der Brug 2007; Rosenblum 2008).

Driven by political developments, the debate about militant democracy is likely to increase in intensity. This compilation, including contributions by leading figures in the field, expands and enriches the research agenda on how democracies ought to combat extremism. It focuses on normative questions, but also features an interdisciplinary range of contributions from political scientists, legal scholars and philosophers. In addition to capturing the current state of play in the field, the chapters of this volume outline new ideas on militant democracy.

A great deal of research on militant democracy is focused on the practice of party bans, so much so that the two are often used as synonymous. Yet, party prohibitions are a fraction of what militant democracy can contain. In the first chapter of this volume Jan-Werner Müller draws attention to a much less known aspect of militant democracy: restrictions on individual rights. This is not an abstract problem. Article 18 of Germany's Basic Law – the most paradigmatic militant constitution – allows the forfeiture of individual rights if these are used to fight the liberal democratic order. The European Court for Human Rights has also found individual rights restrictions at times justifiable from a human rights perspective. Moreover, a range of disturbing developments in the last few years, in particular the spread of citizenship deprivation as an acceptable practice to combat terrorism, make the examination of *individual* militant democracy important and timely.

The question posed in the chapter by Müller is whether complete exclusion from the political process – for instance through a lifelong forfeiture of participation rights or through citizenship deprivation as a kind of 'civic death' – can be justified as a militant democratic measure, or whether there is a limit to how much exclusion is legitimate for broad militant democratic reasons. The author argues that militant democracy should remain restricted to a repertoire of measures aimed at weakening (or outright prohibiting) *organised* anti-democratic activity. Restricting individual rights should be permissible only in exceptional circumstances, against resourceful individuals who are about to subvert democracy, and even then they should be limited in scope and time and adjusted as much as possible to the individual case.

Individuals may be relevant not only as potential targets but also as agents of militant measures. The second half of Müller's chapter deals with *vigilante* militant democracy, that is, a situation where individuals take up the responsibility of defending democracy against anti-democratic actors. Like with individual rights restrictions, such a possibility of legitimate resistance and civil disobedience in order to preserve the free democratic order is foreseen in the German Basic Law. Yet, Müller is very sceptical about the possibility of exercising self-restraint in these cases. Therefore, he argues that acts of civil disobedience might be justified only when individuals believe that the institutions charged with militancy have genuinely failed to comprehend a threat; in addition, they should always be highly constrained and publicly explain under what conditions disobedient civilians would rest their case. At the end, the case for involving individuals as either targets or agents of militant measures is too risky; it complicates further the already difficult task of balancing the urgency to act in defence of democracy with the calm needed to act in a limited and constrained fashion.

Peter Stone shares a similar concern about the role of individuals in the rise of extremism. In Chapter 2 he draws attention particularly to the practice of voting. On one hand, voting is the core mechanism of modern democracy and a key expression of democracy's fundamental norm: equality. It is the equal counting of citizens' votes that distinguishes democratic from non-democratic elections, he argues. On the other hand, voting is one of democracy's weakest points. This is because voters are entitled to make their choices using whatever criteria seem relevant to them. Thereby they risk making bad choices, which for Stone is a failure to fulfil the *public-service purpose of voting*: to properly evaluate candidates and to judge who is the most fit for office, including who can best protect self-government among free and equal citizens.

To use the vote in such a manner, as a responsibility to select officials who will govern according to the demands of democratic equality, is the task entrusted to every individual voter. Conversely, the success of extremist parties is the result of voters making bad choices, choices that contravene the principle of democratic equality. Therefore, Stone argues, voting processes should be regulated in such a way to prevent democratic 'autophagy', a situation where equal voters elect a government opposed to democratic equality.

To defend democracy, voters should be nudged to vote in accordance to the principle of democratic equality. This requires introducing some sort of accountability at the level of the electorate. Stone's main proposal for insulating the vote is to introduce possibilities for increased *deliberation among voters*. Asking citizens to publicly provide reasons for their electoral judgements may produce indirect pressure against reasons and choices that are socially undesirable. One measure in this direction discussed (and rejected) is to 'unveil' the vote, i.e. to make voting choices public; this would address the problem created by the fact that secret voting renders votes invisible and unaccountable for. Other ideas are 'deliberation days', randomly selected mini-publics, or randomly selected voters ('enfranchisement lotteries'). The chapter concludes by highlighting deliberation as a barrier against political extremism, one that protects and advances democratic equality.

Chapter 3 continues the thread of contributions to this volume which are sceptical about party bans. Alexander S. Kirshner praises legislation that restricts the ability of local constituencies to introduce policies on political participation with discriminatory effects on minorities. He brings up the example of the US Voting Rights Act of 1965. It imposed a federal control over state changes in electoral policies preventing a historical tendency to thwart the capacity of African-Americans to vote. This type of militant policy is grounded in the idea that citizens have equal interests in participation. It is a militant policy because it prevents violation of this equality. And it is a 'good' militant policy because it does not violate the participation rights of anti-democrats in the process of defending the participation rights of minorities. It targets anti-democratic *actions*, not anti-democratic *actors*.

Further, Kirshner suggests that political rules are not and should not be neutral with regard to political outcomes. What they should do is secure equal and proportional respect for political actors' equal interests to participation. This means that protecting the right to vote of minorities who are about to be disenfranchised is more important than protecting the right of anti-democrats to disenfranchise them. This example serves to highlight that inaction may carry higher moral costs than militant democratic action. If militant policies violate some democratic principles along the way, this is justified since they promote higher-valued principles, namely the equal interest in participation.

Does a sortition-based system advance this principle? Kirshner answers that it does: it is founded on the equality of individuals' interests. However, he warns that this system too is vulnerable to anti-democratic advances. Those who design and implement sortition mechanisms might design and implement them in an inegalitarian fashion. Therefore, they need to be checked. Because anti-democrats will continue to exist no matter which democratic institutions are in place, we cannot eschew facing the paradox of militant democracy.

The chapters discussed so far – and most research on militant democracy for that matter – consider the use of militant measures in relation to extremist and, in particular, anti-democratic parties. Yet, many are also tempted to extend them to fight off populism, a rather problematic move according to Cristóbal Rovira Kaltwasser. In comparison to extremism, populism is a more ambivalent phenomenon, he argues in Chapter 4. Despite important differences between left and right populists, all of them pose as democrats par excellence. They respect popular sovereignty and have the support of electoral majorities. Yet, their conception of democracy relies on a peculiar understanding, according to which nobody has the right to act against the wishes of 'the people'. In their polarised view of society, the elites are always bad and corrupt, while the people are virtuous and right. Moreover, 'the people' are assumed to have a unified will, a view that rejects diversity, individuality and opinion difference. As a result, populists are at odds with *liberal* democracy, which is defined by pluralism, protection of minorities, constitutionalism and oversight of government by unelected institutions. These theoretical observations are confirmed by numerous empirical examples of how populist governments tend to turn democracies into semi-authoritarian and illiberal regimes. In this light, militant measures against populists seem justified.

Nevertheless, Rovira Kaltwasser disagrees with militant restrictions against populism. True, populists are a danger for 'democratic self-destruction', a situation where democracy provides its internal enemies with the means to destroy it. But militant democracy creates a danger of 'democratic self-injury', i.e. a harm inflicted upon the liberal and democratic nature of a regime in the very effort to defend it. This involves not only curtailing individual rights and freedoms, but also democratic legitimacy itself, especially if popular populist parties that enjoy support by electoral majorities are banned. In addition, implementing militant measures has a boomerang effect: it makes the populist discourse more visible and validates populist claims that the elite is a corrupt enemy of 'the people'. Last, but not least, militant democracy draws its normative legitimacy from the assumption that there is societal agreement on fundamental questions, such as what democracy means, who constitutes the demos and who are democracy's enemies. In other words, it assumes that everyone accepts *liberal* democracy as a regime worth defending. This public consensus, as the emergence of populism shows, does not exist. As a result, Rovira Kaltwasser concludes, we should focus not on banning populist parties but on fostering a populism-averse political culture and other long-term strategies.

Chapter 5, by Anthoula Malkopoulou and Ludvig Norman, offers an elaborate support for long-term strategies of democratic self-defence. The authors propose to expand the debate on how to respond to anti-democratic measures beyond militant democracy, which has too narrow a focus on legal sanctions and other repressive measures. More specifically, they charge the discourse on militant democracy for reproducing 'a largely exclusionary elitist notion of democratic government'. Militant democracy's elitism, they claim, builds on the mistrust of popular self-government, the capacity of people to govern themselves. Although they admit that Loewenstein is the only extrovert advocate of political elitism, the authors find more recent, liberal, accounts of militant democracy also guilty of espousing a preference for unelected institutions over popular judgement and political inclusiveness.

The critique that Malkopoulou and Norman launch against militant democracy – understood as a practice of rights restrictions – is based on the principle of non-domination. Their view coincides, to some extent, with the ideas of Hans Kelsen. Like him, they accept that a majority that excludes a section of the voting population is illegitimate. Excluding anti-democratic parties is, well, undemocratic, like the exclusion of just about any other political actor. Still, the authors disagree with Kelsen's conception of democracy, which is too procedural and formal. It leaves out considerations for social and structural inequalities that disable citizens from exercising their formal rights.

To avoid the pitfalls of both militant and procedural approaches to extremism, Malkopoulou and Norman turn to a less discussed variety of democratic self-defence, which they call 'social democratic'. Drawing on twentieth-century thinkers such as Alf Ross and Hermann Heller, they pitch the idea that 'extremism results from the perceived impossibility of certain groups of the population to channel their socio-economic demands through the political system'. This view justifies a twin focus on *political inclusion* and *social integration* as the best response to extremism. Using non-domination as a guiding principle, the authors develop their social democratic approach to extremism without falling back to substantivist notions of socialist democracy. The key for them is to combine institutions that enable political contestation with policies that address repressed socio-economic demands and inequalities. This strategy against extremism is not only less elitist than militant democracy and less formal than Kelsenean proceduralism, but also less legalistic than the both of them.

By contrast, Chapter 6 offers a defence of militant democracy. In it, Stefan Rummens argues that, in view of the hegemonic nature of tolerance, it is both necessary and legitimate to limit the tolerance that we show towards antagonistic challengers. Unlike ordinary *agonistic* adversaries, who share our commitment to tolerance, *antagonistic* opponents reject and aim to eliminate tolerance. As a result, our political relation with each of these groups is qualitatively different. The struggle with the former is – in Mouffe's terms – a *non-hegemonic* struggle, whereas the struggle with the latter is a *hegemonic* 'all or nothing affair'. In other words, the enemies of democracy pose an existential threat to tolerance, which justifies taking a different and defensive stand against them. To be sure, our aim should not be to eliminate the intolerants, but to curb *the threat* that they pose to the practice of tolerance.

In order to proceed, Rummens argues, one should recognise that the dilemma between a proceduralist and a militant position is a false dilemma. Liberal democracy has both substantive as well as procedural aspects, he says. As a result, we can defend a concentric containment of extremist actors, a 'guideline of decreasing tolerance', meaning that we can give more leeway to extremist actors in the periphery of the political system (the informal public sphere) but should be increasingly intolerant for extremist actors closer to the centre of decision making (parliament/government). The leeway granted to extremists in the periphery of the system is in line with the procedural dimension of democracy; it helps in tracking all the ideas and concerns of the citizenry. At the same time, the intolerance of extremist views that are close to power makes sure that their views are not translated into laws and policies and, thus, do not jeopardise the substantive values of liberal democracy.

Lastly, Rummens takes issue with some of the critiques of militant democracy. The first is that defending democracy involves a moralisation of politics in which the enemies of democracy risk being dehumanised. The second refers to the inevitable arbitrariness in determining who constitutes democracy's enemies. The third and fourth have to do with militant democracy's elitism and neglect of the more structural causes of extremism. Rummens responds to all these accusations by underlining the distinct qualities of the concentric model, which is on the one hand self-limiting and inclusivist and on the other firm in protecting core liberal democratic values.

In Chapter 7, Giovanni Capoccia turns our attention to debates on militant democracy within the field of comparative politics. He notes that, following the seminal work of Karl Loewenstein in the 1930s and 1940s, and a brief period of interest in the 1950s, the theme of militant democracy receded from the comparative politics discipline, and has experienced a revival only in recent years. Surely, comparativists have by no means ignored key issues that are at the core of militant democracy, such as the treatment of extremist dissent, and the repression of the opposition by state actors in democratic regimes. Capoccia argues, however, that these studies have mostly adopted a theoretical perspective that, explicitly or implicitly, considers such phenomena as outside the boundaries of democracy. In so doing, this research has, at times, let a specific normative conception of democracy drive the empirical analysis.

To illustrate these points, the chapter discusses the influential research programme in comparative politics that analyses *political tolerance*. Originating in the US in the 1950s, research on political tolerance moved away from the 'old institutionalist' type of research in political science towards the new paradigm of behaviouralism. Thus, it focused on individual attitudes towards policies that restrict the rights of expression and participation of unpopular groups. Yet, the tolerance literature normatively identified democracy with a model of an unrestricted 'marketplace of ideas'. As a consequence, all policies that restricted ideas and rights were considered anti-democratic, even when targeted at actors who openly advocated anti-democratic views. In addition, militant democracies were lumped together with transitional or illiberal democracies, while anti-democrats were discussed on an equal footing with homosexuals and other such potential targets of intolerance. These conceptual and theoretical codes of tolerance research made it difficult to carve out a conceptual space for militant democracy as '*an independent phenomenon that happens in, and varies across, fully fledged democratic regimes*'. What followed was a lack of attention to the comparative analysis of rights-restricting policies.

The chapter concludes by arguing for the potential utility of various branches of institutionalism in providing a much-needed theoretical framework for the comparative analysis of causes and consequences of militant democracy. Knowledge of a country's legal framework is crucial for determining whether attitudes towards rights restrictions betray support for democratic norms or the opposite. For example, in countries with a militant democratic constitution, citizens' support for rights restrictions may be proof of commitment to democracy rather than the opposite. This goes to show that a comparative body of knowledge on the rights-restricting policies enacted in democracies would improve the interpretation of empirical findings in comparative research on political tolerance. What is needed is an analytical focus of comparative politics research on *institutions* and policies of militant democracy.

Chapter 8 by Tore Vincents Olsen discusses militant democracy in the context of the European Union (EU). This is a very timely contribution in light of the recent EU decisions to act against the governments in Hungary and Poland. The chapter explains why and how the EU should respond to actors that violate EU values in a manner that is consistent with liberal democratic values. EU values *are* liberal democratic values. They include 'respect for human dignity, freedom, democracy, equality, the rule of law and respect for human rights'. They are articulated in the Treaty of the European Union, and they provide a basis for applying a value theory of democracy on the EU. As a result, EU values should guide the design of EU institutions and procedures; more importantly, democratic outcomes can be constrained to conform to these values.

The authors argue that when these values are violated in an EU member state, the citizens of other EU member states are affected. This is because EU citizens are 'tied together in relations of potential domination'. To prevent such domination, they must be assured a status of equal democratic co-rulers on issues of common European concern.

Having established why and how the EU is legitimated to act against anti-democratic governments in member states, the question that remains is through which policies. Olsen and Barsøe are critical of existing sanctions mechanisms on the grounds that they impose a logic of collective responsibility on member states and assume that minorities and other targets of anti-democratic governments are somehow co-responsible for the state of their national democracy. Although democratic minorities have some remedial forward-looking responsibility to mobilise against anti-democratic governments, they do not have equal responsibility with their governments for the democratic backsliding, nor the capacity to reverse it.

Therefore, EU sanctions should not target entire member states but their (anti-democratic) governing parties. For example, EU funds should be withheld from governments and channelled to other political parties. Or, the ejection of member states from the EU Council should be replaced by personal embargos against individual members of the government. In any case, since sanctions should ensue from a violation of the EU's liberal democratic values, these values must be described more systematically in order to prevent an arbitrary application of sanctions.

Another chapter concerned with the practical application of militant democratic measures is Chapter 9. There, Bastiaan Rijpkema asks how to detect groups that constitute a democratic threat – for instance, what concrete measures does a party have to propose to be deemed 'anti-democratic'? And how does one actually recognise an anti-democratic party in time, that is, *before* it is in a position to damage democracy? This chapter proposes a fine-tuned 'detection mechanism' of anti-democratic parties. It presents a set of criteria that aims to evade the pitfalls of a to-mechanic checklist approach, but that, at the same time, is clear enough to protect against the misuse of party bans.

Rijpkema's criteria for detecting anti-democratic parties are based on a normative definition of *democracy as self-correction*, i.e. the unique ability of democratic citizens to revise past decisions. Democracy as self-correction is grounded on three principles: (a) regular evaluation of policies, (b) political competition, and (c) free speech. Parties should be considered a threat to democracy when they are found to violate one or several of these principles, which enable citizens to self-correct.

Inspired by the example of Hungary, and echoing similar reflections in the chapter by Rovira Kaltwasser, Rijpkema asks an additional question: is 'anti-democratic' as a criterion that defines contemporary popular threats still relevant? Perhaps 'anti-liberal' (or 'anti-rule of law'), and not so much 'anti-democratic' forces, are what constitute the foremost threat to democratic politics today. Indeed, we see contemporary right-wing populists taking aim at the 'liberal' in 'liberal democracy'. In Hungary, we see Viktor Orbán explicitly arguing against (political) liberalism and for an 'illiberal state', contending that such a system can still be democratic, though 'illiberal'. In line with this thinking Orbán has, among other things, restricted the powers of the constitutional court, installed loyalists in neutral institutions and redrawn the electoral districts to his (strong) benefit. Despite these observations, Rijpkema concludes that, empirically speaking, some of the so-called 'illiberal democrats' in practice also exhibit anti-democratic tendencies. Besides, the problem that 'illiberal democrats' and anti-democrats pose to militant democracy is fundamentally the same: at what stage is intervention justified? Within Rijpkema's theory, this is only the case when parties seek to impair democracy's self-correcting capacity, and not when the 'liberal' in 'liberal democracy' is threatened.

In Chapter 10, András Sajó offers his views about the contemporary dangers posed to democratic constitutionalism. Like the previous chapter, he is especially concerned about takeovers of government by populist 'illiberal democrats', who obtain or intend to obtain power in order to perpetuate control by using the means of electoral democracy. Under the cover of majority support, populists threaten to undo liberal constitutional laws, which protect minorities against the tyranny of the majority (see also Rovira Kaltwasser above). His native Hungary easily comes to mind. In this context, the author asks: to what extent can constitutional self-defence be developed as a militant preventive system? He identifies two types of preventive or *militant constitutionalism*, which can counter the threats posed by the rise of populism. The first is a set of rights restrictions, which makes it unlikely for democracies' enemies to win power through elections. The second is a set of measures that limit the possibilities to abuse government power. However, both sets of constitutional measures are difficult to apply to populist parties, because the latter have gained power legally and legitimately.

Indeed, these are *desperate* times for democrats, Sajó claims. Even though constitutional self-defence has had a long tradition, its institutions are full of loopholes. Take for example constitutional *amendment* procedures: in theory they can make changes to the constitution very difficult, but in practice illiberal amendments can always be pushed through by means of referenda and similar tools. Other constitutional protections against autocracy should be activated: guardianship of the constitution, term limits, electoral system checks, limitations to the use of referenda, multi-layered constitutions. Still, none of these constitutional self-protecting measures will be effective if the commitment to militant democracy is missing. Therefore, preventive constitutionalism requires further measures, such as entrenchment of key clauses or guarantees of the independence of the judiciary.

Is a militant configuration of the legal and institutional framework sufficient? Sajó thinks it is not. Admitting that the success of populism and illiberalism is above all a problem of mentality and not of the law, the chapter goes on to discuss how to raise militant barriers to the formation of the populist *mindset*. By way of illustration, it is difficult to regulate populist speech because it does not fall squarely in the category of hate speech or incitement to violence. What constitutional democracies should do in this respect is to foster rational political debate. And they should do so, Sajó observes, before populists are in power and take control of the media.

In the final chapter Svetlana Tyulkina rekindles an optimistic view about militant constitutional democracy and its capacity to deal with emerging threats. Democratic self-preservation is an 'instinct' inherent in the nature of every democratic state, she claims. Therefore, it is neither illegitimate nor surprising that every democratic state features aspects of militancy, whether they are expressly stated in the constitution or not.

Indeed, militant measures are not always part of the constitutional text, and rightly so. For example, Spain's 2002 Law of Political Parties is a regular piece of legislation allowing party bans. In addition, many anti-fascist laws listed by Loewenstein have by now migrated to the domain of criminal law. Tyulkina makes a case for extending the scope of application of militant democracy to a wider range of threats, not just anti-democratic parties but more elusive actors such as religious fundamentalists, global terrorists and illiberal populists. In the face of these threats, do states have a positive obligation to defend democracy?

To answer, Tyulkina turns her attention to public international law. She argues that international treaties not only favour a substantive view of democracy, but also establish a positive obligation for states to preserve democracy and guard its institutions. For example, clauses that allow militant rights restrictions are included in the International Covenant on Civil and Political Rights (ICCPR), the EU's admission criteria for new member states (the 'Copenhagen criteria') and the Council of Europe's membership requirements. Moreover, case law of the European Court of Human Rights indicates that states may be obliged to ban violent or racist political parties.

Drawing on public international law, Tyulkina argues that international institutions, such as the Council of Europe and the EU, have the same capacity as national actors to apply militant measures. They can oblige member states to impose legal mechanisms in defence of democracy, on the basis of these international institutions' foundational laws, jurisprudence or soft law. Therefore, Tyulkina concludes, international institutions should be less hesitant and more proactive than at present in protecting democratic structures of their member states, especially in addressing the rise of populist political movements.

To varying degrees, all the chapters in this volume deal with conceptual aspects of militant democracy. They offer different views about what militant democracy is, although most see it as a practice of rights restrictions with the purpose of defending democracy against its internal enemies. Defined in these terms, many authors in this volume accept it as a necessary feature of liberal or constitutional democracy, albeit for different normative reasons. Some, however, reject it and suggest refocusing on the principle of resistance against democracy's enemies, not the practice of sanctions. This point is shared by many contributors to this volume, militant democrats or not, who argue that we should refrain from narrowing down militant democracy to rights restrictions and party bans. Militant democratic theory provides a solid ground for expanding the scope of democratic self-defence, and this volume offers a contribution in this direction.

Note: In some chapters, gender-specific terms are used to ease the text flow. These should be understood as referring to both genders unless explicitly stated.

ONE

Individual Militant Democracy

Jan-Werner Müller[1]

One could have arrested a few of us in 1925, and everything would have been finished and over.

Joseph Goebbels, 1940

Militant democracy has traditionally been treated as a matter of institutions: states take militant measures against political parties or associations in order to protect democracy from actors who might subvert or outright destroy democracy (but who do not engage in conduct punishable under criminal law). To be sure, restrictions on free speech – usually part of the repertoire of techniques for defending democracy – mostly apply to individuals, rather than institutions;[2] but, broadly speaking, the fact remains that organisations of some sort have been both the agents and the objects of militant democracy.

This essay asks about militant democracy targeting individuals – and also about individuals adopting militant measures against threats to democracy. This is clearly a highly fraught subject, and there are good reasons why theorists of democratic self-defence have generally shied away from considering what, for shorthand, I shall be calling *individual militant democracy* (for the purposes of this chapter I shall use 'militant democracy' and 'democratic self-defence' interchangeably, setting aside the standard distinction between the former as repressive and the latter as also including softer elements such as civic education). When individuals have their rights restricted or in some other manner are excluded from the political process, it not only gets much more *personal*, so to speak (with particular persons being stigmatised), the main problem is that citizens' legitimate interests in political participation might be permanently harmed: being excluded from the political process would appear to be an obvious instance of being dominated, that is to say, being at the will of others without any means of controlling their conduct (Pettit 2012).[3] Put more bluntly: it's one thing if my favourite quasi-fascist party has been banned; it's another thing if *I* personally have been banned from ever giving political speeches, demonstrating, standing for office or, for that matter, voting – in short, if I can feel with good reason that I have been entirely removed from the realm of politics, and that my standing as a citizen has been permanently diminished.

As Alexander S. Kirshner has pointed out, even anti-democrats have a range of political interests (they are not all single-mindedly, ascetically focused on abolishing democracy); hence banning individuals, so to speak, would prima facie appear to be a highly problematic move within militant democracy (Kirshner 2014). This is one reason why theorists, as well as public lawyers, have generally insisted that *actions* ought to be subject to militant democracy, and never *actors* (Invernizzi Accetti and Zuckerman 2017); states should, if anything, ensure *orthopraxy*, and not *orthodoxy*, as Julian Rivers has put it (Rivers 2018). Otherwise we might well end up with Chinese-style 'citizen scores' or even be thrown back into a Lockean universe where those consistently unwilling to follow what Locke called 'the Rule of Reason' are eventually cast out among the beasts.

Practitioners tend to concur with this line of reasoning: in its 'Code of Good Practice in Electoral Matters', the Council of Europe's Commission of Democracy through Law (generally known as the Venice Commission [2002]) proposes a clear principle when it comes to individuals being excluded from the political process: one's right to vote should only be removed on the basis of a criminal law (or mental incapacity), and the decision has to be made by a court. Since militant democracy, by definition, is about conduct *not* already covered by the criminal law, measures such as disenfranchisement or other deprivations of basic political rights on the basis of some kind of anti-democratic attitude would appear to be plainly illegitimate.

Yet the legal possibility of banning actors, and not just actions, exists in a number of countries. And not least in the one polity which is often considered the paradigmatic example of a country with a successful track record of militant democracy: the Federal Republic of Germany, where Article 18 of the Basic Law provides for the forfeiture of basic political rights if such rights are being used to fight against liberal democracy. Moreover, individual rights restrictions for political reasons which amounted to banning actors and not just actions have come before the Council of Europe's Court, the European Court of Human Rights (ECHR) – and the judges have sometimes found it justifiable to declare them compatible with Europe's human rights regime. For good measure, adopting a historical perspective, one can also find plenty of examples of such individual militant democracy, from ostracism in ancient Athens to present-day mechanisms of impeachment (on the understanding that officials can be impeached, even if they have *not* engaged in criminal conduct) (Whittington 2017; Tribe and Matz 2018).[4]

These not always very well-known facts make it less fanciful to examine the question under which conditions (if any) such militant democracy with individuals as targets could ever really be legitimate. There is also the particular concern that we might live in an era where individual (quasi-Ceasarist) leaders appear as perhaps the greatest threats of all to democracy. Models focused on ideologically committed, somehow 'extremist' mass parties, as they were prevalent in the twentieth century, might be more misleading than helpful – as might be the pervasive tendency to draw an analogy between defending democracy and criminal prosecution, a tendency which remains dominant in American discussions (Issacharoff 2015: 23).

Individuals as the actors *implementing* militant democracy would also appear normatively very fraught indeed. As even its defenders would concede, militant democracy is always in danger of damaging the very thing it seeks to protect. A democracy overzealous to defend itself, or so a long-standing worry suggests, might well go too far with rights restrictions and exclusions, and, at the very least, bring about the very authoritarianism it seeks to avoid.[5] A typical precaution to prevent this outcome is to build checks and balances into the very process of deciding on, and implementing, militant measures.[6] The institutions ultimately making the decision to 'go militant', usually a constitutional court, are supposed to be insulated from both popular and party-political pressures, mostly to avoid a situation where majorities target vulnerable minorities or where parties start to outlaw their competitors. It is hard to see how individuals could ever be in a similarly constrained (and also a similarly accountable) position. Hence the long-standing worries about militant democracy being arbitrary would appear to be compounded, if it seems like individuals can simply take democracy-defence into their own hands.[7] In short: if one has concerns about militant democracy, one should be especially anxious about anything smacking of what we might call *vigilante militant democracy*.

As with militant democracy directed *against* individuals, it turns out there actually exist plenty of practices of democracy-defence *by* individuals, even if they are not always presented, let alone generally understood, that way. I am thinking in particular of civil disobedience and, as an ultimate measure, resistance in contexts where parts or even most of the state has already been taken over by anti-democratic forces. As outlandish as the latter might sound, it is worth emphasising that, yet again, the paradigmatic example of militant democracy contains precisely resistance as part of a repertoire of techniques to save democracy: the Basic Law of the Federal Republic of Germany features an article explicitly legitimating resistance for the sake of defending the so-called free-democratic political order. In an era when talk about 'popular resistance' has become inflationary even in long-established democracies, it is particularly important to assess the legitimacy of disobedience and resistance as militant measures.

In this chapter, I shall argue that there is a space for militant democracy both against and by individuals – but that such a space has to be very constrained, and also clearly has to be limited to exceptional circumstances.[8] In particular, militant democracy aimed at individuals has to be hemmed in by three considerations: first, beliefs and their expression, no matter how radically anti-democratic, cannot plausibly be subjected to militancy by states (for incitement to violence or to hatred, there are already criminal statutes in many democracies). Rather, there has to be a pattern of behaviour that makes it plausible that an individual is intentionally subverting, or at least is just about to subvert, democratic institutions – and that such efforts are possibly having an effect.[9] That charge is prima facie much more plausible in case of powerful individuals. So militancy applies to what we can call *resourceful* persons (we might be talking about financial resources, ownership of media, but also personal charisma, or celebrity status, or, for that matter, links to significant organisations).[10] The worry that sanctioning such individuals might make them martyrs in the eyes of their supporters is justified – but, then again, a democracy can hardly have its actions dictated by how a group of citizens with anti-democratic inclinations view such sanctions.

Second, if democracy is a political system dedicated to the advancement of freedom and equality, then individual militant measures have to be as respectful of equal individual autonomy as possible; they cannot fundamentally deny the standing of an individual as holding democratic citizenship (and as a democratic co-author of the laws) if they wish to participate in democratic institutions.[11] Militancy should only affect as small a set of political rights as possible, and leave as much autonomy as possible (for instance by prohibiting an individual from standing for office, but not disenfranchising, let alone denationalising, them). It should also be strictly limited in time. Democracy, after all, is built on the idea that citizens can and do change their minds; hence it is plausibly understood as a form of institutionalised uncertainty (Przeworski 1991). Any militant measures that assume that citizens are just not capable of changing their political beliefs, that they are 'irredeemable' (in Hillary Clinton's infamous words), contradict one of the core elements of democracy.[12]

Third, while Kirshner is absolutely right that even those presently hold-ing anti-democratic convictions have an interest in political participation, it is important to see that such a basic interest generates not one *general* right to participate, but a multiplicity of specific rights with diverse duties placed on others (including, but not limited to, the state) (Waldron 1989). Any-thing like a blanket removal of an individual from the political process is to be rejected in favour of a nuanced approach that involves at most the tem-porary forfeiture of specific rights (and the attendant lifting of some duties). Such measures should be tailored as closely as possible to the individual case; ideally, restrictions should clearly be linked to specific problematic behaviour (even though, for reasons I shall discuss below, that ambition cannot always be fulfilled).

Such an approach mitigates the worry that a democratic state ultimately responds to anti-democratic actors in a *symmetrical* fashion, mirroring the very anti-democratic conduct of its declared enemies. This concern is par-ticularly acute in our historical moment: after all, those threatening democ-racy today hardly ever officially reject democratic ideals; rather, they will suggest that some groups (be they 'corrupt elites' or certain minorities) do not properly belong to the demos at all (the very move that I think is best called populist, which is to say: a claim to a monopoly of representing the supposedly 'real people', while holding that all those who do not support the populists' ultimately symbolic construction of the 'real people' are out-side the people *tout court*).[13] It is not the case that populists in general do not believe in democracy or freedom, so that, as Rawls had hoped, the 'liberties of the intolerant may persuade them to a belief in freedom' (Rawls 1971: 219). Rather, they believe that only some are the proper people who should enjoy freedom and equality. Here a militant response is in danger of sound-ing like 'because you exclude, we exclude you' – an untenable position that gives credence to the concern that militancy will end up undermining democracy itself. By contrast, an approach that disaggregates the interest in participation and then selectively restricts rights in the face of plausible threats is less likely to end up with such a fateful symmetry.[14]

Let me also preview the arguments about militant democracy *by* indi-viduals. Ideally, such militancy should be confined to exerting pressure on states to actually become more militant; there ought generally to be no short cuts by civilian, i.e. non-state actors, to restrict the rights of other citi-zens in anything like democracy-saving 'self-help measures' (especially if these other citizens have not yet themselves infringed any rights). Where individuals believe that a majority, and, more particularly, the institutions charged with militancy, have genuinely failed to comprehend a threat, highly constrained acts of civil disobedience might be justified – with a publicly articulated account of under what conditions civil disobedients would rest their case. Finally, resistance is an outlier in matters of militant democracy: it assumes that a state has already at least partially been taken over by anti-democratic forces; hence, this approach is unlikely to count as pre-emptive in accordance with conventional understandings of militant democracy. But a situation is imaginable where a state has simply been weakened in many of its defences; it could be completely taken over by anti-democratic forces next, but resisters might still be in a position to prevent such an outcome.

As has been said many times, the problem with all such scenarios is that one assumes the best about the actors engaging in militancy: they will restrain themselves; militancy will involve both government and opposition members; executives will not take militancy as an occasion to score partisan points, etc. If all these conditions hold, one is led to think that such a democracy is probably secure enough not to need militancy in the first place. Hence the real paradox of militant democracy is this: democracies that need militant democracy probably won't have it, because the actors cannot agree on such a model (or, where it does exist, militancy does damage to the democracy); whereas polities that would do fine even without militant democracy can agree on having it, but probably will never truly need it.[15]

This chapter does not dispute this basic insight, but still holds that militancy is important to think about, because the line between political systems (or cultures) that really need it and those that don't just isn't always as clear as this neat paradox makes it out to be. It hardly needs mentioning that in recent years, complacent assumptions about what makes for 'consolidated democracies' have been profoundly shaken. We are not in Weimar any more. But we are also not quite where we thought we were in terms of solid, self-assured liberal democracies.

Should Individuals be Targeted by Militant Democracy? Forfeiture of Rights, Denationalisation, Political Trials

Most accounts of militant democracy include not just criteria as to what kind of political content might be taken to indicate threats to democracy; they also emphasise that the likelihood of those threats materialising needs to be taken into consideration when deciding whether militant measures are justified.[16] Prima facie, single individuals would appear to pose much less of a danger than individuals acting in concert, let alone individuals forming stable organisations. Jonathan Quong, in an important article on the rights of 'the unreasonable' (broadly speaking: those who deny their fellow citizen's freedom and equality), has emphasised that only the systematic reproduction of unreasonable beliefs, which could then endanger what he calls the 'normative stability' of a liberal polity, should be prevented by restricting the rights of the unreasonable (Quong 2004). In the same vein, the 'concentric circles' model of containing anti-democratic extremism which has been proposed by Stefan Rummens and Koen Abts emphasises that the justification for restrictive measures kicks in when anti-democratic actors get closer to power (Rummens and Abts 2010); by contrast, individuals should enjoy extensive free speech rights in order to voice 'grievances' that could then be addressed by non-extremist parties. Again, it is hard to see how individuals *qua* individuals, disconnected from political parties or mass civil society organisations, could really get close to power in most contemporary representative democracies. When prominent individuals have been fined for inciting hatred or for Holocaust denial – think of Jean-Marie Le Pen or Geert Wilders – what mattered was surely the fact that these were leaders of politically significant parties.[17]

Here I want to say more about the empirical example mentioned at the beginning of this chapter. The German Basic Law envisages in Article 18 the possibility of forfeiting a range of basic rights – the right to free expression (freedom of the press in particular), the freedom to teach, freedom of assembly, freedom of association, protection of privacy for mail and telephony, the right to property, and also the right to asylum.[18] Only three institutions have the right to apply for such a forfeiture of rights: the federal parliament (Bundestag), the federal government, and the executives of the individual states comprising the German federation. Once an application reaches the Constitutional Court, the authorities may search a defendant's house, seize property, and in other ways investigate possible abuses of fundamental rights. If the Court agrees, the minimum period during which a right or multiple rights are forfeited is one year. Not surprisingly, Article 18 is usually presented as a direct reaction to the fate of the Weimar Republic, with the implicit assumption that militant measures, had they been available at the time, might have saved the Republic (Möllers 2010; Deutscher Bundestag 2012).

Four attempts have been made so far to deprive individuals of basic political rights. All concerned right-wing extremists; all have failed. Tellingly, the Constitutional Court – the only institution that can decide on a forfeiture of rights – has generally emphasised that the danger of an individual overthrowing the basic democratic order is small, or simply non-existent.[19] In one case, the neo-Nazi in question appeared to have retired from political life already; in another, the right-wing extremist publisher of a newspaper was deemed no actual danger for West German democracy; and with two neo-Nazis, the Court argued that, after their criminal convictions and time in prison, one could expect that they would no longer engage in anti-democratic political expression and conduct.

These cases in the end yield little guidance as to how one should think about the forfeiture of rights. The Court has emphasised the importance of individuals actually posing a threat to the democratic order, but there is little indication of what the criteria for judging single citizens to be a plausible danger actually are. Moreover, there is not much of a sense of which rights exactly would be forfeited and whether there needs to be an internal connection between the conduct of individuals and the rights lost; more particularly, it is unclear where a line should be drawn between doing something morally wrong on the basis of a right and doing something politically dangerous with a right (after all, as Jeremy Waldron famously argued, rights must be understood as rights to do wrong [Waldron 1993]). Clearly, rights can be used to engage in criminal activity, but the proper response to such activity would appear to be specific forms of punishment, not a permanent forfeiture of a whole range of rights. Put less abstractly: yes, I can use freedom of speech to incite hatred of a particular minority, but then proper punishment awaits me (possibly including a temporary forfeiture of my right to liberty, at least in some jurisdictions), not a permanent ban on voicing opinions.[20] Moreover, I am not necessarily judged as posing a permanent danger. It seems that the German Constitutional Court also does not want to adopt a view according to which individuals could somehow conclusively be seen as politically bad (and threatening) characters.

By contrast with these failed cases against individuals, two political parties were banned in the 1950s: the Socialist Reich Party, a de facto neo-Nazi organization, and the Communist Party of Germany. In January 2017, a party, the extreme right-wing NPD, was declared hostile to the constitution but was not dissolved (while parliament was encouraged by the judges to draft legislation allowing special measures to be applied to the NPD, in particular through restrictions on party financing through the state). Less well-known is the fact that almost routinely extremist associations (*Vereine*) are banned in Germany (by contrast, parties are privileged by the constitution and afforded special protections on account of their crucial role in democratic will-formation); since the Basic Law came into force, more than 500 associations have been dissolved by the executive.

All these findings would seem to support the general belief that if one is willing to have militant democracy at all, then militant measures should be aimed at organisations, not at individuals.[21] Most accounts of democratic self-defence include a call for proportionality: militant measures must be proportional to the threats posed, and individuals on their own would hardly ever seem to pose an existential threat to a democracy. Furthermore, the ban of an organisation automatically affects a number of individuals anyway; practically, it would simply be too burdensome to go after every member of an anti-democratic organisation individually (especially if the organisation was not banned and thus could keep giving individuals ideas about adopting anti-democratic attitudes, so to speak, and generally attract them to the cause).[22]

And yet: there are actually instances when the state passes a more comprehensive judgement on a citizen's character – and even decides on what one might call a civic or political death penalty as a consequence. And there seems reasonable disagreement about the legitimacy of states taking such a stance. Think, most obviously, of prisoners' voting rights.[23] Democracies take a range of very different approaches to this question, from no disenfranchisement to disenfranchisement for the entire prison term or even beyond. Different justifications for such disenfranchisement have been advanced, including the notion that prisoners have forfeited the 'moral authority' to vote (an argument invoked by a court in the UK's defence of the state's restriction of a prisoner's voting rights), as well as the state's legitimate aim of promoting 'civic responsibility' and 'respect for the rule of law'.[24]

Note that these justifications are rather different: with the former, disenfranchisement is not primarily a form of punishment; rather, a legislature holds that a society wants particular individuals to have absolutely no say whatsoever in the way it is governed – on account of their moral character. However little difference one vote makes, the view is that the process is somehow tainted if it includes citizens who have forfeited their moral authority to affect the manner in which we live together as a political community; democratic authority is only assured if that particular individual is not part of the demos, at least as far the latter's role in the political process is concerned. Loss of moral standing thus translates into forfeiture of the right to influence our collective fate (see also Morris 1991).

In the second case, the forfeiture of rights seems more straightforwardly a matter of punishment with a view to deter and to educate citizens about the fact that crime will incur a whole range of disadvantages (even if there are no reasons to believe that the prospect of disenfranchisement will act as an incentive not to commit a crime in the first place).[25] The approach is pedagogical; it is not about assuring the purity of democratic authority, so to speak.

The ECHR has accorded states a wide margin of appreciation in what in recent years has turned out to be a highly controversial, symbolically fraught issue (Dzehtsiarou 2017). In what is probably the most well-known case dealt with by Strasbourg, a British prisoner convicted for manslaughter was denied the vote, according to the Representation of the People Act 1983; the latter holds that 'a convicted person during the time that he is detained in a penal institution in pursuance of his sentence . . . is legally incapable of voting at any parliamentary or local election'. The ECHR decided against the UK government, but not because disenfranchisement constituted a violation of the Convention's right to free elections per se. Rather, it found fault specifically with the 'automatic and blanket restriction on convicted prisoners' franchise' adopted by the British parliament.[26]

Strasbourg also emphasised that in previous rulings 'uncitizen-like conduct' and 'dishonorable' behaviour had been accepted as reasons for denying a citizen the right to vote.[27] Such a connection between politically dishonorable behaviour and a public downgrading of one's civic status (short of loss of citizenship altogether) goes back to democratic Athens, which featured the institution of declaring a citizen *atimos* – without honor – justifying a loss of rights. And, after the Liberation, the French Republic introduced the crime of *indignité nationale* for those who had collaborated with the Germans under the occupation. Those convicted incurred the penalty of *dégradation nationale*: a citizen was declared 'unworthy' and stripped of basic political rights (Simonin 2008), a measure which leading French politicians sought to reintroduce in the wake of the attack on *Charlie Hebdo* in January 2015.

The problem at the point of the Liberation was clearly not pre-emption, or, put more bluntly, power – there existed no realistic possibility that collaborators would somehow enter government and re-establish Vichy-style authoritarianism. Rather, it served as a kind of political pedagogy mixed with concerns about historical justice; the law that attributed 'infamy' to a citizen had primarily an expressive function (as would a reintroduction of *indignité nationale* for convicted terrorists today).

Now, once 'un-citizenly' conduct has been admitted as a possible justification for forfeiting rights, one might be led to wonder (warning sign: slippery slope!) why a complete loss of citizenship should not also be an option. Denationalisation has in fact been debated (and practised) extensively in recent years. One French president, François Hollande, sought to include it in the Republic's constitution; one British Home Secretary quietly kept proceeding with it for years, on grounds that have not exactly been transparent.[28] To the extent that there have been explicit justifications of this practice (which, in theory, is severely limited by the UN Conventions on Statelessness),[29] the main one has been about security: known terrorists are supposed to be removed from the country. Another motivation has been punishment. And, finally, less obviously, there has been the notion that denationalisation can serve as a symbolic distancing of a democratic state from some of its citizens: one effectively disowns the national and their conduct (Macklin and Bauböck 2015). Closer to the concerns in this chapter, there has been the idea that citizens who commit acts of violence or even just *intend* to commit them for political reasons have themselves effectively severed any kind of civic bond. This thought is rarely spelt out; it appears to rely on some underlying notion of reciprocity: someone committing crimes on the basis of ideas fundamentally incompatible with the polity is said to have taken themselves out of the political community altogether, even if they have not formally renounced citizenship (see also Miller 2012).

Normatively, such measures make no sense within a militant democracy framework (and, in most cases, are indefensible *tout court*). Not because losing or, for that matter, giving up citizenship is always wrong: of course, citizens can hand back their passport voluntarily (not least if they actually object to the political direction their home country is taking); moreover, there are circumstances in which denationalisation might be justified, because individuals effectively have no ties to a country (think of descendants of emigrants inheriting passports down the generations, so to speak, without having any connections to the emigrants' homeland [López-Guerra 2005]). But these scenarios have nothing to do with militant democracy. If a citizen engages in politically motivated violence there are criminal punishments (and militant democracy does not enter the picture at all); if a person advocates the violent overthrow of democracy there might be criminal sanctions, depending on the free speech legislation of the country in question (and militant democracy does not enter the picture at all). But if someone propounds anti-democratic principles, or perhaps also starts organising others on the basis of such principles, it is hard to see how such actions could possibly justify anything as drastic as loss of *all* rights by virtue of loss of nationality (not to mention the fact that only those with dual nationality could be subject to such measures). Such measures would clearly fail to respect the autonomy of the citizen in question; they would not take the necessary nuanced approach that disaggregates the interest in political participation and might legitimate the restriction of some rights, but not the temporally unlimited forfeiture of *all* rights. Depriving an individual of citizenship leaves no possibilities of showing moderation, not least because the person in question has no access to the state anymore – which is the very intention of denationalization on the basis of security concerns.

So does all this not push us in the direction of rejecting militant democracy targeting individuals who have not committed any criminal acts altogether? Not so fast. Thinking back to ostracism in ancient Athens, one is reminded that the basic idea then was that a particularly powerful individual might pose a threat to democracy – even if that individual had not committed any acts yet that could be construed as political crimes. Moreover, there are plenty of examples of prominent politicians, and sometimes even ordinary citizens, who have been banned from standing for office, without losing their other basic political rights. Are these so obviously illegitimate measures?

We need to make two shifts in our discussion. First, as has already been suggested a number of times, we need to unbundle what Kirshner has called the right to participate (López-Guerra 2017). There might be valid reasons to restrict particular individual rights and yet not have a citizen end up in a situation that could plausibly be described as domination. Second, we need to move away from the typical images of democratic self-defence familiar from the twentieth century: ideologically-driven mass movements that appear easily classified as 'extremist'. We should give at least some thought to the possibility that seemingly 'mainstream' individuals might do as much, if not more, damage to democracy – especially if they are well resourced, or can call on a strong personal following (or the possibility that 'mainstream' parties come under the control of actors who end up taking party and perhaps even an entire polity in an undemocratic direction). We should also consider impeachment as an example of individual militant democracy, as those subject to it do not necessarily have to have committed criminal offenses, they just have to have engaged, for instance, in an abuse of public office, which may well include de facto attempts to subvert a democratic system as a whole – though, to be sure, most provisions for impeachment do include a requirement of the office-holder having violated actual laws, as opposed to vaguer language such as 'betrayal of public trust' or 'bringing the office into disrepute'.

It is hard to see how in modern representative democracies one could replicate something like the Athenian ostracism, where sometimes the wealthy were banned simply for being wealthy, as they posed a potential threat to the democracy – but sometimes also powerful rivals of leaders who were somewhat less popular and who could be removed from the scene without bloodshed (Malkopoulou 2017). It is not hard to see, however, that particular citizens, if they exhibit a pattern of behaviour which suggests that they will use their wealth in ways to subvert democracy or seek financially to profit from public office (or avoid criminal sentences by using the immunity granted by the office), could be barred from standing in elections, or be held accountable through impeachment or impeachment-like procedures. Such an approach would not be quite comparable to ancient ostracism, where the character of the person to be ostracised was not necessarily impugned and where political ideas were not judged illegitimate and in any way 'punished' (Forsdyke 2005; Malkopoulou 2017). By contrast, such militant measures today would be based on a holistic (and cumulative) judgement, informed by the past conduct of an individual (Whittington 2018).

Now, a critic might say that such an approach does not truly fall into the category of militant democracy, where the realisation of an anti-democratic ideological agenda is to be thwarted. Based on recent experiences – Berlusconi, Trump – I would argue that this focus on ideology is too narrow. It also tends to forget that during the twentieth century (and, for that matter, today) many actors threatening democracy actually went out of their way to profess allegiance to democratic values; they did not always do us the favour of openly advocating authoritarianism. Especially if we take militant democracy to be concerned with *action*, we might want to say that what matters are *patterns of action* over time – and if these patterns suggest that an actor appears to be intent on undermining democracy, then prohibiting the relevant *actor* from exercising a circumscribed set of rights (ideally, just the right to stand for office) may well be justified. Unlike with the issue of voting for prisoners, there is a clear link here to patterns of action in the past, and there is ideally an internal connection between such patterns and the specific rights being temporarily forfeited.[30]

If 'political trials' did not have such a bad name, one might describe the approach here as one advocating political, but not partisan, trials (Posner 2005). Some actual institutional practices fit this characterisation: impeachment in the US involves a judgement by political peers, as does the procedure whereby the European Council decides to suspend the membership rights of an EU member state in breach of fundamental values of the Union (primarily democracy, the rule of law, and human rights).[31] But one could envisage institutions that give greater weight to jurists and experts: election commissions or even special tribunals which judge the fitness of particular individuals for office or, even more broadly, a prominent role in democratic life.[32]

Obviously, the potential for abuse would be significant here – capturing that particular election commission might be tantamount to controlling the political process and might effectively destroy democracy itself. In less dramatic cases, it might be a problem that a self-declared 'outsider' could be kept out by such a commission – and hence have his or her story confirmed that corrupt elites are preventing the real champion of the people from gaining office.

This is a difficult question of institutional design. What we might call the *enemy test* (would we ever want such an institution in the hands of our political enemies?) on one level yields an obvious result. Still, a well-designed institution would make for a balance of political forces or at least pluralism in such a way that abuses become at least very unlikely. Then again: if actors in a democracy are so reasonable that they can craft such a pluralist institution, the likelihood of militant democracy being necessary is probably very small anyway. But it is not zero: democracies change over time, polarisation is not a constant.[33] It can happen that the powerful start acting against democracy from within; that, broadly speaking, is the kind of scenario for which this kind of individual militant democracy appears appropriate.

This leaves one obvious difficulty: if the approach is supposed to respect autonomy, if militant measures have to be nuanced and focus on particular rights restrictions that do not ride roughshod over the general interest in participation (and, ultimately, not being dominated) – then how could that ambition be realised in practice so that citizens can have clear expectations under what conditions they might regain all their rights? Here the danger of loyalty oaths, McCarthyite hearings that amount to political persecution, and the effective outlawing of dissent, etc., loom large. By definition, if the basis for specific rights restrictions is a pattern of action in the past, that pattern will have ceased once the restrictions are in place. Must an individual then (more or less abjectly) profess belief in democratic values in front of a political tribunal or even explicitly repent – a distinctly unattractive, deeply illiberal vision?

I can think of two answers. One is that it's actually not so obvious that the pattern will have ceased even after rights restrictions: those fanatically devoted to anti-democratic ideas (or fanatically devoted to using the political process for personal gain, for that matter) might well try to use surrogates or otherwise to continue their scheming in ways that are devious, but ultimately can be detected. Admittedly, such an expectation appears to rely on the cartoonish image of the single-minded, ascetic anti-democratic which Kirshner has rightly criticised; I share the criticism, but it would also be problematic to exclude the possibility of such actors appearing altogether a priori.[34]

Second, there is nothing illiberal, let alone completely illegitimate, about the idea of a hearing as such (and resulting judgement of a threat that an individual might pose to democracy). After all, it's a routine procedure in confirmations of judges and all kinds of state officials. While rights restrictions are not to be thought of as a form of punishment, the expectation that a panel of experts, judges, political peers, or, for that matter, ordinary citizens comes to a judgement as to whether a particular individual still poses a threat to democracy could well be likened to a parole hearing (without thereby accepting the analogy between militant democracy and criminal prosecution).

Should Individuals Execute Militant Measures? Civil Society, Civil Disobedience, Civil or Uncivil Resistance

Should individuals, as opposed to institutions, play an important role in defending democracy? Traditional models of militant democracy have often been criticised as elitist, since they are supposedly suffused with a deep distrust of 'popular participation' (Malkopoulou and Norman 2018). This is not an unreasonable worry: Karl Loewenstein, the original theorist of militant democracy in the mid-1930s, harboured deep reservations about the fitness of the masses for modern politics. In line with the clichés of nineteenth- and twentieth-century mass psychology, he charged them with being overly emotional, a fact which had allegedly made them particularly susceptible to fascism (which Loewenstein judged to have no real ideological content; it was simply a political technique to gain power on the basis of – emotional – mass mobilisations). Less obviously, militant democracy has sometimes been pursued in what could seem like a rather technocratic vein: take the right militant instruments out of the toolkit of militant democracy, apply them correctly – problem solved. In other words, citizens should just leave the challenge of some people having a problem with democracy to the institutional machinery of militant democracy; no need to get very much involved (or, for that matter, concerned, if the machine is well oiled and produces the right result in terms of keeping democracy safe).

In response, both theorists and practitioners of democracy defence have long argued that repressive legal measures ought to be complemented with education as well as broader attempts to address what is sometimes perhaps too glibly described as the 'underlying causes' of some citizens turning against democracy (Capoccia 2005; Rummens and Abts 2010). What has been stressed less is the possible role of civil society: individuals – civilians, if you like – can mobilise to show their opposition to parties and movements that they think pursue anti-democratic agendas.[35] Government and civil society activity obviously do not exclude each other: for instance, in October 2000, German Chancellor Gerhard Schröder launched an appeal for an 'uprising of the decent' (*Aufstand der Anständigen*) after a synagogue had been attacked.[36]

Now, civil society action undoubtedly can aim at defending democracy – but it is not strictly speaking an instance of militant democracy, if we take the latter to involve the restrictions of rights. One possible course of action that individuals can undertake and that can result in restricting the rights of others – one that has played no real part in discussions of militant democracy traditionally – is civil disobedience. According to Rawls's classic definition, civil disobedience must be based on conscience and aim at publicly breaking the law to bring an injustice to the attention of a majority which as yet has failed to see that injustice (Rawls 1971; see also Habermas 1985). In that classic model, disobedients are supposed to display 'fidelity to the law', while at the same time their actions must presumably be sufficiently drastic to make a public pay attention. Now, what if civil disobedience effectively becomes a way of drawing the majority's attention to a threat to democracy that has not been properly appreciated? What if it becomes a way to put pressure on governments to initiate measures of militant democracy?

The obvious question in response is: why aren't legal means enough to accomplish such goals? Citizens concerned about actors who, in their view, pose a threat to democracy can be out on the streets, they can blog, they can write to parliamentarians, etc. The question of course applies to all acts of civil disobedience: why not just legal protest? One possible answer is that engaging in unlawful acts and then taking the punishment increases the credibility of the claims being made by civil disobedients. That argument can go only so far, though: presumably the claims about injustice (or threats) still need to be plausible and bear the weight of a conscientious decision to break the law; some kind of existential investment in politics cannot substitute for what may be lacking in the moral arguments being addressed to a majority.

A second, more promising, notion is that acts of civil disobedience can directly respond to the injustice – and, if done well, can make the injustice more visible than would ordinarily be the case, even with well-crafted protests. Both Gandhi and the leaders of the American civil rights movement carefully staged their law-breaking in such a manner that the authorities' responses made the public (in some cases a global public) perceive the injustices – as well as the pernicious political ideas behind the injustices – much more clearly.[37]

Blocking or even breaking up a demonstration by anti-democratic actors – assuming that the demonstrators have a permit – might be an example of this approach. The anti-democrat actors' rights would be restricted, and, possibly, the injustice inherent in their ideas might become more visible in clashes with counter-demonstrators: it is revealed, for instance, that they really are full of hatred against particular minorities and prepared to engage in horrific violence. Of course, a state that has not initiated militant measures against the presumed anti-democrats will be compelled to guarantee the latter's right to demonstrate. And, presumably, governments will not want to feel they are being blackmailed into militant action by civil disobedients, or, put differently, self-empowered vigilantes for democracy preservation.

Nevertheless, in particular cases, if civil disobedience is well crafted and well executed, it might sway public opinion more generally to put pressure on a government to restrict the possibilities of presumed anti-democratic actors more generally. This might especially be the case if the latter are locally concentrated (and had thus far not been so clearly visible to a general, national audience).

Having said that, one of the assumptions of classic accounts of civil disobedience clearly can no longer be taken for granted in many democracies: Rawls, Habermas and others did not yet live in an age of highly fragmented public spheres, where a notion of appealing to *the* public has become highly implausible (see also Smith 2011). Both what civil disobedients and what, in this case, presumed anti-democrats do and say seems always already framed normatively in and for their separate publics. This does not pose a particular challenge to the use of civil disobedience in a militant democracy context, but it certainly makes it less likely that such efforts can succeed in polarised political cultures – bringing us back to the basic point that in less polarised societies, militant democracy might be more easily practised, but is probably not really needed, whereas in much more conflictual settings, militant democracy is much more difficult to establish as legitimate.

There is a further concern here that applies to practices of civil disobedience generally, but that might be particularly acute for civil disobedience in the name of defending democracy: under what conditions, if any, are those engaging in civil disobedience willing to accept a majority's decision not to adopt the view of civil disobedients that an injustice needs to be righted? If the quality of the public sphere is low, it is easier to make the case that the majority has not really had the opportunity yet to understand that case. But what if it is in reasonably good working order? Will civil disobedients just keep going to jail? And what about the situation we are particularly interested in here: will they persist with attempts to restrict the rights of what they take to be actors posing public threats to democracy, even if a majority (and, let's say, the institutions officially tasked to undertake militant measures) reject their views about the dangers involved in leaving the rights of these actors unrestricted? Presumably, it strengthens the case of civil disobedients if they specify some conditions for ceasing their law-breaking (after all, lawful protest still remains a possibility then); moreover, it makes it less likely that they can be accused of actually undermining democracy in the process of supposedly defending democracy.

One might also ask: should the constraints on state institutions specified earlier in this chapter also apply to individuals implementing militant measures on their own? While civil disobedients might peacefully infringe the rights of others, there is every reason for them to signal at the same time that they retain faith not just in the law but also in a basic capacity for autonomy, as far as their fellow citizens with apparently anti-democratic attitudes are concerned. In short: they should not treat such citizens as 'irredeemable'. They should thus also not fall into the trap of symmetry described earlier.

However, civil disobedients – as civilians – do have more leeway in how they treat other citizens, as long as what they do can plausibly be said to bring out particular injustices or the threats posed to democracy. A state cannot really provoke or, let's say, ridicule particular citizens, Saul Alinsky-style. For civil disobedients, by contrast, these might be fair tactics; unlike with classic accounts of civil disobedience, it is not so much unjust structures to which attention needs to be drawn but actors with unjust (and specifically anti-democratic) deigns. Or, put another way, civil disobedients might go very far in actively denying some citizens appraisal respect; what they cannot do is somehow communicate a message that recognition respect is also to be withheld in a democratic polity (Darwall 1977).[38]

One last instance of individual militant democracy that I wish to discuss is resistance in moments when the state itself might have been partially captured by anti-democratic forces. As mentioned above, language justifying such resistance for the sake of preserving democracy can be found in the German Basic Law. The relevant clause was only included in 1968, alongside highly controversial provisions for emergency powers, which gave the impression that, politically, the introduction of potentially authoritarian elements into the constitution had to be balanced with an explicit empowerment of individuals willing to face up to authoritarianism (Johst 2016).[39] The constitution makes it clear that all other means of countering anti-democratic forces must have been exhausted before one is entitled to engage in acts of resistance. It also implies that, unlike in the case of civil disobedience, violence might be used.

Critics have long held that a 'right to resistance' has no place in positive law; it is at best a (redundant) remnant of pre-modern times. Once the liberal rule of law is established, such a 'right' is actually no right at all (Raz 1979). Language invoking it might have at best a pedagogical function to make citizens think about what should, in any case, be a very, very remote scenario: the codification of the right is supposed to give a moral boost to individuals who see their democratic world being destroyed, but who can take heart that, if they were to succeed in reversing that destruction, re-established liberal democratic institutions would thoroughly vindicate their conduct.

Again, the obvious danger here is the scenario of individuals empowering themselves to violate the rights of others when in fact there is no threat to democracy, or the destruction of democracy is not nearly as advanced as the resister claims. By definition, anyone invoking the right in the face of functioning liberal democratic institutions is likely to be judged as simply having committed a politically motivated crime.

Conclusion

Militant democracy is always curiously suspended between politics and law. Ultimately, its only justification is the prevention of major harm – most obviously the harm done to individuals in the course of massive human rights violations after a takeover of a democracy by authoritarian forces. Militant democracy claims that there is a space beyond criminal law where such harm needs to be prevented by excluding certain actors from the political process. Of course, if one rejects the proposition that such a space can exist, one necessarily will be against the very idea of militant democracy. Those who see such a space have, for the most part, thought of organisations as the proper targets of militant measures. The most obvious reason is that organisations are much more likely to cause harm. But banning organisations is also much more clearly compatible with respect for individual citizens' autonomy (whose character is generally not judged by such bans).

Nevertheless, I have argued that individuals may, under certain conditions, also be subject to such measures – but that such an approach must be handled with the utmost caution. Something like a permanent banishment of an individual from the polity – literally or figuratively, in the case of a complete forfeiture of political rights – cannot be justified. However, not all participation rights are equally important. There is a space for temporarily restricting some rights as a result of a pattern of action that suggests a particularly resourceful individual is intent on undermining or destroying democracy outright. Some forms of impeachment – when impeachment is also forward-looking, taking into account the damage that might be done in the future by an irresponsible office-holder abusing their powers – can be justified in similar fashion.

Individual militancy needs to remain respectful of autonomy, leaving open the possibility of anti-democratic actors changing their minds (or, rather, changing their conduct – the depths of their character are not the issue, and in a sense not our business). Attempts at exclusion of minorities by such actors should not be met with seemingly symmetrical measures to exclude these anti-democratic citizens completely; again, the most plausible approach is to disaggregate the general interest in political participation and restrict rights (or otherwise exclude from the political process) selectively and temporarily only.

I have also argued that sometimes militant democracy might be under-taken by individuals. By definition, all actions by individuals opposing presumed anti-democrats within the confines of the law are welcome and normatively unproblematic. De facto restricting the rights of others through civil disobedience for the sake of bringing a threat to democracy to the attention of democratic majorities (and, ultimately, the institutions charged with militancy) might also be justifiable. Civil disobedients should remain respectful of the autonomy of those they judge a threat to democracy; and they should also resist the temptation of responding to moral exclusions in a symmetrical fashion. Finally, a very special case is individual resistance in situations where democracy is already partially destroyed. In theory, it is conceivable that individual resisters restrict the rights of others in what might well already look like a civil war situation, with a view to defending, or perhaps rather re-establishing, democracy.

Notes

1. This chapter was written largely during a research stay at the Wissenschaftsze-ntrum Berlin; many thanks to Britta Volkholz for research assistance. I am also grateful to Anthoula Malkopoulou, Alex Kirshner and the participants of the NYU Colloquium in Legal, Political, and Social Philosophy, especially Sam Scheffler and Jeremy Waldron, for very helpful comments.
2. I say 'mostly' because of the attribution of free speech rights to corporations in the US, and because there have been militant measures to shut down entire newspapers and websites.
3. The counter-position here is that those who refuse basic elements of liberal democracy are no longer owed justifications by liberal democratic governments (Quong 2004).
4. Impeachment is a form of excluding an individual from the political process, but not necessarily a rights restriction – unless a person is banned from stand-ing for office again.
5. To be sure, few democracies will commit outright suicide in order to prevent death; much more likely are scenarios where parts of the population, usually vulnerable minorities, no longer enjoy the benefits of a proper democratic life – somewhat analogous to the ways in which anti-terror measures usually only hit some hard (leaving majorities with the illusion that deeply illiberal policies actually change little and can be justified) (Waldron 2003). But this concern also applies when it comes to the question how much of a threat a party or even an individual pose: a party might be insignificant at the national level, and yet have local strongholds – to the point where citizens feel completely intimidated. Under such conditions, a ban might well be justified, as a state speaking against the party nationally is experienced by the relevant citizens as

effectively powerless (Brettschneider 2012). But in federal systems, where *only* federal institutions can initiate a ban (as in Germany), this situation might also create particular political and legal difficulties.

6. It might seem that the practice of giving a monopoly of militancy to one institution – usually a constitutional court – contradicts this point. The fact is, though, that the procedures leading up to a decision for militancy involve checks and balances. Moreover, the targets of militancy have extensive opportunities to defend themselves against the charges; *audi alteram partem* is ensured.

7. The common charge of arbitrariness against militant democracy is more complex than is usually suggested. Contrary to what Invernizzi Accetti and Zuckerberg argue, it is not subject to the same paradoxes as the demos problem (Invernizzi Accetti and Zuckerman 2017), since militancy does not aim to fix the boundaries of the people per se (with the possible exception of denationalisation, discussed in this chapter). One possible form of arbitrariness has to do with the definition of the constitutional core that is to be defended: powerful actors might include elements in such a core about which there is perfectly reasonable disagreement. A second form is the conflation of 'protection of the state' with 'protection of democratic core institutions and practices' – which is more or less what happened in the early years of militant democracy in West Germany (Rigoll 2017); the lie identified by Nietzsche 'Ich, der Staat, bin das Volk' becomes a different lie: 'Ich, der Staat, bin die Demokratie'. And a third form has to do with application: unless one assumes a duty of militancy (i.e. all possibly anti-democratic actors *must* always be banned), it becomes a matter of expediency, or just day-to-day politics, as to who in the end is made subject to militancy (since there is no duty to ban, there also is no possibility of individuals taking state institutions to court because they failed to initiate a ban). Having said that, the Venice Commission explicitly calls for a 'political filter' or space for discretion as a part of a legitimate form of militant democracy – so as to avoid overly restrictive practices such as in Turkey, where bans basically have been automatic and, in the eyes of the Venice Commission, far, far too frequent (Venice Commission 2009).

8. To be sure, that's easier said than done. Arguably, militant democracy has a way of expanding on its own: just think of the *Radikalenerlass* in 1970s' West Germany, which eventually made it possible to fire train drivers because they were suspected of communist sympathies, or the UK's current 'Counter-Extremism Strategy' which appears to be more about protecting 'British values' than actually countering threats to democracy (Rivers 2018).

9. Even in *Brandenburg*, there is a hint of what kind of pattern of conduct might be thought of this way: while 'mere abstract teaching' cannot be restricted, 'preparing a group for violent action and steeling it to such action' is another matter. It is the 'steeling' part that is particularly interesting: presumably, 'steeling' is a matter of repeated instruction by a leader; it aims at anti-democratic action, but that action is clearly not imminent.

10. The point about media suggests that individual and institutional militant democracy cannot and should not always be completely separated. For an excellent account of what it can mean to prevent or not prevent the rise of an anti-democratic resourceful individual, see Elster (2018).

11. I am indebted to Corey Brettschneider for discussions on this point.

12. This certainty about individuals' supposedly unchanging character determining electoral choices is often invoked to justify felon disenfranchisement: it is alleged, for instance, that felons will vote to change the criminal law in such a way that a society's order as a whole is undermined. Many variations of this argument are rehearsed in *Richardson v. Ramirez et al.*

13. This is a telegraphic version of my argument about populism in Müller (2016b).

14. One might object that populists in power also do not go all the way with their anti-pluralism and practical exclusions: it is enough that they systematically deny the legitimacy of an opposition, treat some citizens as de facto second class, and, at most, selectively withdraw citizenship to strike fear into potential dissenters.

15. I am indebted to Christoph Möllers on this point.

16. Not always. In the KPD judgement, the German constitutional court held that the likelihood of a party gaining power was actually irrelevant for a decision on banning – a view that today would clearly be out of line with the approach of the ECHR.

17. This logic can also work the other way around, though: if one of the major normative concerns about militant democracy is that it arbitrarily cuts short, or at least distorts, a collective democratic learning process or forms of democratic experimentalism (Frankenberg 2004), then it is clear that banning parties is particularly egregious, while taking individuals out, so to speak, might be less of a concern, given the limited influence that individuals ultimately have over these processes (not counting genius democratic theorists who change the course of history with their innovative theorising).

18. Note that the list does not include the possibility of forfeiting one's right to religious liberty – a fact particularly salient in light of suggestions by German politicians in recent years that Article 18 should be applied to individual militant Islamists. On the other hand, note the inclusion of a right to property, which implies not only that property by anti-democrats can be seized; it also hints at the not-so-obvious suggestion that somehow the right to property can be abused in such a way that it destroys democracy. One might think of situations in which shortages are artificially created in order to undermine the legitimacy of a democratic regime.

19. There has long been a legal debate as to whether it is really the likelihood of actors destroying democracy that justifies militant measures or whether an intense 'fighting' attitude – *Kampf* – is crucial. At the very least, in the second case under discussion here – concerning the right-wing extremist publisher of the *Deutsche National-Zeitung* – there could be little doubt that he exhibited

such a fighting attitude and was determined to continue the *Kampf* into the indefinite future.

20. It has been argued that a plausible interpretation of Article 18 can actually cannot justify an extended forfeiture of rights; all that really happens is that in the case of an abuse of a right, the duty on the state to refrain from interfering with the individual is lifted on just this particular occasion (Schnelle 2014).

21. When a party is dissolved, members and voters of that party obviously lose representation in the political process, but what Kirshner has called a right to participate is not forfeited per se: these citizens can form a more moderate party; they can vote for an existing party whose programme at least partly covers what they might see as their core political preferences; they can also keep up the advocacy of the party's positions individually. It is also imaginable that the citizens in question themselves modify their anti-democratic attitudes (or that they don't – and simply retreat from political life, while of course retaining all other benefits of citizenship).

22. In Germany, it is a criminal offence to be a member of a prohibited party or a party that obviously serves as a substitute for the prohibited party.

23. Another example would be the preventive restriction of some of the basic rights of individuals deemed close to Islamist extremists: even though they may never have engaged in criminal activity, such individuals can, for instance, have their right to free movement restricted (electronic surveillance, confiscation of passport, duty to report to state agencies, etc.).

24. *Hirst* v. *UK*, *Sauvé* v. *Canada*.

25. An unusual argument for denying prisoners the right to vote was advanced before the ECHR by the Latvian government: it argued that prisoners connected with criminal structures – presumably a polite way of saying 'mafia' – could use their votes to bring to power individuals also connected to said criminal structures. See *Hirst* v. *UK* 2. Of course, one can also turn this reasoning around: by disenfranchising prisoners/felons, it is much less likely that anything will ever be done to put an end to the shameful prison-industrial complex in the US.

26. In the eyes of the UK's critics, the relevant provisions could be traced back to the Forfeiture Act 1870, which in turn was derived from earlier notions of 'civic death'.

27. *H.* v. *Netherlands*, *X.* v. *The Netherlands* (sic!).

28. According to Patrick Weil, between 2006 and 2015 the British Home Secretary stripped at least fifty-three British subjects of their nationality (Weil 2017). At least two were subsequently killed through American drone strikes. The UK now has an extremely low threshold for citizenship deprivation; it is sufficient that the Home Secretary be 'satisfied that such deprivation is conducive to the public good'. Since 2014, it has been possible to take way British nationality from a naturalised citizen – even if they are immediately rendered stateless – as long as the Home Secretary has 'reasonable grounds' for believing that the

person in question could acquire the citizenship of another country. Theresa May, during her time as Home Secretary, usually stripped British subjects of their citizenship when they were outside the UK, making it impossible for the latter to initiate any review of the decision.

29. As long as governments respect the international conventions against stateless-ness, they can only apply the particular punishment of citizenship deprivation to dual nationals – an obvious form of discrimination.

30. But notice how the approach suggested here differs from that of the Venice Commission, for which the relevant conduct must also have been subject to criminal law.

31. See Article 7 TEU.

32. Or even a greater role for lay people: Article 90 of the Italian Constitution envisages a complicated impeachment procedure for the president, one which at one of its multiple stages empowers not only the fifteen judges of the Constitutional Court, but also sixteen citizens from outside parliament to make a decisive judgment.

33. From the point of view of democratic theory, polarisation is not the problem as such: democracies are always divided; the whole point of the exercise is that we can deal with our divisions. Polarisation turns into a potentially existential threat to democracy when one side systematically starts denying the legitimacy of the other (a process that started years before Trump in the case of the US).

34. Detecting the pattern again and again does not have to be equivalent to making an immutable character judgement; nothing prevents a state from giving yet another chance after the expiry of specific rights restrictions.

35. One might object that when it comes to civil society – and concrete measures such as counter-demonstrations – we are not really talking about individuals, but about collectives and, in many cases, organisations that initiate concrete measures. True, what was often referred to as 'the sheer significance of our numbers' during the civil rights movement in the 1960s matters a great deal. But in theory it's still possible for one individual to take action against undemocratic forces. Think of the self-immolation of a Polish citizen in front of Warsaw's Palace of Culture in October 2016. He had handed out leaflets accusing the ruling Law and Justice Party of violating the constitution, effectively destroying the constitutional court, and restricting the rights of individual citizens. It's arguable whether this example fits better into the category of resistance discussed at the end of this chapter.

36. Militant democracy has often been charged with being elitist because the ultimate judgement on rights restrictions is delegated to a court. Yet we know that courts can be very sensitive to what jurists take to be public opinion. So, what they decide might not be out of line with majority concerns – but the worry is then also that the trouble with militant democracy is not that it is insufficiently participatory, but that it is exercised mainly against unpopular and vulnerable minorities.

37. It is important to insist that civil disobedience be non-violent – or else the logic of provoking the authorities to overreact, reveal the ugly truth about the system, etc., becomes indistinguishable from terrorist strategies.
38. I am grateful to Ulrich Wagrandl for suggesting the use of this distinction in the context of militant democracy (see Wagrandl 2018).
39. The federal states of Hesse and Bremen contained such a right from the beginning.

TWO

Democratic Equality and Militant Democracy*

Peter Stone

Introduction

A *militant democracy*, as defined[1] by Karl Loewenstein (1937a, 1937b), employs a variety of practices to discourage or combat the rise of extremist, anti-democratic political parties. There are several instruments that a militant democracy could conceivably employ. (For a list, see Tyulkina 2015a: 55n11). It could, for example, ban such parties outright. It could overtly discriminate against such parties – by denying them campaign funding on an equal basis with other parties, for example. Or it could impose regulations on such parties that, while facially neutral, pose special problems for them. This is effectively what the UK's Equality and Human Rights Commission (EHRC) did when it forced the British National Party (BNP) to amend its membership rules, which excluded non-whites (Kirshner 2014: 61–62). Obviously, interventions of this sort pose challenges only to racist parties.

Most militant democrats admit that democracies must proceed cautiously in deploying militant measures. All citizens in a democracy – including those who may hold political views hostile to democracy – have rights to political participation, and militant democracy practices may potentially trespass on those rights. Moreover, those practices may backfire. Politicians, after all, are not angels, and established political actors may use militant measures against newcomers to the political scene, not to combat extremism or preserve democracy, but to entrench themselves by restricting legitimate forms of competition (Tyulkina 2015a: 29).

For this reason, militant democrats must proceed with caution, with a continuous recognition of the potential benefits and costs of anti-extremist measures. They can display this caution in several ways. One way to do this is to target specific identifiable weaknesses in existing democratic institutions, and craft militant democracy measures to combat these weaknesses. Democracies, after all, have strong points and weak points. Certain institutional features of democracy may encourage the growth of extremism. Other features may enhance the ability of extremist parties to harm the democratic system or prevent established actors from moving against rising extremist forces until it is too late. Some have argued, for example, that proportional representation encouraged the rise of Nazism in the Weimar Republic, by paralysing the government and leaving it unable either to combat extremism directly or to solve the social problems contributing to the rise of that extremism (Hermens 1941). This claim is highly disputable, but, if it were true, it would suggest an obvious area in which militant democrats should concentrate their attention, either by opposing proportional representation or by identifying ways in which its extremist-friendly properties could be counteracted.

In short, militant democrats display proper respect for the potential dangers inherent in militant democracy by working to strengthen democracy at its weakest points. This chapter identifies one such weak point in the contemporary practice of voting. This practice obviously lies at the heart of modern democracy; unlike proportional representation, it can be found in every modern system calling itself democratic. And so, identifying the specific ways in which the practice of voting (especially under the Australian, or 'secret', ballot) constitutes a weak point is of critical importance to any theory of militant democracy. If militant democrats properly understand how extremist parties can exploit the voting process, then they will be equipped to devise ways in which to minimise the possibility of this exploitation. There is probably no way to insulate a democracy's voting system (or any other part of its democratic process) from extremist threats without compromising its democratic nature. But there may be ways to minimise the extent of this compromise and maximise the insulation effected.

Section 2 examines the practice of voting. It argues that the practice is in tension with the foundations of democracy, in ways that leave room for the growth of extremism. Section 3 then considers several possible institutional remedies for this deficiency. The chapter concludes by emphasising the importance of deliberation to democracy – not only for its own sake, but for the contribution it can make to militant democracy.

The Two Faces of Voting

Modern democracies elect most significant political officials via voting, under something resembling universal adult suffrage. All citizens are eligible to vote, and it is the votes, within a system of electoral rules,[2] which determine which political officials are selected. Modern democracies employ other selection methods as well. Sometimes they allow political officials or civil servants to select certain types of officials, notably agency heads and judges. At other times they dispense with elections entirely and allow voters to decide directly through procedures of initiative and referendum.[3] Rarely, they select officials randomly; this is particularly the case with juries, although randomly-selected mini-publics or citizen juries are playing an increasingly prominent role (more on that later). But election remains the central method of modern democracy; it is free and fair elections of leading political officials that distinguish democracy from its rivals today.[4]

In an election, citizens take part on an equal basis. Each citizen is entitled to one vote, and each citizen's vote counts equally. The identity of the voter, as well as her or his various personal qualities – race, gender, sexual orientation, political opinions, etc. – do not matter for purposes of the election; all that matters is her or his vote. One could permute the votes cast in a particular election[5] any which way one likes, assigning the ballot of voter x to voter y, the ballot of voter y to voter z, etc., and the outcome of the election will remain the same.[6] This rule is not a necessary property of voting rules. It is perfectly possible to imagine a system in which the votes of, say, graduates of elite universities count for more than those of other, less-educated voters.[7] But today such a system is widely regarded as anathema, as fundamentally undemocratic. In a democracy, each vote is supposed to count equally in an election. The question, then, is *why*?

There is no universally accepted theory of democracy in the political theory world today. Most political theorists, however, identify democracy as a practice having an intrinsic, non-instrumental[8] value. This value is generally cashed out in terms of a conception of *democratic equality*. According to such a conception, all citizens are to be regarded as equal partners in the enterprise of governing the polity in which they live.[9] Some of them may be smarter than others, others may have more skills or education or wealth, but *qua* citizens all of them have equal entitlements as participants in the political process. As such, all citizens possess certain fundamental rights. Many[10] of those rights enable their participation in political decision making, such as the right to (political) speech and the right to petition the government. The right to vote is a quintessential example of such a right. Whatever their other differences, citizens are equal when it comes to voting. The fact that each citizen's voice counts equally in the voting process is an expression of this fundamental democratic equality.

None of this is to say that democracy requires the widespread use of elections. As noted before (note 4), democracies in the distant past made relatively little use of elections (but when they did, it was usually consonant with the demands of democratic equality). Other small-scale democracies have relied heavily upon direct democratic participation. Democracy does not require elections, but it does require than when elections are used, they respect democratic equality by ensuring that all votes play an equal role in determining electoral outcomes.

Democratic equality is thus the key value that underlies elections, as well as other democratic practices. It is this value that explains why certain institutions, including elections, count as democratic, and more importantly, what gives them their *value* from a democratic perspective. Majority rule, deprived of any other context, is as stupid as it sounds. The same applies to any other democratic decision-making rule.[11] In a democracy, the many are not supposed to win and the few not are supposed to lose merely because the former can, by virtue of their numbers, force the latter to comply.[12] Rather, elections are justified because they are an appropriate way for democratic citizens to come together as equals and assign public responsibilities. The use of such procedures constitutes an expression of a polity's commitment to democratic equality.

A polity that values democratic equality is thus committed to elections in which citizens take part as equals. They are equally part of a joint project for determining how their society is to be run. And a critical part of that determination is the selection of certain types of political officials. Elections provide a method for citizens to select these officials in accordance with democratic equality. In doing so, they allow citizens the opportunity to offer their best judgements regarding which officials should serve the polity. Citizens are entitled to make this judgement any way they wish, using whatever criteria seem to them most reasonable. This is a critical component of the democratic part of the system. Bernard Manin defended this point in his book *The Principles of Representative Government*. Elections, according to Manin, have a democratic and an aristocratic component. They are partially aristocratic because, by their very nature, they involve judging some citizens more fit than others to hold office. They are partially democratic because they allow each citizen to decide for her-/himself what this 'fitness' involves. This is part of what distinguishes an election from, say, a civil service examination (Manin 1997).[13]

A polity may not always be justified in selecting officials in a manner that reflects both of these components. Where the aristocratic component is not justified, sortition makes more sense, as it reflects a stronger commitment to equality, one that does not recognise some as better suited for office than others (Stone 2016). Where the democratic component is not justified, there exist some objective grounds for selection that preclude allowing

individuals to select on any basis they please. Something like a civil service examination is appropriate under such conditions. But when a polity
decides to fill a particular office via election it thereby expresses a belief
that the two components are appropriate to the circumstances. The decision
does not make sense otherwise.

When an election takes place, citizens may be justified in judging one
candidate more fit for office than another according to any criteria they
think relevant. This does not mean, however, that they are justified in voting any way they please. Elections entrust voters with a specific form of
public service. Voters serve the public by identifying, as best they can, the
best candidate for office. That candidate will be the one best qualified to
contribute to the ongoing project of citizens governing themselves under a
relationship of equality. By assumption, some candidates will do this better
than others. There may be no way to specify a clear formula for evaluating
candidate qualifications. But this does not mean that there are not good or
bad choices. And a voter fails to perform her or her duty to the public when
she or he fails to evaluate candidates properly.[14]

A voter could fail to perform this duty in two different ways. First, she
or he could fail to scrutinise candidate qualifications in a reasonable manner. She or he could decide flippantly, without paying serious attention
to the election or the candidates featured in it. It is difficult to specify just
what would count as a reasonable level of scrutiny on the part of a voter.
From a purely instrumental perspective, even a public-spirited voter cannot justify scrutinising candidates carefully before voting – or even voting
at all, for that matter. One vote, in a mass election involving thousands or
millions of voters, is almost certain not to be decisive.[15] This is the phenomenon Anthony Downs identified as 'rational ignorance' (Downs 1957).[16]
It does not depend upon voters being stupid – quite the contrary. Ignor-
ing instrumental considerations like these completely would represent
'hyperrationality' on the voter's part (Elster 1989). But non-instrumental
considerations, such as a commitment to public service, may reasonably
lead citizens both to vote and to pay attention to elections. (Indeed, some
such non-instrumental considerations must be involved. People do, after
all, vote.[17]) There is a limit to how much scrutiny even public-spirited citizens should reasonably bring to elections, given their miniscule chances of
influencing the result. But the proper level of scrutiny is well above zero,
and voters who fail to attain it are failing to do their jobs.[18]

Second, a voter could pursue ends unconnected to the goal of the voting
process. This goal, which follows from the demands of democratic equality,
is to contribute to the ongoing project of self-government, the government
of a society of free and equal citizens, by selecting officials most likely to

protect and advance such a government. Obviously, there are many other goals a voter might advance in casting her or his vote. A voter might vote for the candidate most likely to provide personal benefits – through pork barrel projects targetted at the voter's constituency, for example. Or a voter might vote for the candidate who favours citizens like her-/himself. Such a candidate does not work for the ongoing project of self-government among free and equal citizens. Instead, the candidate treats only some citizens ('real Americans') as full members of the project, with others of lesser or no consequence. The voter who votes this way fails to act in a manner consistent with democratic equality, the value that justifies the equal right to vote in the first place.

Democratic equality, then, explains why every citizen in a democracy should enjoy the equal right to vote in an election (assuming that the democracy believes an election is justified for a particular office). Democratic equality further enjoins the voter against using that vote any which way she or he pleases. In effect, a democracy entrusts each voter with a mission, a job to perform, just as it entrusts other officials (selected through election or sortition or whatever) with jobs to perform. The fact that the office of 'voter' is not one voluntarily assumed by citizens is irrelevant to this point (Stone 2016). At the same time, voting by its very nature empowers the voter to carry out this mission in whatever manner she or he thinks appropriate. The voter must exercise her or his best judgement in selecting candidates according to the demands of democratic equality. But the process of exercising judgement is not visible in the election – the votes are. The vote itself provides no clear evidence as to whether citizens performed their duties satisfactorily or not. Furthermore, there is no sanction imposed upon citizens for poor use of their judgement in voting (just as there is no sanction for juries who acquit or convict in a questionable manner.) In that regard, the voter's judgement truly is sovereign, however badly she or he employs it.

In contemporary democracies, voting is almost always combined with the Australian (or 'secret') ballot,[19] by which the votes citizens cast are never made public. The public never learns how any specific voter voted, although it of course learns the total numbers of votes received by each candidate. While the Australian ballot is not specifically demanded by the logic of voting, it is fully compatible with this logic. This does not mean, however, that the practice is required by the value of democratic equality – indeed, there may be times when democratic equality demands 'unveiling' the vote (Brennan and Pettit 1990), a topic considered further in the next section.

The process of voting, whether accompanied by the Australian ballot or not, is a natural expression of democratic equality. This does not, however, mean that the process generates no dangers for democracy. In a mass election, the process whereby voters reach their judgements regarding candidates may be completely opaque. This opacity provides an opening for extremist parties into the democratic process. Such parties, by their very nature, reject the value of democratic equality upon which democratic political systems rest. As a result, a vote for such a party is by definition incompatible with this value. Each citizen, however, votes according to her or his own personal judgement, a judgement rendered invisible both by the nature of the voting process (which allows her or him to vote any way she or he wishes) and by the Australian ballot (which renders her or his specific vote invisible). Citizens are thus placed in a position whereby their votes can empower extremist parties. This runs counter to the value of democratic equality that justifies voting in the first place, but the voting process does not in itself generate any obstacles to this. This constitutes the heart of the danger of democratic 'autophagy' – the danger that an electorate may employ its votes to elect a government committed to abolishing the democracy. The electoral success of extremist parties represents a serious failure, on the part of voters, to respect democratic equality – even though this success is made possible by the democratic equality those voters enjoy.

Protecting Democracy from Elections

The electoral process – a process whereby citizens employ their judgement to select candidates for political office, a judgement 'veiled' by the Australian ballot – is subject to potential exploitation by political extremists. This poses dangers to democracy, up to and including the extinction of the democracy itself. Elections generate only one barrier against political extremism – the good judgement of the voters themselves. Under ordinary circumstances, this will be sufficient – no democracy could survive any length of time if it was not.[20] But when democracies come under strain, other measures may prove necessary. Hence the potential contribution of militant democracy measures. Such measures, however, should be carefully tailored to the dangers they seek to prevent; otherwise, they risk becoming the democratic cure that is worse than the disease. This concluding section, then, examines several countermeasures a democracy could employ against the risks posed by the nature of the electoral process, as well as their expected benefits and costs.

Militant democracy measures can be distinguished along several different dimensions. They can be *targeted* or *untargeted*, *soft* or *hard*, and focused on either the *demand* or the *supply* side of electoral politics. Targeted measures explicitly single out extremists for negative attention;

untargeted measures are facially neutral but affect extremists more strongly than anyone else. Hard measures either ban or require certain activities; soft measures induce good behaviour without commands or prohibitions.[21] Supply-side measures focus on potentially threatening political parties or movements; demand-side measures focus on the citizens who might be attracted to them.

This chapter will not attempt to classify and analyse every proposed militant democracy measure, even those focused upon the electoral process. Nor will it draw sweeping generalisations as to the types of measures a militant democracy can employ. Such measures, like many democratic institutional mechanisms, are highly context-dependent. It is therefore difficult to recommend one bundle of features in the abstract. About the only generalisation I will offer here is that other things being equal, untargeted measures are better than targeted measures. By definition, targeted measures must single out particular parties or citizens in order to take action against them. This process is easily subject to abuse by political actors, and even when it is not abused it can potentially cast a negative shadow upon political activity that discourages legitimate as well as illegitimate political activity. Instead of generalisations, I will focus my analysis upon several specific militant democracy measures to see what they might offer, under the right circumstances, in terms of combating the dangers of extremism in electoral politics.

Perhaps the most obvious way to protect against citizens voting for anti-democratic parties is to prevent those parties from running for office in the first place. Democracies can ban extremist political parties from competing in elections. This option – which is *targeted, hard* and *supply-side* – is perhaps more associated with the idea of militant democracy than any other (Tyulkina 2015a: 19). But while this may be the most obvious option, it is also one of the most controversial. Party bans cut against the right of political association that stands at the very heart of democracy.[22] Moreover, powerful political parties can exploit party bans to marginalise or eliminate their political opponents. Given these risks, this is a weapon of militant democracy that should be employed sparingly, or not at all.

A democracy can, of course, impose restrictions upon extremist political parties short of outright prohibitions (Tyulkina 2015a: 87–88). These (targeted, supply-side) restrictions can be hard or soft. One option is to restrict the types of political appeals a party can make during a political campaign. India, for example, bans parties from campaigning on the basis of racism or other forms of bigotry, even though it allows racist statements from parties outside of the campaign season (Tyulkina 2015a: chapter 6).[23] As with party bans, such measures are at least partially consistent with the spirit of democratic equality; they prevent parties from seeking votes in a manner contrary to the values which justifies the voting in the first place. The effectiveness of such measures, however, is again a subject of dispute; India has not been particularly successful at damping down Hindu extremism. It is hardly surprising that such measures should prove of limited effectiveness. If such measures are applied outside political campaigns, then they effectively become bans on hate speech, another controversial tool of democratic societies. If they are not so applied, then they merely require racist parties to pretend not to be racist for short periods of time. And once again, such restrictions are subject to abuse by political parties eager to hamstring potential competition.

Both party bans and party restrictions target parties representing values that are at odds with the value of democratic equality – the value which justifies, among other practices, elections. Both pose intrinsic and instrumental dangers to democracy – intrinsic because they affect the right of political participation, and instrumental because they are subject to abuse. Both types of danger result from the fact that these practices single out some types of parties and not others – in other words, that they are targeted measures.[24] It is in the interest of democracy for polities to draw as few distinctions as possible between different types of party. The whole point of an election, after all, is to allow the voters to decide, using their own judgement, who is to hold office. While there is no reason to assume that this judgement should be unlimited, attempts to restrict this judgement – to decide for the voters who is worthy of election – are worth keeping as a last resort. It is therefore important to ask whether untargeted measures – measures that do not distinguish 'good' and 'bad' political parties – can provide sufficient protection for democracies against extremism.

Both party bans and restrictions on party activity attempt to preserve democracy by directly reducing the supply of anti-democratic political activity. The natural alternative to reducing the supply is reducing the demand – decreasing the number of people led to support such parties. This method has the advantage that it can be done without singling out any particular party. There are several measures a democracy could take which affect voters. Perhaps the most obvious of these measures (untargeted, soft) is to eliminate the Australian ballot – to 'unveil' the vote and make citizen vote choices public. This option is endorsed by Geoffrey Brennan and Philip Pettit, who see in it a way to encourage citizens to vote in a 'discursively defensible manner' (Brennan and Pettit 1990: 311). This generates a soft form of accountability, by creating circumstances under which citizens feel pressure not to vote in ways indefensible to their fellow citizens. Unfortunately, this proposal encourages other forms of citizen responsiveness to outside forces, many of them not so pretty. Without the secret ballot, voters become susceptible to bribes or threats from interested parties. The dangers to democracy posed by such forces in a world where votes are public – especially when there are extremist, potentially violent political parties on the rise – easily outweigh the potential benefits from increased publicity in such a world.[25]

The remaining (soft, untargeted) measures to be considered all involve increasing the likelihood of meaningful deliberation on the part of voters. Deliberation can have positive instrumental effects, especially in the face of diversity, which can enable the 'wisdom of crowds' (Surowiecki 2005; see also Landemore 2012). But more fundamentally, deliberation is of great intrinsic importance to democracy. A critically important way that citizens demonstrate respect for each other as equal participants in the democratic project is by giving reasons for the democratic decisions they favour and listening to the reasons offered in return (Cohen 1989). As a result, deliberation, like majority rule, has a natural connection to democratic equality (although the exact nature of the connection remains underspecified, and worthy of further study).

Moreover, deliberation generates a form of accountability among voters, or at least those who participate in the deliberative process. Deliberation does more than simply provide voters with access to information and reasons for and against the options facing them. It also introduces the 'civilizing force of hypocrisy' into the political process (Elster 1998). The deliberative process forces its participants to put forth reasons for their positions in terms they could reasonably expect others to accept. By this process's very nature, it rules out naked appeals to self-interest, group chauvinism, etc. But it is psychologically uncomfortable to put forward reasons which one simply doesn't believe. The process of putting forth reasons thereby generates a form of pressure upon people to act in accordance with the reasons they provide.[26] The result might not be the hard form of accountability created via formal sanctions, but it still involves real costs becoming attached to undesirable forms of behaviour. This is a soft form of accountability, but it is a form of accountability nonetheless.[27]

Deliberation does not favour all parties equally. Extremist parties rely heavily upon demagogy, including fearmongering and crude appeals of loyalty to clan, caste, nationality, race or religion. This fact was recognised from the start by militant democrats. Karl Loewenstein, for example, associated democracy with reason and fascism with emotionalism (Loewenstein 1937a, 1937b). For Loewenstein, this connection was sufficiently powerful as to provide potential justifications for restrictions on democratic participation. A technocratic regime, argued Loewenstein, still counts as 'democratic' because of its reliance upon reason (and the presumably benevolent intentions of the technocrats running it). Democratic theorists today, by contrast, view technocracy as a clear breach of democratic norms, although possibly a necessary one under the right circumstances. They also view mass participation and reason as much more compatible than Loewenstein did. Nevertheless, most democratic theorists today accept the association of emotionalism with democratic extremism, and reasoned deliberation with democratic equality.[28] They recognise that deliberation among equals can potentially disarm the most potent mechanisms by which extremists build mass support. On a playing field based upon the respectful exchange of reasons, extremists are at a definite disadvantage.

All of this suggests that democratic deliberation, among its other virtues, has the advantage of increasing the likelihood that voters will vote in a manner compatible with the value of democratic equality. A militant democracy, then, should seek to enable citizen deliberation whenever it can do so at reasonable costs. Many sceptics have noted the significant costs associated with mass deliberation, but there are some proposals for promoting deliberation on the table that may prove cost-effective. At the one end are proposals to create forums for mass deliberation directly. Bruce Ackerman and James Fishkin's 'deliberation day' is one such proposal (Ackerman and Fishkin 2004). Such forums are obviously expensive and can be criticised for mobilising exactly the sort of concerned citizens least likely to benefit from added deliberation. There may be other methods of increasing deliberation that cost less and that reach a wider spectrum of voters.

One alternative method of encouraging mass deliberation makes use of deliberative forums on a smaller scale. Randomly-selected mini-publics,[29] which bring together cross-sections of the polity to deliberate about one or more public issues, are classic examples of this. The empirical literature on such mini-publics suggests that they are indeed capable of generating high-quality deliberation. But all this deliberation can accomplish little if the broader public is not paying attention. The contribution of mini-publics thus depends heavily upon the extent to which other public institutions, such as political parties and the mass media, serve as 'transmission belts' to the public by raising awareness of mini-publics and the conclusions they reach.[30]

If randomly-selected mini-publics do so well at encouraging deliberation, perhaps they can play more ambitious roles in the political process. One such role is that of 'guardian of the political process' (Delannoi, Dowlen and Stone 2013). Mini-publics could be employed to create and enforce the rules of the political game – for example, the rules governing legislative ethics. Such tasks cry out for an agent above the fray of day-to-day politics; mini-publics definitely fit the bill. Mini-publics could also undertake tasks more directly tied to militant democracy. They could, for example, be used to judge whether extremist parties had broken the rules of the political game (e.g. through hate speech). Indeed, if a militant democracy feels compelled to resort to hard measures against political parties – for example, party bans – it would be well advised to consider employing mini-publics to enforce these measures. Doing so would minimise the chance of such measures being abused by established political actors.

Perhaps the most extreme proposals along these lines would substitute randomly-selected mini-publics for the electorate as a whole. This could be done in two ways. One is the 'enfranchisement lottery', in which only a randomly-selected subset of eligible voters receives the chance to vote in an election (López-Guerra 2010). The other is to dispense with elections entirely for certain offices and entrust mini-publics with tasks normally reserved for elected officials. This could mean creating randomly-selected mini-publics to work alongside elected legislatures and other elected officials in the policy-making process (e.g. Leib 2004; Barnett and Carty 2008; Callenbach and Phillips 2008; Sutherland 2008; Buchstein and Hein 2009; Zakaras 2010; Guerrero 2014). Or it could mean eliminating elections entirely, and relying exclusively upon randomly-selected officials, although this position has few proponents (but see Burnheim 2006).

Obviously, when mini-publics substitute for elected legislatures, either partially or entirely, the opportunity for electorates to be seduced by extremist parties disappears. Moreover, the deliberative nature of mini-publics renders them less susceptible to similar forms of seduction. The delegation of decision making to a mini-public in effect shrinks the size of the electorate. With a small number of voters (a few hundred at most), meaningful deliberation – a force anathema to demagoguery – becomes much easier to ensure. Even if participants cannot be forced to speak their minds, they can be required to attend mini-public meetings at which arguments are exchanged. And if they choose to participate, then the civilising force of hypocrisy kicks in, by both limiting the arguments they can reasonably make and then generating internal pressure to conform to the arguments made.

Bypassing the electorate in this manner is potentially compatible with democratic equality on two grounds. First, both universal suffrage and the random selection of mini-publics assume that each voter has an equal claim upon casting a vote in the decision-making process. Under universal suffrage, every citizen's claim can be satisfied; when a mini-public is employed, only a small subset of the claims can be satisfied. So long as a lottery is used to select participants for the mini-publics, the underlying conception of democratic equality remains the same in both cases (Stone 2016). Second, random sampling is capable of generating a sample that statistically resembles the population as a whole to a high degree of accuracy.[31] To the extent that the mini-public 'looks like' the public as a whole, the former shares in the legitimacy enjoyed by the latter.[32] These arguments are independent of each other, and neither commands universal assent in the democratic theory literature,[33] but either would be sufficient to justify this form of electoral shrinkage (setting aside other potential benefits of mass electoral participation, such as increased political legitimacy).

Despite all this, many militant democrats might balk at the idea of replacing elected legislatures with randomly-selected ones, even if elected legislatures work alongside them. (Loewenstein himself might not have had such reservations, at least if the replacement generated a more deliberative and rational politics.) As noted before, elections have an inherently aristocratic component; they are supposed to select the *best* officials, on the assumption that not just any citizen will suffice. Replacing elected decision-making bodies with randomly-selected ones would mean giving up on this aristocratic component.

The enfranchisement lottery avoids this problem. It retains elections, entrusting ordinary citizens with the selection of the best officials. But it entrusts this responsibility, not to the entire electorate, but to a random sample selected from it. Reliance upon a random sample, I would argue, respects the democratic equality that voters enjoy just as much as reliance upon the entire electorate. But the reduction of the size of the electing body makes meaningful deliberation a much more realistic possibility.

Whether this advantage suffices to justify the enfranchisement lottery depends critically upon the purpose(s) to be served by election. If the sole purpose of an election is to select the best officials, while resisting the siren song of extremist forces, then election under enfranchisement lottery might well outperform mass election. But if elections serve other purposes as well – if they are necessary, for example, to generate mass consent to election outcomes – then the enfranchisement lottery may well not suffice. The case for the enfranchisement lottery, then, depends crucially upon the full theory of democracy upon which elections are to be grounded.

I conclude not by endorsing any particular militant democracy measure but by emphasising the importance of deliberation to militant democracy. Deliberation has received a great deal of attention in recent years as a vital component of democratic equality. At the same time, sceptics often deny that meaningful deliberation can play a central role in a large-scale democracy. This chapter offers an additional reason for opposing such scepticism. Deliberation is not only valuable as a component of democratic equality, it also generates a unique barrier against political extremism, which by its very nature does not thrive under the cool glare of reasoned argument between political equals. This barrier is all-the-more necessary due to the specific vulnerability to extremism created in democracies by electoral politics. And while other barriers against extremism can be created in the electoral process, many of them have the potential to compromise the democratic equality which justifies their imposition. Deliberation, by contrast, not only fails to compromise democratic equality, by its very nature it advances that equality. The methods of institutionalising deliberation in mass democracy discussed here are but examples; other possibilities can be imagined. Militant democrats would do well to prioritise analysing these methods, as they could potentially strengthen modern democracy at one of its weakest points.

Notes

* An earlier version of this chapter was presented at Workshop WS20: 'Should the People Rule? Conceptualizing Democratic Institutions', Joint Sessions of Workshops, European Consortium for Political Research, 10–14 April 2018. This chapter was drafted during time spent at Stanford University as a visiting scholar. I am grateful to everyone at the political science department there – especially Josh Ober – for making the visit possible. Work on this chapter was supported by a grant from the Arts and Social Sciences Benefaction Fund at Trinity College Dublin.

1. I use the term 'militant democracy' to refer to a democratic regime featuring some set of anti-extremist practices. A 'militant democrat' is someone who advocates militant democracy – who believes that democracies should be militant. A theory of militant democracy purports to explain why and how militancy is appropriate for democracies. There are alternative understandings of militant democracy. Malkopoulou and Norman (2018: 442), for example, use the term 'democratic self-defence' to describe democratic anti-extremist practices in general. They confine the term 'militant democracy' to those forms of democratic self-defence that place 'a fundamentally anti-participatory and elitist logic at the centre of anti-extremist politics, one that identified political participation of the masses as an intrinsic part of the problem' (p. 444). I do not employ this more restrictive definition here.

2. Those rules may, of course, prevent voters from electing certain types of candidates, such as representatives of extremist parties. This is a key militant democracy measure.

3. Elsewhere, I argue that democratic citizenship should be viewed as a type of political office, charged with such responsibilities as electing officials and making decisions through referenda (Stone 2016).

4. This has not always been the case. Ancient democracies relied centrally upon *sortition*, or the random selection of political officials. This was so much the case

that Aristotle associates sortition with election and election with aristocracy. On the replacement of sortition with election in the democratic imagination, see Manin (1997).

5. I assume, of course, an election within a well-defined constituency. Obviously, in an election with multiple constituencies, things work somewhat differently. My opinions regarding the candidates of other constituencies do not affect the outcome of the election at all – only my opinions regarding the candidates of my own constituency matter. The problem of constituency definition is particularly vexing to contemporary political science (Rehfeld 2005).

6. In terms of social choice theory, election rules routinely satisfy the *anonymity* condition. This condition must not be confused with the *neutrality* condition, under which the identity of the option for which votes are cast does not matter. There is no necessary relationship between these two conditions. See Austen-Smith and Banks (2000: chapter 3).

7. Great Britain did, in fact, employ a similar scheme until 1948, permitting university graduates to cast votes for parliament in multiple constituencies. This scheme is sometimes mistakenly identified with that of John Stuart Mill, who did favour weighted votes for the well-educated (Thompson 2015: 101).

8. This is not to deny democracy's instrumental value. Amartya Sen, for example, famously argued that elections enable voters to punish governments that fail to prevent disastrous outcomes, such as famines (Sen 1983).

9. Cf. the distinction drawn by Joshua Cohen between a democratic form of government and a democratic society, in which the latter is characterised by a condition of equality (Cohen 2003: §2.2).

10. Political equality may entail other equal rights – for example, the right to be left alone in matters of deep personal significance, such as religion. Joshua Cohen cashes this idea out in contractarian terms. No citizen could reasonably agree to a political system which offered no guarantees regarding freedom of religion and similar 'non-political' rights (Cohen 1994: §II.A.3).

11. It is arguable whether democratic equality requires any specific voting rule, beyond merely requiring that all votes count equally. Majority rule certainly has many desirable properties (May 1952), and some have argued that majority rule is a uniquely democratic way of making decisions (e.g. Schwartzberg 2013). But it is difficult to extend majority rule to three or more options without allowing arbitrary factors to shape the outcome, at least in part (Riker 1982). The argument presented here does not turn on this point.

12. This is not typically how the world works. Quite the contrary – governments are routinely controlled by organised minorities that enforce their will upon disorganised majorities. But critics of democracy often view it as simply the mirror image of this. This is the picture of democracy that lies behind complaints of ochlocracy, or 'mob rule'. A democracy is supposed to represent something more than that.

13. Manin focused upon representation, but his argument applies to elective offices that may not be properly described as representative – to elected presidents, for example.

14. A conception of democratic equality thus imposes restrictions, not simply upon how a democracy should make decisions but upon the types of decisions it should make. To this extent, at least, any satisfactory democratic theory – and theory resting upon a conception of democratic equality – must be both procedural and substantive. See Cohen (1994, 2003) on this point. Tyulkina (2015a: 37) points out the relevance of this idea for militant democracy.

15. Although the 2017 state legislative elections for the Commonwealth of Virginia demonstrate that single votes definitely can have an impact. In those elections, which unexpectedly put control over the Virginia House of Delegates into contention, one race resulted in a tie, requiring the winner to be selected randomly. See Trip Gabriel, 'Virginia officials pull Republican's name from bowl to pick winner of tied race', *The New York Times*, 4 January 2018, https://www.nytimes.com/2018/01/04/us/virginia-tie.html. Ties do take place in elections (Stone 2011: §1.1) but they are still quite uncommon, especially when the number of voters is large.

16. The extent of rational ignorance can be exaggerated, even if the phenomenon clearly exists. Voters can, to some extent at least, rely upon cues from better-informed sources. See Lupia and McCubbins (1998).

17. Citizens seem to vote at least partially out of a desire to express either certain political commitments or a certain political identity. See Brennan and Lomasky (1997). For an argument that political scientists have neglected political identity as a critical factor in determining voting behaviour, see Achen and Bartels (2016).

18. This raises a question of non-ideal theory – whether it is better for ill-informed voters to vote at all. Jason Brennan (2009, 2011) argues forcefully that they should not. For a response to Brennan, see Arvan (2010).

19. What one might call 'veiled' voting (cf. Brennan and Pettit 1990).

20. This barrier may be a particularly uncertain if the democracy is new or in the process of being institutionalised. Not surprisingly, many political scientists view militant democracy measures as most appropriate for newly-formed democracies (e.g. Tyulkina 2015a).

21. Cf. the distinction drawn by Tyulkina (2015a: 19) between 'direct' measures, which 'prohibit certain actions against democracy or impose obligations to identify those actions in a preventative way as well as to promote pro-democratic beliefs and attitudes', and 'indirect' measures, which 'modify rules concerning decision-making'.

22. It is, however, unclear just how far this right of political participation extends. Kirshner (2014) argues forcefully for a (non-absolute) right to vote for extremist political parties, arguing for it in terms of the 'right to do wrong' (Waldron 1981). But political rights, unlike civil rights, directly impact upon the rights of

others. There is no way for you to put a Nazi into office without impacting my rights. Space prohibits further consideration of this problem here.

23. Many Eastern European countries, by contrast, take the opposite approach, imposing no specific restrictions upon parties but prohibiting hate speech both inside and outside the campaign season (Tyulkina 2015a: 92).

24. A militant democracy could in theory target *citizens* as well as parties – by banning certain citizens from voting or running for office, for example. The objections offered here against targeting parties apply even more strongly against targeting citizens.

25. Brennan and Pettit are shockingly dismissive of the possibility of large-scale bribery and intimidation under public voting. Such an attitude may conceivably have been justified given the relatively healthy state of democracy in 1990, but it is certainly not justified now.

26. At the very least, people do not want to be caught acting in ways inconsistent with the arguments they have made. Even when people are content to be hypocrites, they do not like to be called out as hypocrites. But determining whether citizens have voted in ways inconsistent with their expressed reasons would require 'unveiling the vote' (see above).

27. Deliberation is primarily a demand-side tactic; it leads voters to vote more responsibility and to be less susceptible to demagogic appeals. But it can have knock-on effects on the supply side. The civilising force of hypocrisy works on parties as well as voters. If demagogic appeals are less likely to work, then would-be demagogues might become less likely to make them. Extremist parties, in a deliberative polity, would presumably have to couch their rhetoric in more reasonable-sounding and less 'raw' terms to have any chance of success. This might not eliminate the threat of such parties completely, but it would raise the overall tone of the political conversation.

28. The latter association is probably more controversial than the former one. Some political theorists (e.g. Sanders 1997) argue that the emphasis upon deliberation in democratic decision making works against marginalised groups lacking in deliberative skills.

29. The term 'mini-public' was first employed by Fung (2003) in a more inclusive manner than I employ here. Goodin and Dryzek (2006) narrowed the focus to something like what I have in mind. Fung drew upon the work of Dahl (1989), who used the term 'minipopulus'.

30. Farrell (2013: 114) argues that Ireland's Convention on the Constitution was successful as a mini-public precisely because it included elected officials alongside randomly-selected ordinary citizens. This resulted in politicians with an investment in the outcome of the Convention giving them serious reason to champion its results. This may have influenced the successful referendum on behalf of marriage equality that endorsed the Convention's recommendations.

31. This will be the case so long as either participation in the mini-publics is mandatory or stratified random sampling is employed. The latter, while often employed by real-life mini-publics, compromises the first form of compatibility between

mini-publics and electorates, as different citizens in effect wind up with different chances of being selected.

32. This argument is critical to James Fishkin's case for 'deliberative opinion polls' (Fishkin 1993, 1995, 2011). For a critique of Fishkin, see Garry, Stevenson and Stone (2015).

33. For a general argument that defenders of mini-publics would do well to focus upon the first argument and not the second, see Delannoi, Dowlen and Stone (2013).

THREE

Militant Democracy Defended

Alexander S. Kirshner

Introduction

Article 21 of the German Basic Law (*Grundgesetz*) establishes that anti-democratic parties are unconstitutional, rendering them liable to be declared illegal and banned. The banning of a party is the paradigmatic example of militant democracy; it is the practice political theorists and constitutional lawyers have in mind when they write about militant democracy. And it's the practice critics of militant democracy focus on when they inveigh against it. There is, however, no reason to assume that party bans justified by reference to a group's beliefs are the only way to militantly defend democracy.

Consider the US Voting Rights Act of 1965 (the VRA). The US isn't considered home ground for militant democracy. But it has a well-known, frankly dispiriting, record of allowing groups and parties to weaken self-government. Those groups and parties have famously laboured to keep African-Americans and other minorities from exercising political power. The VRA was aimed directly at these practices; it was fashioned to secure democracy against an internal threat. And it did so via political restrictions. It famously blocked certain states and localities from establishing their own electoral policies. Jurisdictions that had thwarted minorities' capacity to vote in the past were required to have changes to their electoral laws pre-cleared with the Federal Department of Justice or a federal court, specifically the DC District Court. Those bodies would determine whether the electoral laws had a discriminatory purpose or would have a discriminatory effect.[1] In this way, the VRA's restrictions prevented further anti-democratic activity. The VRA is clearly a militant policy.

The VRA boasts several elements that ought to be of interest to students of militant democracy. First, its restrictions were not enforced on the basis of a group's ideology or beliefs – i.e. the target was not parties claiming to be anti-democratic. Instead restrictions were established in response to actions, actions intended to establish or actually establishing discriminatory limits on individuals' capacity to participate. Second, neither its creation nor enforcement were advanced by the unchecked decision of an executive. It was developed and adopted by the US Congress, which readopted it several times. And the law is applied by legal professionals, whose decisions are subject to legal review. Third, the VRA's manifest success demonstrates that militant policies can work (Davidson and Grofman 1994; Lublin 2007). By 'work', I do not mean that no one still seeks to disenfranchise African-Americans – such a claim is obviously false (*N.C. State Conference of the NAACP v. McCrory*, 831 F.3d 204 (4th Cir. 2016)). Instead, I mean that it made the US more democratic – the US features fewer discriminatory practices as a result of the law. Fourth, beyond its practical effects, the policy and its repeated reauthorisation amounted to a public political sign that discriminatory disenfranchisement was intolerable. Finally, the policy reflects a concern for the interests of citizens targeted by discriminatory laws *and* for citizens whose preferred electoral rules are rejected via the VRA. For instance, jurisdictions subject to pre-clearance could challenge the decisions of the Justice Department. And citizens in those jurisdictions were not excluded from further participation even though they had attempted to undercut the rights of others. In this sense, the VRA was a compromise – an attempt to advance the legitimate interests of both democrats and anti-democrats.

It is my intuition that a militant policy of this sort, not a party ban, would avoid most of the critiques hurled against efforts to defend self-government. Further, I believe many of those opposed in principle to militant democracy would likely embrace the VRA. In my book, *A Theory of Militant Democracy: The Ethics of Combatting Political Extremism*, I investigated these intuitions, considering whether restrictive policies might be consistent with democratic principles and how those principles might in turn limit the practice (Kirshner 2014).[2]

Summarising roughly, I argued that those opposed to democracy possessed the same interests in participation as those who embraced it. Defensive action, in this view, would not be justified merely if opponents of democracy participated in political life. Instead, militant policies should block individuals from invidiously violating the democratic rights of others. And I argued that those policies should be informed by the paradox of militant democracy – the possibility that both inaction in the face of a threat to democratic rights *and* action taken in defence of those rights could leave a polity less democratic. Instances of the first problem arguably mark much of the history of the US – e.g. when anti-democratic actors kept African-Americans from participating and ostensible demo-crats did little to halt that villainy. Instances of the second problem occur when militant policies unjustifiably or disproportionately infringe on the legitimate moral interests of those subject to those policies – e.g. party bans that limit the participation of those who pose no threat to the dem-ocratic interests of others. I called this approach the *self-limiting theory of militant democracy*. By weighing the legitimate interests of both demo-crats and anti-democrats, one might successfully manage the challenges posed by the paradox of militant democracy. My project stands in sharp contrast to approaches calling for principled inaction no matter the toll, and to approaches demanding unyielding repression of those who do not espouse the democratic faith.

In the sections that follow I weigh several challenges to my approach to militant democracy. Unsurprisingly, I find all of them lacking. First, I con-sider the claim that militant policies are necessarily unfair to their targets. Anti-democrats are wronged, in this view, when the political process does not allow them to realise their goals. Second, I investigate whether norma-tive accounts of militant democracy are merely covers for the self-interested or merely arbitrary actions of political actors, actors whose true aim is not to expand or defend democracy but to hobble their opponents. Third, and finally, I consider whether the paradox of militant democracy might be resolved by recognising the weak foundations of the 'right to participate'. Some argue, for instance, that sortition-based or lottocratic systems may pro-vide a way out of the morass of militant democracy. Others claim that there is no 'paradox of militant democracy'. Anti-democrats, individuals who aim to wrong others, simply do not have a legitimate right to exercise power over others – i.e. a right to participate. They are not wronged when they are excluded from the political process. Before weighing these arguments, the next section briefly outlines my assumptions.

Assumptions

What is at stake when citizens are kept from participating fully in the demo-cratic process? By democratic process, I mean the familiar, flawed, competi-tive, roughly majoritarian political processes characterising actually existing democracies (often referred to as minimal democracies) (Przeworski 1999). For convenience, I will group the interests at stake into two broad categories: instrumental and intrinsic.

Instrumental interests concern the outcomes of political processes – like laws and judicial decisions. These interests include one's economic situation, one's legal capacity to follow a religion and so forth. There is a common, and I think wholly credible, belief that if groups are excluded from participating their instrumental interests are likely to suffer – i.e. since they are excluded no one will seek to advance their interests and others will seek to advance their own interests at the expense of the excluded.

Intrinsic interests are advanced because democratic processes have certain characteristics. They are not advanced because of the outcomes of those processes. Here are two examples. I believe citizens are equals, that no one is, intrinsically, the boss of anyone else. In other words, I believe in the import of relating to one another as equals (Anderson 1999). Given the coercive nature of political procedures, I believe citizens have an interest in political institutions that instantiate that idea. Individuals will therefore suffer in some important respect just in case members of one group possess two votes and members of another possess one vote. Advancing our interest in relational political equality does not turn on whether a particular decision is wise or good, but on how it is achieved – i.e. did everyone possess the same formal power over the outcome (Kolodny 2014; Viehoff 2014). Democratic processes also advance our interest in political agency, a second intrinsic interest (Stilz 2016). Just as we have an interest in making our own decisions, we have an interest in being able to justifiably view the political world, a world that makes legally obligatory demands on us, as, in part, of our own making. A key way in which we can exercise our agency is by formally participating in a political process – e.g. casting a vote, running for office and so on.

Intrinsic interests are advanced via political processes. But, obviously, individuals' opportunities to advance these interests can be undercut by those processes – e.g. a democratic decision might disenfranchise Jewish citizens. Political rules that block certain groups from participating keep them from advancing those interests – i.e. if the opportunity to formally participate in the political process, to vote, is essential to equal standing and you do not possess the opportunity to vote, then your interest in equality is not being advanced.

For the purposes of this chapter, I will assume that members of a political society have interests of roughly equal weight at stake in the political process (Brighouse and Fleurbaey 2010). I will assume further that we evaluate institutions for managing conflicts among individuals' interests via a roughly contractarian process of reflection – whether the institutions could be rejected reasonably (Scanlon 2000). Finally, I assume that, taken together, these assumptions, if defensible, would ground a claim or right to participate for democrats and anti-democrats alike.

Militant Democracy Wrongs Anti-Democrats

In my view, militant democrats are democrats. They accept that democrats and anti-democrats have the interests discussed above. They accept that advancing those interests requires the opportunity to contribute in meaningful ways to decision making about basic aspects of the life of the community. And they accept that citizens ought to have a wide range of ends they can advance through the political process. What is not required is a legal pathway to make any decision at all. In my view, for instance, your claim to participate is not burdened unjustifiably if you face a legal obstacle keeping you from unjustifiably burdening my democratic interests.

But some scholars suggest that equal interests in participation entail an equal claim to have one's projects realised as law or policy (Lenowitz 2015; Mudde 2015). In this view, as I understand it, the political system must be neutral among projects or plans in order for the political system to be democratic. If my particular project, say a system of universal healthcare, is not possible given the structure of the political system, then I am not being treated as an equal. Unlike others who might see the possibility of realising their political ends, I cannot. And this is wrong.

If correct, this would be a reason to think that policies associated with militant democracy, such as the VRA or bans on political parties, are undemocratic. The VRA blocked elected legislators from disenfranchising their fellow citizens – it was not neutral among political ends. And a party ban would also be subject to the same challenge. These policies keep actors from fully realising their goals through the political system. Therefore, such policies do not treat anti-democrats as full citizens.

Is that view correct? I don't see how it could be. The idea that a claim to participate requires a political system to make any outcome possible seems mistaken. One can imagine all sorts of non-institutional factors that limit possible outcomes. Suppose I was British. And suppose that I and a majority of my fellow citizens wanted a British person to be the first human to travel to the moon. Of course, Neil Armstrong, an American, was the first person to walk on the moon. Would my claim to participate, my right to rule, be diminished in any sense if my dream of British lunar dominance could not be achieved? Of course not. Any account of democracy that generated a positive answer to this question would find all political systems unbearably undemocratic. Simply put, no political system, no matter how ideal, can facilitate the achievement of any political outcome. This interpretation of political equality is broken.

Perhaps those who offer this argument have a different view in mind. The object of our interest should not be the actual likelihood of success but whether formal political institutions impact the likelihood of success. Formal political institutions should not make any political outcome more or less likely. But this too seems mistaken, clearly so.

Suppose I am subject to a political system in which decisions are made via majority rule and in which each citizen can cast a single vote (a rule which I assume is plausibly democratic). Suppose I believe earnestly that it would serve the commonweal if everyone gave me all of their money. A system of majority rule makes achieving this outcome unlikely relative to other political systems (compare it to a system where a monarch is selected annually by lottery). Does a majority-rule system unjustifiably set back my interests because it is biased against my preferred outcome? It isn't at all clear that under the system of majority rule my legitimate interests are set back because I cannot hope to have all the money. Notwithstanding this limitation, I am treated as an equal and I can join with others to impact political outcomes of great import. I can rule (with others).

Perhaps the source of concern with militant democracy isn't that someone's preferred outcome is unlikely to occur or that it is made less likely by the political system's formal rules. Perhaps the real source of concern are rules explicitly limiting what I can achieve via the political process. To be clear, an explicit restriction on a particular outcome may not make that outcome less likely than an informal restriction. For example, I strongly suspect that the US government would be more likely to restrict my freedom of speech, notwithstanding the existence of the First Amendment, than it would be to achieve equality of economic opportunity or racial justice – even though these outcomes are not barred by law. The issue, therefore, is not the incapacity to achieve some outcome through the political process, but the fact that a blockage is formal, entrenched by law.

So why might a formal restriction matter? Perhaps because it is something someone did, someone actually formalised the restriction and others have to enforce it. The actions of the enforcers, one might think, evince disrespect for those whose activities are targetted.[3] Anti-democrats are picked out for special sanction. For that reason, a policy aimed at keeping actors from disenfranchising others might suggest that anti-democrats are not full members of the polity.

There are several reasons to be sceptical of this claim. First, let's assume that these formal restrictions are disrespectful and that this disrespect is a potential source of moral concern. In our case, the restrictions aim to protect the democratic interests of other citizens. Accordingly, to identify a legitimate institutional response, we have to weigh the disrespect entailed by militant policies against the disrespect entailed by violations of individuals' participatory claims. In other words, we have to consider the disrespect generated when political actors are kept from invidiously disenfranchising their fellow citizens *and* the disrespect entailed when individuals are invidiously disenfranchised. Under what circumstances would it make sense to grant greater weight to the former? Not many surely. Note that those who find themselves inhibited by the militant policies I have defended can almost always still participate in political life. Their activities are inhibited mainly in that they are kept from violating others' rights. They can still vote, form parties, join political coalitions and so forth. Any sense in which those subject to these policies are not full members of the community, the sense of disrespect communicated, is of a very limited sort. By contrast, when individuals are disenfranchised because of their race or religion, the sense of disrespect communicated is more severe.

Here's a deeper reason to be sceptical of the respect argument: no disrespect is conveyed when citizens are kept from illegitimately violating the interests of other citizens – or at least no disrespect that ought to be the subject of moral concern. To see this, consider the following example.

Imagine a political system allowing one vote for each citizen with the capacity to contribute to common decisions (i.e. not small children). All else being equal, if we assume voters are qualified and have roughly equal interests at stake, there is nothing disrespectful about a system based on one-person-one-vote. In fact, we are likely to conclude that such a system instantiates the equal status of democratic citizens. Now imagine that someone tries to cast two votes. She honestly believes she is twice as virtuous and twice as wise as her fellow citizens. In this case, the poll workers would not be acting disrespectfully if they refused to allow this citizen to cast two votes (indeed, we might think the woman was acting disrespectfully). In sum, if you accept the basic premises of arguments in favour of democracy, than one-person-one-vote will not strike you as offensive.

The preceding argument is uncontroversial. But it has important implications. Rules and regulations aimed at maintaining a one-person-one-vote system should be no more controversial than turning down someone who aims to vote twice. What distinguishes them? Nothing. Of course, some efforts to protect such a system are disrespectful and unjustifiable – imprisoning anyone who ever thought that their fellow voters were morons would seem to be self-defeating. But as I have argued at length, not all defensive systems suffer from this kind of flaw. The VRA is an clear example. It limits the capacity of some citizens to determine various rules regarding their political system but does not exclude them from the political process. Here's the upshot of our work: if we have good reasons for thinking that a democratic system is respectful, we will have good reasons for thinking that some efforts to maintain and protect that system will be respectful. And if this final critique fails, the claim that anti-democrats are mistreated necessarily by efforts to defend democracy is likely to fail too.

Militant Democracy is Inevitably Unprincipled

In this section, I treat three related arguments alleging that militant policies are inherently unprincipled. Here's the first. Informed by the writings of Carl Schmitt, some authors claim that restrictive efforts to defend democracy are necessarily arbitrary (Invernizzi Accetti and Zuckerman 2017; Schupmann 2017). To make sense of this critique, I assume that arbitrary means unprincipled. If militant policies are necessarily arbitrary they will be undemocratic because they are unrelated to democratic principles.

In their essay, 'What's wrong with militant democracy' (2017), Carlo Invernizzi Accetti and Ian Zuckerman contend that democratic theory's boundary problem poses a fundamental challenge to the justification of militant democracy. The problem is straightforward – to make a decision democratically we must have a mechanism for determining who can participate in the decision-making process (Espejo 2011). That mechanism cannot be determined democratically since determining who might participate necessarily precedes the decision-making process. Deciding who can participate requires some bootstrapping, and efforts to defend democracy are inevitably debates about who has a legitimate claim to participate – debates about that bootstrapping. By implication, the outcome of debates about militant democracy are always unprincipled. 'The reason the arbitrariness is inherent is that the decision over who to exclude from the possibility of participating in the democratic game is ultimately a decision over the boundaries of the political community itself, which cannot coherently be taken by democratic procedures and therefore cannot be subsumed under any prior norm' (Invernizzi Accetti and Zuckerman 2017: 183).

This concern is open to two different interpretations: strong and weak. The first is self-defeating, the latter is far less persuasive than it appears. The strong interpretation assumes there is no principled answer or answers to the boundary problem (note: this assumption is inconsistent with the assumptions I made at the beginning of this chapter). All decisions touching on who is a member of the demos will be arbitrary, equally so. But if that is correct, it doesn't undermine, set back or limit democracy if ostensible anti-democrats are excluded from the political process, even if they are excluded arbitrarily. Why not? Because the democratic process will be comprehensively arbitrary whether or not they are excluded. If the strong view is correct, militant democracy is not problematic or arbitrary, democracy itself is problematic and arbitrary. By implication, the criticisms advanced by authors like Invernizzi Accetti and Zuckerman will not serve to undermine militant democracy. In sum, the strong interpretation requires us to throw the baby out with the bath water. And it implies that the VRA had no possible impact – the de facto enfranchisement of African-Americans made the US no more democratic than their exclusion.

My suspicion is that Invernizzi Accetti and Zuckerman would resist this interpretation of their argument. Presumably, they haven't spent time pondering the limitations of militant democracy because they think it doesn't matter whether militant policies are employed. An alternative understanding of the boundary problem, one weaker than the view developed in the previous paragraph, might makes more sense of their approach. In the weaker view, the boundary problem has not been finally answered. But we might still be able to speak confidently about certain cases, cases covered by different principled ways of thinking about the problem. For instance, when individuals, like African-Americans, are legal members of the community, are subject to laws, are counted for the purposes of districting, are qualified in relevant ways and have fundamental interests at stake in the political process, we might accept that those individuals have a *pro tanto* claim or right not to be excluded from the political process because of their skin colour. And we might conclude that excluding them would make the political process less democratic. We might come to this conclusion even while admitting that there are many non-core cases in which the boundary problem stops us from arriving at settled answers (e.g. when do immigrants or non-citizens have a justified claim to participate?).

The weaker understanding of the boundary problem might revivify Invernizzi Accetti and Zuckerman's concerns. For instance, they might admit that many voters have a non-arbitrary claim to participate but they could still argue that debates about militant democracy are, as an empirical matter, always about non-core cases, cases in which there are no principled answers. In this way, militant democracy will be arbitrary. And in their essay, Invernizzi Accetti and Zuckerman point to cases that seem to support this case. In particular, they express unease about the discretion and judgement involved with crafting and applying militant measures:

> the justification of militant democracy cannot rest on the assumption that it will be employed only by people who happen to share our substantive normative views. Indeed, smuggling such premises into the justification of

militant democracy actually obscures their primary danger, namely that, as instruments of exclusion, they can be exercised by whoever happens to hold power against political opponents. (Invernizzi Accetti and Zuckerman 2017: 188)

There are several, fundamental problems with this alternative strategy. As an empirical matter, it isn't the case that efforts to undermine democratic rights always or necessarily focus on individuals at the periphery of the boundary problem, like non-citizens. Consider the long-time exclusion of African-Americans. And it isn't the case that militant policies will always disenfranchise anti-democrats – e.g. consider the VRA.

Invernizzi Accetti and Zuckerman and others who make arguments of this sort also fail to recognise that the threat of unprincipled behaviour is just as likely to cause governments to forgo action. They are laser-focused on the costs of action, but do not consider the cost of inaction. And inaction in the face of attempts to disenfranchise part of the population may be just as harmful as the unjustified restriction of anti-democratic activity. Just as we cannot assume that the tools of militant democracy will be employed by angels, so, too, we cannot assume those tools will be spurned by angels.

Perhaps critics of militant democracy actually accept that inaction could also be damaging. They just think that a world in which militant policies were not on the books would be a world in which malign actors would be *less likely* to undermine the rights of their fellow citizens. This is a complicated empirical claim and the actual effect of militant institutions in one polity, at one time, might be different than in another. Invernizzi Accetti and Zuckerman certainly provide no evidence to support this probabilistic claim. Again, American history provides a powerful rejoinder. For much of its history, the Supreme Court concluded that legal debates about the republican or constitutional character of the country's political system were non-justiciable. That is, the court agreed with Invernizzi Accetti and Zuckerman. There was simply no principled way of determining whether various political schemes were consistent with a republican scheme of government, even though the aim of many schema were clear: to keep black people from participating and having their interests served by the government. What can we draw from the Supreme Court's treatment of voting rights? It is entirely possible for individuals who believe there is no principled way to assess the legitimacy of political rules to use that conclusion to undermine the democratic process.

The preceding conclusion is a sign that something is fundamentally amiss in this kind of critique of theories of militant democracy. Obviously we will be able to find instances in which efforts to defend democracy will reflect arbitrary decision making. But our aim should be to determine whether and under what conditions it might be consistent with our reasons for valuing democracy to defend popular government. That critics like Invernizzi Accetti and Zuckerman ultimately recommend what they take to be a non-arbitrary standard confirms this point. They claim that efforts to defend democracy should focus on how individuals act, not what they say. But this is the exact thesis I defend in my book, a thesis they claim is mistaken.

Here is an alternative reason someone might conclude that militant democracy is inherently unprincipled: it requires political officials to make difficult judgements. By difficult, I mean that no single course of action will self-evidently be the only course of action consistent with one's principles. Determining whether a group has violated the rights of others, whether they might do so imminently and whether an intervention will improve upon the status quo requires tough choices, choices that, inevitably, will be contestable. And given the difficulty of making such choices, one might conclude that it is impossible to do so in a principled manner. Instead of mechanically applying the rules laid out in a constitution or electoral law, political officials will have to make choices and those choices, inevitably, will be arbitrary.

Presumably, those who invoke this kind of critique of militant democracy have a vision of democracy and politics in which judgements and difficult choices can be avoided. Perhaps inaction, in this view, doesn't require any judgements at all. That view is mistaken. Laws and policies require political officials and participants to determine how they apply in the real world. Lawmakers cannot anticipate the variety of real situations to which legal rules are applied. These are hardly original observations. And, notwithstanding fears about the arbitrary use of judgement by political officials, we have developed a variety of mechanisms to manage this issue – public hearings, access to courts, the right to appeal to higher courts and so forth. These checks are intended to ensure, to the degree feasible, that officials act in ways consistent with the principles that motivated the laws. Of course, one might think that such protections are not applicable in the context of militant democracy – since targets of militant policies are claimed to be outside the political body. But that isn't true. Countries like Germany, the UK and the US use overlapping mechanisms to police the use of militant practices.

Let's return to the VRA. The act was necessary because those opposed to black suffrage kept on finding new ways to disenfranchise their fellow citizens. If excluding people on the basis of their skin colour was blocked, anti-democrats introduced grandfather clauses. If that was arrested, new policies were created. What was required was a strategy allowing the federal government to head off these new policies. What was required was a policy allowing officials to use their judgement to identify whether new political rules would unjustly keep Americans from voting. Critically, the act included several instruments to check the judgement of those overseeing the policy – impacted jurisdictions had a choice, they could have their policies 'pre-cleared' via the courts or the Justice Department. And the decisions of those bodies were subject to appeal. The VRA demonstrates that militant policies can depend on non-arbitrary forms of judgement.

There is a final version of the 'it's arbitrary' critique of militant democracy – that it can only be justified by an appeal to raison d'état. The idea here is that there is nothing 'democratic' or principled about restricting individuals' political participation. Democracy is about equality, voting and majority rule. Restricting participation is inconsistent with that ideal. Accordingly, when individuals claim to embrace democracy while seeking to limit the participation of neo-Nazis, for instance, they are merely trying to advance their narrow self-interest, they are acting politically. The logic of this claim depends on an assumption: there is no principled justification for militant democracy consistent with democratic practice. But that is a very weak assumption. Democrats don't merely embrace majority rule, they think majority rule and democratic institutions, more broadly, are valuable because they advance and instantiate some important interests. Democracy or majority rule, in this view, are not valuable in themselves but because they reliably advance or instantiate those interests. And when individuals unjustifiably keep others from advancing those interests – by, for instance, removing them from the voting rolls – then efforts to block such projects will not, by definition, be unprincipled. They can be consistent with our reasons for embracing democratic procedures in the first place (Kirshner 2010).

There is No Right to Participate

The best way to understand the normative landscape of militant democracy is to focus on the right to participate. At least that is what I argued in *A Theory of Militant Democracy*. My thought was that the interests grounding the right to participate are the interests set back when anti-democratic parties unjustifiably undercut the political process. And those are the same interests potentially set back when militant policies inhibit participation. Focusing on a 'right to participate' raised several concerns. I treat two of them in this section.

Here's the first. Voting is often treated as the central feature of the right to participate. But as Peter Stone argues in this volume, we might ask: would the paradoxes I have identified also be raised if I admitted that there was no right to vote? What if citizens merely had a right to take part in a fair, democratic process, like a lottery (López-Guerra 2010; Stone 2011; Guerrero 2014)? In other words, perhaps questions about banning parties, for example, would not arise in a system in which some or all representatives were selected via a fair lottery? And perhaps, as Professor Stone notes, the make-up of those bodies and the effect they would have on partisan incentives might dampen urges to subvert the democratic process.

Suppose that were right; suppose a sortition-based system really would effectively inhibit the drive to undermine democratic institutions. We would have a ready method for brushing aside the paradox of militant democracy – the idea that action or inaction might weaken democratic systems. Why is that? Because a sortition-based system would not obviously violate citizens' interest in relational equality. And a sortition-based system might do as good a job advancing individuals' instrumental interests. One might be concerned that, relative to an electoral system, a lottocratic arrangement will limit individuals' opportunities for formal participation, since only those selected for a representative body will exercise formal influence in the political process. But even in a sortition-based regime one might still be able to satisfy one's interest in active participation by protesting, organising efforts to engage one's fellow citizens and publishing one's thoughts in print and online.

This is an attractive picture. But there are two reasons, I think, that it will not successfully resolve the paradox of militant democracy. Notwithstanding all of their ostensibly commendable attributes, sortition-based systems will be unlikely to rid the world of opponents of democracy. There will still be individuals who believe that their own views and interests should be privileged institutionally. To my knowledge, none of the skillful advocates for lottocratic systems has claimed that it would be the answer to all of society's ills. And none has claimed that it would remove the impulses and interests that cause individuals to reject political egalitarianism. In other words, we have to assume that anti-democrats, those who seek to undermine or thwart the achievement of egalitarian institutions, would still exist.

What does this mean? Imagine a federal system of representation in which positions in national and local assemblies are determined via some fair, random procedure. And imagine that in one local assembly the majority of representatives are anti-democrats. As a result, they pass a law precluding citizens of a certain race or religion from being selected during the next lottery. Other citizens in the polity will now face the paradox of militant democracy – how do they respond to these anti-democratic acts? Perhaps a majority in the national assembly could block the bad actions of the local assembly, establishing some law invalidating the local assembly's work. Presumably the local assembly would identify some new method to achieve the same end. The sortition-based national assembly would face the same kind of difficulties confronted by an elected national assembly, the US Congress, when it faced just these sorts of difficulties in the twentieth century. Our fictional, national, sortition-based body will have to determine what intervention is called for and whether it should sanction those who have actively disenfranchised their fellow citizens. This body will confront the paradox of militant democracy. This hypothetical case suggests that once we admit that anti-democrats will inhabit sortition-based systems, we will have to admit that the paradox of militant democracy will retain its force.

Here's another reason to doubt that the paradox would be eradicated by sortition-based institutions. As in the preceding paragraphs let's assume a lottery-governed polity would feature anti-democrats. It is implausible to assume that lottery-based institutions generate anti-democrats, that no anti-democrats would exist without those institutions. Accordingly, we should assume that they will exist before the establishment of those sortition-based institutions. And we should assume they will impact the form of those institutions. The existence of anti-democrats explains, at least in part, why representative regimes like the US have the inegalitarian, undemocratic shape that they do, the shape that defenders of lottery-based systems of representation often decry. And if anti-democrats have a hand in designing sortition-based institutions, then we should be confident that those institutions will be hampered by the same kinds of challenges confronted by familiar, electoral regimes. In sum, establishing sortition-based institutions might improve on the status quo, as its many defenders suggest. But those institutions are unlikely to obviate the paradox of militant democracy or the need to think about how to manage it.

A different concern about the right to participate cuts more deeply. J. S. Mill famously argued that formal participation in a political process is not akin to self-regarding behaviour or collective action engaged in voluntarily; political participation involves exercising a small measure of coercive power over others (Mill 2008; López-Guerra 2014, 2017). Accordingly, it is subject to a different justificatory standard than merely exercising power over oneself. To be legitimate, *my* participation should advance *your* interests – for instance, by securing attractive outcomes or instantiating a society in which individuals relate to one another as equals. In this view, individuals have a claim not to be invidiously excluded from participating in political life. But no one has a right to participate, understood in the normal sense.

If someone is excluded from the political process because they aim to use that process to harm others, they have not been wronged. Anti-democrats seem to fall into this category. And this raises the question of whether the paradox of militant democracy arises when their participation is restricted. If there is no right to participate, then anti-democrats who are reasonably disenfranchised or kept from participating suffer no obvious wrong.

This take on 'the right to participate' differs in important ways from the 'right' I defended in *A Theory of Militant Democracy*. I am not going to arbitrate between these distinct views – doing so would take me far afield from my purpose. Instead, I am going to show that even if one accepts that there is no right to participate, the paradox of militant democracy still retains its bite and that anyone interested in defending democracy will still have to weigh both the costs of action and inaction.

For instance, imagine that leaders of the Imaginary Party have undermined the democratic process – making it difficult for the poor to register to vote. Constructing an appropriate sanction, one would have to consider the following factors. Many Imaginary Party members do not support or have only limited involvement in the wrongs identified. That even those committed to bad ends may possess perspectives whose expression can advance the commonweal (especially if they are kept from violating the interests of others). One will have to weigh Imaginary Party supporters' legitimate interests, interests distinct from the ends of their party, that will likely suffer if they are disenfranchised from the political process. For instance, if supporters of the party are disenfranchised, elected officials will systematically and unjustifiably overlook their material interests or sacrifice them in the interest of those who can participate. In sum, even if no one possesses a 'right to participate' militant action will still carry the possibility of overreach and may set back the legitimate interests of non-democrats. Militant policies may still keep a democratic political system from achieving its ends. In other words, the paradox of militant democracy will still keep its grip on militant democrats. And then we ought still to favour an approach like the one I outlined in *A Theory of Militant Democracy*.

Conclusion

Defending democracy against popular challenges requires tough choices. Those who want to preserve or extend the democratic character of a society's political institutions will have to consider the interests of those threatened by anti-democratic action and those who support it. They will have to weigh both the costs of action and inaction. They will recognise the likelihood that by defending the interests of anti-democrats, by ensuring that they can participate, they make the achievement of some valuable political ends more difficult (since their achievement may be opposed by anti-democrats). Still, I believe this is the most defensible way of thinking about militant democracy.

In this essay, I have considered three kinds of arguments, each aimed at simplifying the complex challenges posed by anti-democrats in democratic regimes. Some argued that any efforts to defend democracy are illegitimate or arbitrary. Others that the interests of anti-democrats are immaterial to right action. I found each view lacking – because they were self-defeating or because they were unlikely to simplify successfully the challenges I believe democrats presently face. If this is correct, then democrats face a challenging task – how to bolster democracy without disenfranchising its opponents. The VRA is a stunning example of how such a challenge can be met. Today, that great law is the subject of a sustained legal assault, an assault that serves as a testimony to its import and influence (*Shelby County* v. *Holder* 1133 S. Ct. 2612 (2013)).

Notes

1. Section 5 of the VRA, the focus of my analysis, was effectively voided by the Supreme Court in 2013: *Shelby County* v. *Holder* 1133 S. Ct. 2612 (2013).
2. There are a number of excellent works considering the legitimacy of militant practices. These include, but are not limited, to Rosenblum (2007), Rummens and Abts (2010), Müller (2011a).
3. On the communicative effect of state action, see Brettschneider (2010).

FOUR

Militant Democracy Versus Populism

Cristóbal Rovira Kaltwasser[1]

Introduction

Populist forces with diverse programmatic proposals have become increasingly influential across the globe and therefore we have seen growing concern about the consequences of populism. Despite important differences between leftist and rightist populist actors, all of them maintain a complex relationship with liberal democracy (Mudde and Rovira Kaltwasser 2012). Liberal democracies are characterised by defending not only popular sovereignty but also unelected institutions that seek to provide and secure common goods. By contrast, populist forces have a very peculiar understanding of democracy, according to which nobody has the right to act against the wishes of 'the people'. Unsurprisingly, various scholars have argued that there is an elective affinity between populism and illiberalism (Krastev 2007; Plattner 2010; Pappas 2014; Mudde and Rovira Kaltwasser 2017). Consequently, one could see turning to 'militant democracy' – adopting a radical approach towards those who allegedly are at odds with liberal democratic procedures – as a particularly fruitful way to deal with populism. This chapter aims to analyse the extent to which this is the case. Can we safeguard liberal democracy from populism by adopting a militant defence of unelected institutions, limiting the manoeuvring room of populist forces and even banning them if necessary? This contribution answers this question in the negative. The main argument to be presented is that, when it comes to dealing with populism, militant democracy is self-defeating for at least three reasons.

First of all, although employing militant policies against the internal enemies of democracy seems to be a smart strategy to safeguard democracy, one has to consider the high legitimacy costs of the very implementation of these policies. After all, the application of militant democratic mechanisms implies curtailing fundamental rights to a segment of the electorate. Second, if a militant democracy limits the political participation of populist forces, the validity and visibility of the discourse of the latter will probably increase. Not without reason, populists will claim that 'the establishment' is a corrupt entity, since it does not give voice to (a section of) 'the people'. Third, and finally, militant democracy implicitly assumes that there is wide consensus among both the population and the elite on what democracy means and who constitutes the demos. Nevertheless, this is a problematic assumption and the very rise of populism reveals that within societies there are constituencies with very peculiar understandings of both democracy and the boundaries of the demos (Rovira Kaltwasser 2014; Mudde and Rovira Kaltwasser 2018).

The rest of this chapter is structured in five sections. We begin by explaining the notion of militant democracy by tracing its origins in the work of Karl Loewenstein and by showing its implementation in post-war Europe. After this, we analyse the contradictions of militant democracy, in particular the paradox of democratic self-destruction and the paradox of democratic self-injury, since the study of these paradoxes help us to better understand the promise and perils of militant democracy. In the next section the concept of populism is briefly discussed, putting special emphasis on the ambivalent relationship between populism and liberal democracy. Subsequently, we argue that militant democracy usually produces more harm than good when it comes to dealing with populism. Finally, the chapter concludes with some reflections on the alternatives available to cope with the rise of populism.

What is Militant Democracy?

Democratic regimes are characterised by allowing political participation and public contestation (Dahl 1971, 1989). While the former refers to the right of the population of a given association to take part in the political process (e.g. by deciding in free and fair elections who should govern), the latter describes the possibility of building political forces that express different views and compete against each other to obtain votes (e.g. by developing political parties that are able to access the executive and legislative powers). This basic definition of democracy is widely shared among political scientists, and there is also wide agreement from both scholars and practitioners that democratic regimes are not necessarily stable arrangements that last forever (e.g. Dunn 2005; Tilly 2007). Thus, the issue of democratic breakdown, erosion and consolidation has received vast attention.

Among the challenges that democracies have to face, one of the problems that generates increasing worry today is the emergence of populist forces that can use the two dimensions of the democratic regime – political participation and public contestation – to subvert the rules of the game and potentially end up constructing a (competitive) authoritarian regime. Examples are numerous: from the Chavista and now Maduro government in Venezuela to Viktor Orbán's Hungary and the Trump administration in the US. What these three instances have in common is the coming into power via democratic means of populist leaders who have a radical rhetoric and seem to spare no effort in undertaking institutional reforms that hurt the (liberal) democratic regime. Although the future of these three cases is uncertain, there is little doubt that contemporary Venezuela is a competitive authoritarian regime, Viktor Orbán's Hungary is an illiberal democracy and the Trump administration is, to say the least, putting liberal democracy under stress in the US.

However, the very idea that democratically elected forces can use free and fair elections to erode – and in extreme cases even overthrow – the democratic regime is an old preoccupation in political thought. Ever since Plato's warning about the possibility that democracies can transform into tyrannies, scholars have been reflecting on the ways to deal with the internal enemies of democracies. By allowing ideological pluralism, democratic regimes can give birth to intolerant political forces that might exploit freedom of association and free elections to violate the democratic process. This is why Plato and many others have argued that experts, or so-called 'guardians', should make the most important decisions in order to avoid democracy degenerating into rule by mob. There is perhaps no better example of how the toleration of intolerant forces is a dangerous phenomenon than the collapse of the Weimar Republic and the rise of the Nazi regime in Germany. As has often been noted by pundits and academics alike, Joseph Goebbels, Hitler's propaganda minister, claimed that it 'will always remain one of the best jokes of democracy, that it gave its deadly enemies the means by which it was destroyed' (quoted in Tyulkina 2015a: 11). In effect, Hitler was able to become prime minister in 1933 thanks to the support of the Nazi Party and once in power he needed little time to abolish the democratic rules of the game and establish a dictatorship, with catastrophic consequences for the whole world.

The emergence of Nazi Germany generated a profound discussion among academics of the time and one of the sharpest observers was someone directly affected by Hitler's regime: a Jewish legal scholar called Karl Loewenstein, who fled to the US in the early 1930s and coined the concept of 'militant democracy' (*streitbare Demokratie*). As the notion of militancy indicates, democratic regimes of this sort adopt a confrontational strategy against those who are interested in coming into power to subvert the rules of the game and install an authoritarian government (Flüman 2015: 97–99). According to Loewenstein, tolerating intolerants is a dangerous approach that generates more harm than good, and, in consequence, the best way ahead consists in fighting fire with fire. In his own words:

> [. . .] democracy is at war, although an underground war on the inner front. Constitutional scruples can no longer restrain from restrictions on demo-cratic fundamentals, for the sake of ultimately preserving these very funda-mentals [. . .] Constitutions are dynamic to the extent that they allow for peaceful change by regular methods, but they have to be stiffened and hard-ened when confronted by movements intent upon their destruction. (Loew-enstein 1937a: 432)

In summary, 'militant democracy' can be defined as a type of liberal demo-cratic regime that is characterised by the provision and employment of legal mechanisms that seek to protect the regime from challenges to its contin-ued existence by curtailing the rights of those who allegedly aim to overturn democracy by using democratic procedures (Flümann 2015: 105; Tyulkina 2015a: 15). The key aspect behind this conceptualisation lies in the fact that the regime is provided with institutional devices that allow for *pre-emptive* actions against the internal enemies of democracy. Instead of waiting to see what the intolerants can do once in power, militant democracy anticipates their potential arrival by limiting their manoeuvring room. Although dif-ferent militant strategies can be employed to confront the internal enemies of democracy, the application of ad hoc legislation to restrict the political rights of political forces that exploit democratic procedures to undermine democracy is the one that has received wide attention in the political sci-ence literature (Capoccia 2013: 208), particularly when it comes to debat-ing about the promise and perils of banning radical political parties (e.g. Capoccia 2005; Bale 2007; van Spanje and van der Brug 2009; van Spanje 2010).

The concept of militant democracy became relevant not only in aca-demic discussions about the reasons for the emergence of the Nazi regime, but also in practical debates about how to (re)build democratic systems that can avoid the potential rise of extremist forces that can seize power by democratic procedures to create an authoritarian regime. The paradigmatic

example is none other than post-war Germany, as it adopted a constitutional setting that explicitly defines the regime as a 'militant democracy'
and includes two important characteristics. First, the constitution of the
Federal Republic of Germany establishes that the principles laid down
in Articles 1 to 20 are unamendable, since they are crucial to protecting
human dignity and securing democratic self-preservation.[2] This is what is
normally called the 'eternity clause' (*Ewigkeitsklausel*) and refers to the irre-
vocability of those elements that secure the liberal democratic character of
the constitution (Capoccia 2013: 211). Second, the constitution of the Federal Republic of Germany offers militant democratic mechanisms to deal
with extremist forces. The most important mechanism lies in the capacity
of the Federal Constitutional Court to outlaw political parties and declare
them illegal. While the constitution of post-war Germany affirms the central role of political parties for the proper functioning of democracy, it also
establishes that those parties that 'by reason of their aims of the behaviour
of their adherents, seek to undermine or abolish the free democratic basic
order or to endanger the existence of the Federal Republic of Germany shall
be unconstitutional' (Tyulkina 2015a: 67).

Importantly, the militant democratic character of Germany's post-war
constitution has not been an empty rhetoric since it has been applied
on two occasions: to ban the Socialist Reich Party (SRP) in 1952 and
to declare unconstitutional the Communist Party of Germany (KPD) in
1956. While the former was relatively straightforward and did not cause
much sensation, the latter was highly controversial as the trial sparked
a public debate about not only the justification of party bans but also
their effectiveness to fight against political radicalism (Thiel 2009a: 121).
There have been other attempts to forbid political parties in post-war
Germany, particularly against the so-called Nationalist Democratic Party
(NPD), an extreme-right party founded in the mid-1960s that has been
able to enter some regional parliaments, primarily in eastern German
federal states after the reunification of the country. Nevertheless, the
Constitutional Court decided not to ban the party in question, but in the
last trial (2013–2017) the Constitutional Court claimed that the NPD
has an unconstitutional attitude.

Although Germany is usually seen as the paradigmatic example of a
militant democracy, it is worth considering that Western European countries after the Second World War became very distrustful about the notion
and praxis of popular sovereignty, to the point that the regimes that were
created after 1945 should be conceived of as a new type of political order.
As Jan-Werner Müller (2011a) has indicated in his ground-breaking study
about the history of ideas in Europe, post-war Europe is characterised by the

construction of democratic regimes that were highly constrained, mostly by unelected institutions, such as constitutional courts. The constitutional ethos that came with such democracies was positively hostile to ideals of unlimited popular sovereignty, as well as the "people's democracies" and later "socialist democracies" in the East, which in theory remained based on the notion of a collective (socialist) subject mastering history' (Müller 2011a: 5). Post-war European democracies introduced two important innovations: the welfare state and the EU. Whereas the former was intended to inhibit the return of fascism and communism by guaranteeing the material well-being of citizens, the latter was thought to install further constraints on nation-state democracies via the construction of new unelected institutions. In this sense, it is not far-fetched to suggest that contemporary democracies, particularly in the European context, have an affinity with the militant democracy model, to the point that most constitutional orders around the world do include provisions to deal with the internal enemies of democracy (Tyulkina 2015a).

Two Paradoxes of Militant Democracy

So far, we have explained the origins of the notion of militant democracy, and we have shown also how this notion has manifested in the real world, particularly in post-war Europe. Nevertheless, militant democracy remains a disputed concept in the scholarly debate not only in relation to real-world applications, but also because of an ongoing theoretical discussion about its internal contradictions. To better understand this theoretical discussion it is important to identify two paradoxes haunting militant democracy: the paradox of democratic self-destruction and the paradox of democratic self-injury. It is worth briefly examining these two paradoxes since they have important consequences for analysing the extent to which militant democracy is an appropriate method to cope with populism or not.

The paradox of democratic self-destruction describes the fact that democratic regimes are the only ones that provide its internal enemies with the means to overthrow it. By contrast, authoritarian regimes spare no effort in using all available means to combat their opponents. In fact, dictatorships persist not only by building a government coalition that secures enough power to guarantee regime survival, but also by applying two mechanisms of control that are crucial for keeping adversaries in check: repression and co-optation. While the former is employed to generate fear among opponents, the latter is exercised to turn enemies into passive or active supporters of the regime (Svolik 2012). However, democratic regimes cannot proceed in this way since they justify their existence by respect for values such as freedom of association and freedom of speech. The problem is that some political forces might use the freedoms that the regime warrants to destroy democracy from within. In other words, non-democratic actors can employ institutional and legal means to end up erecting an authoritarian regime.

To solve the paradox of democratic self-destruction, some scholars take a pragmatic approach by arguing that the fundamental rights that permit free association and free speech should be seen as a sort of 'safety valve' whereby citizens can raise their discomfort and, in consequence, give information to the political class about the issues that are more pressing for society (Müller 2016a: 252). This means that citizens should have the right to defend their ideas and interests in the public sphere, forcing the political community to debate about what democracy means and who constitutes the demos (Kirshner 2014: 35). However, *normative* political theory generally maintains that a strong constitutional order is needed to prevent majorities implementing reforms that erode the democratic system (e.g. policies seeking to limit minority rights or to generate an uneven playing field between incumbents and opposition). Certainly there is a tension in arguing in favour of tolerating an open debate about the preferences of the demos and simultaneously supporting the existence of unelected institutions that, if necessary, can limit fundamental rights. But according to many normative theorists, this tension is rather artificial because there is a harmonious relationship between popular sovereignty and constitutionalism.

There is probably no better example of this line of reasoning than the work of Jürgen Habermas (1992, 1996), who takes a teleological approach when maintaining that constitutionalism should be seen as a continuously self-correcting mechanism that is able to come to terms with the ideas and interests of the demos. Seen from this light, constitutionalism must be conceived of as a dynamic process that takes into account the collective learning process undergone by the people over time, including the dramatic experiences of past generations that might have led them to constitutionally entrench militant democratic mechanisms to avoid the paradox of democratic self-destruction. Nevertheless, as I have argued elsewhere in more detail (Rovira Kaltwasser 2014: 477–478), the position of Habermas has little empirical validity. Given that he is inclined to assume that constitutional change is exercised mainly by courts (Honig 2001: 799), there is little space in his theory for thinking about the possibility of the activation of the 'constituent power' with enough strength to enact constitutional amendments or revolutions. This phenomenon is particularly pressing when it comes to dealing with populist actors in government, who are often tempted to undertake constitutional revolutions with controversial legacies (Müller 2016b: 60–68; Rovira Kaltwasser 2013).

Take, for instance, the case of Hugo Chávez in Venezuela, a populist leftist leader who won the presidential elections in 1998 and subsequently implemented a series of institutional changes – including the creation of a constitutional assembly that proposed a new constitution, which was ratified in a referendum in 1999 – that seriously limit the capacity of the opposition to compete freely against the supporters of Chávez and allows the government to keep unelected institutions, such as the electoral and constitutional tribunals, under its control. There is no doubt that Hugo Chávez used democratic procedures to undertake major transformations that both him and his successor (Nicolás Maduro) have employed to erect a competitive authoritarian regime (Hawkins 2016; Mainwaring 2012). A less radical example in terms of the negative impact of populist actors in government on the democratic regime can be found in contemporary Hungary, where the Fidesz party and Viktor Orbán were able to undertake a major constitutional change in 2012 which enables them to control key institutions even if the opposition wins elections in the near future (Batory 2016; Müller 2016b: 65–66).

The second paradox that haunts militant democracy is the paradox of democratic self-injury. It refers to the idea that attempts to defend democracy against its internal enemies can generate irreparable damages, to the point that the regime might end up losing its democratic character. Put in other words, the paradox of democratic self-injury refers to 'the possibility that efforts to stem challenges to self-government might themselves lead to the degradation of democratic politics or the fall of a representative regime' (Kirshner 2014: 2). By fighting fire with fire, governments might be able to eradicate the internal enemies of democracy, but there is a fair chance that the regime will become increasingly illiberal and thus harm its own legitimacy. There is a very thin line between restricting political liberties in the name of democracy and giving birth to 'paranoid' administrations that can well destroy democracy in the very process of defending it. Just think about the continuous ban of religious parties in Turkey since the 1980s with the aim of allegedly protecting secularism, despite the fact 'that 90 percent of the population affiliates with one religious group [. . . but the state . . .] insists on keeping all religious matters (including those related to Islam) out of the public domain' (Tyulkina 2015a: 181).

Loewenstein was well aware of the paradox of democratic self-injury, but according to him the price of tolerating the intolerant is too high, and in consequence he is of the opinion that the (temporary) suspension of fundamental rights is justified when dealing with the internal enemies of democracy. 'If democracy believes in the superiority of its absolute values over the opportunistic platitudes of fascism, it must live up to the demands of the hour, and every possible effort must be made to rescue it, even at the risk and cost of violating fundamental principles' (Loewenstein 1937a: 432). Nevertheless, he does not offer clear guidelines on how to avoid government misuse of militant democratic mechanisms. This is why other authors of the time opposed the notion of militant democracy. In this regard, the position of Hans Kelsen is paradigmatic. He argued that one of the tragedies of democracies lies in the fact that they are characterised by tolerating internal enemies, although this might lead to the very collapse of the democratic regime itself. In his own words, '[a] democracy that tries to assert itself against the will of the majority [. . .] has ceased to be a democracy. The self-government of the people cannot rule against its own people [. . .] Who is in favour of democracy should not get tangled up in the fatal contradiction of resorting to dictatorship in order to save democracy' (Kelsen 1967: 68, own translation).

Kelsen's approach assumes that democrats have to tolerate their adversaries in the hope that the political discussion will help to solve the existing controversies. This means that one cannot forbid the existence of the internal enemies of democracy (unless they promote the use of violence), because if this is the case one ends up undermining the democratic principles. A more contemporary interpretation of the paradox of democratic self-injury can be found in the work of Kirshner (2014), who argues that militant democratic mechanisms that are used preventively should be seen as illegitimate. Denying a party the opportunity to compete in elections is very problematic, since we are not certain about the extent to which the party in question represents a comprehensive threat to democracy until it has been able to acquire power. In addition, it could be the case that some parties begin with a very radical impetus, but after a while they moderate and accommodate themselves to the liberal democratic rules of the game (as seen in the evolution of so-called Green parties in Western Europe at the end of the twentieth century). Therefore, the illegitimacy of preventive interventions lies in the fact that they are morally costly as curtailing fundamental rights necessarily means limiting the right to participate in the democratic process. Accordingly, to solve the paradox of democratic self-injury Kirshner proposes the principle of limited intervention: 'militant policies should not be employed in the pursuit of an ideal regime; instead, defensive projects should help attain an intermediate end, an imperfect political system in which capable citizens can play a meaningful role (that is, polyar-chy)' (Kirshner 2014: 7).

An important consequence of Kirshner's principle of limited interven-tion is that the use of militant policies should be seen as a mechanism of last resort, which can be employed only when one has the absolute certainty about the potential threat to democracy posed by their internal opponents. While determining this with certainty is anything but simple, he points out that the size and political influence of anti-democratic move-ments is a key factor to be considered: 'large antidemocratic organizations may require a more extreme response than small, less influential organiza-tions' (Kirshner 2014: 18). After all, if a niche party with dubious demo-cratic credentials enters parliament, it will have limited space of action. By contrast, when a massive party with dubious democratic credentials enters parliament and has enough votes to undertake reforms and/or control the executive power, it will have enough strength to overthrow the democratic regime. Although this is an interesting argument, it is impracticable if one takes into account real-world cases, in which banning a majority party reflects a situation where the establishment of a liberal democratic regime is likely unviable.

A good example of this situation can be found in Argentina during the 1950s and 1960s, a period during which – as Guillermo O'Donnell (1973) rightly argued – democracy became an 'impossible game' in the country. It is interesting to note that O'Donnell's argumentation is linked to the classic work of Lipset (1959), who maintained that democratic regimes can thrive only when two *prerequisites* are present: legitimacy and efficacy. To better understand O'Donnell's line of reasoning, one has to acknowledge three basic assumptions of his argument of an 'impossible game' (see also Linz and Stepan 1996: 196–200). First, during the 1950s and 1960s the Peronist party became the biggest electoral player in Argentina, but it had a rather thin commitment to liberal democracy. Given that the Peronist government from 1943 until 1955 had shown clear anti-democratic practices, there was no other option available than banning the Peronist party in order to pre-serve the democratic regime. Second, the largest anti-Peronist force was the Radical party, which did not have enough electoral strength to win elec-tions unless restrictions were imposed on the Peronists. Nevertheless, even if the Radical party could come to power via elections with the Peronists excluded from the ballot, the latter had sufficient support in the unions and at the mass level to impede effective government by the Radicals. Third, confronted with a deadlock in which a government of the Peronist party would lead to an authoritarian regime and the coming into power of the

Radical party would lead to an ineffective government, the bourgeoisie accepted military rule as the lesser evil in the hope that democracy might become possible later.

What can we learn from this brief analysis of O'Donnell's 'impossible game' argument? This example reveals an uncomfortable state of affairs that occurs in the real world: moments and places where there is no agreement between the people on the necessity of respecting the liberal democratic rules of the game. Under these circumstances, militant democratic policies are of little help since they cannot generate a shared commitment to sustaining liberal democracy, but will rather exacerbate polarisation between constituencies with very different interpretations about what democracy means and who constitutes the demos. In other words, the liberal democratic regime hinges upon prerequisites that it cannot itself guarantee (Böckenförde 1991).

Populism and its Ambivalent Relationship with Liberal Democracy

After having discussed the notion of militant democracy and explained its internal contradictions, it is time to define populism and briefly analyse its ambivalent relationship with liberal democracy.[3] For a long time, academics and pundits alike argued that populist forces emerged in poor societies, while rich countries were seen to be immune to the 'populist virus'. However, the last two decades have shown that populism can arise in both the developed and developing worlds. Populist actors are making headlines today in countries as diverse as Bolivia (Evo Morales), Hungary (Viktor Orbán), Spain (Podemos), France (the National Front) and the US (Donald Trump). While it is true that different types of populist forces have been becoming increasingly influential across the world, populism remains a contested concept in the social sciences. It is therefore important to base any argument on a clear definition.

Let's begin with the most basic aspect: populism is a political ideology.[4] In everyday language, the word 'ideology' often has a bad connotation. Many assume that ideologies are irrational constructions that are created and employed to indoctrinate individuals with the aim of dominating societies. While it is true that some political ideologies (e.g. fascism) have been used for this purpose, it is important to bear in mind that political ideologies are pervasive and part of modern political dynamics. They provide us categories with which to map and organise the political world (Freeden 1996, 2003); consider the relevance of liberalism, nationalism and socialism in the political debate. Ideologies are a set of beliefs or principles defended by individuals and organisations. Hence, to study political ideologies properly, one has to look at both the discourse of leaders and parties (supply side) and the language used in the everyday life of common people (demand side).

In the case of populism, it is a thin-centred ideology that not only claims that society is divided between 'the pure people' and 'the corrupt elite', but also argues that politics is about defending popular sovereignty at any cost (Mudde 2004a). This means that populism is first and foremost a moral worldview, in which 'the people' is depicted as good whereas 'the elite' is portrayed as bad. Seen from this light, it is almost impossible to reach an agreement with the establishment, given that the latter is seen as a perverse and corrupt entity that is only interested in benefiting itself.[5]

Moreover, populism assumes that 'the people' is an assembly of individuals with a united will, which is inalienable. Despite important programmatic differences between populist forces across the contemporary world, all of them propose a peculiar narrative according to which 'the people' is an imagined community with a shared heartland – a version of the past that celebrates an uncomplicated and non-political territory of imagination from which populists draw their own vision of their unified and ordinary constituency (Taggart 2000). At the same time, the very notion of 'the elite' is also a construction that is framed in various ways by different populist forces. They sometimes change their views on who should be included as part of the corrupt establishment or remain silent about certain sectors of the establishment that implicitly or explicitly support the populist project.

To better understand the peculiarity of the populist set of ideas and its difficult relationship with liberal democracy, it is key to analyse its opposites. This helps us to distinguish the boundaries of the populist phenomenon and also to empirically differentiate populism from non-populism. Generally speaking, there are two conceptual contraries of populism: elitism and pluralism. Elitism shares the Manichean distinction between 'the people' and 'the elite' that is inherent to populism, but it inverts the morality given to each of these terms. In effect, the elitist worldview regards 'the people' as dangerous, irrational and vulgar, whereas 'the elite' is portrayed as an intellectually and morally superior group of individuals who should be in charge of government.

As a consequence, elitists are of the opinion that politics should be run first and foremost by experts and 'the people' should have a very limited influence over the political process, since they can be easily mobilised by demagogues. A contemporary illustration of elitism is the approach defended by technocrats, who maintain that solving economic and political problems is exceedingly complex and who therefore argue that the most important decisions should be made by experts rather than by voters (Caramani 2017). Something similar occurs within certain factions of the environmental movement, which take an elitist position when arguing that their worldview is morally superior to the one advanced by the common people, who are seen as ignorant.

In contrast to elitism and populism, pluralism does not believe in the Manichean and moral distinction between 'the people' and 'the elite'. According to pluralists, societies are composed of individuals and groups with very different opinions. Diversity is seen as both an undisputable reality and a political strength, because it forces us to establish a dialogue in order to reach agreements. From this perspective, 'the people' is a constantly changing ensemble of individuals, and, in consequence, the unified will of the people is a fictional entity. Thus, pluralism assumes not a collective entity in singular (i.e. 'a people') but rather a multiplicity of individuals and groups exerting influence within the polity (Ochoa Espejo 2011).

In summary, populism is a specific set of ideas that it is not against democracy per se but rather at odds with the *liberal* democratic regime. The latter is a complex regime, which not only allows the periodic realisation of free and fair elections, but also nurtures unelected institutions in charge of providing public goods and exercising horizontal accountability (Armony and Schamis 2005; Plattner 2010). In fact, the populist ideology is characterised by the defence of the popular sovereignty at any cost. Given that 'the people' are seen as good, honest and pure, while 'the elite' is portrayed as corrupt, fraudulent and tainted, populists are prone to claim that nobody has the right to bypass the popular will. This has important consequences for the type of government that populist actors support both in theory and in practice. They certainly favour democracy defined as the respect of popular sovereignty, but at the same time they have serious problems with liberal democracy, defined as the respect of not only popular sovereignty but also of minorities as well as actors and institutions that seek to oversight the power of those who are in government (e.g. the judiciary, the media, etc.) (Mudde and Rovira Kaltwasser 2012, 2017; Rovira Kaltwasser 2013).

Is Militant Democracy the Right Approach to Cope with Populism?

At this stage we have clarity about the two key concepts discussed in this contribution: militant democracy and populism. Therefore, we are well-equipped to address the question of whether militant democracy is a useful strategy for dealing with populism or not. Although it is true that populist forces challenge the liberal democratic regime, employing militant democratic tools to cope with populism creates its own challenges and generates more harm than good. This is particularly the case when the size and political influence of populist actors is large. There are three main reasons why militant democracy is not necessarily the best approach to cope with populism: (1) the legitimacy costs of militant democracy are far too high when dealing with populism; (2) the implementation of militant democratic mechanisms makes the populist discourse more attractive; and (3) militant democracy takes for granted that there is wide consensus on what democracy means and who constitutes the demos, but the very emergence of populist forces shows that this is not necessarily the case in the real world. Each of these arguments is developed in the following pages.

The first point that I want to advance is related to the high legitimacy costs of militant democracy when it comes to addressing populist forces, particularly if the latter have a significant level of electoral support. By high legitimacy costs I mean that the very application of militant policies brings the paradox of democratic self-injury to the fore. Restricting the participation of certain political forces not only undermines democratic principles but also paves the way for the formation of a regime where political preferences become meaningless as voters cannot select the party that pursues their preferred policies.[6] Imagine that the party in question is supported by a majority of the population and that it will continue to be outlawed unless it makes a profound change to its programmatic stances. In this hypothetical scenario, an important segment of the electorate will realise that democracy is pointless since one's desired goals cannot be realised.

Although the high legitimacy costs of militant democracy are always present, they become exceptionally acute when dealing with populism because its aims are not always and necessarily clearly hostile to the democratic system. Banning populist political forces can be difficult to justify, since they are not against democracy per se but rather at odds with the *liberal* democratic regime. Remember that liberal democracy is built upon a deep distrust of the extent to which 'the people' can govern themselves. As a consequence, and despite their programmatic differences, all populist forces share the opinion that the question of how to control the controllers has become more urgent than ever, because many unelected institutions at the national and supranational level have increasing power to jeopardise the principle of popular sovereignty (Rovira Kaltwasser 2013, 2014). Populists claim, not necessarily without reason, that under certain circumstances unelected bodies can run amok and favour the interests of powerful minorities. By way of illustration, as Wolfgang Streeck (2014) has recently argued, we should seriously ask ourselves if the promotion of austerity measures by the EU reflects the advancing immunisation of capital against democracy.

In addition, populism's discomfort with liberal democracy does not come out of nothing but rather out of failures of democratic representation (Hawkins and Rovira Kaltwasser 2017b; Mudde and Rovira Kaltwasser 2017; Roberts 2017). When segments of the electorate have the impression that their ideas and interests are not being taken into account by established political parties, there is fertile soil for populist forces that will politicise those issues that are pressing for segments of the electorate feeling orphaned. Take, for instance, the emergence of populist radical right parties in Europe, which have put the topic of immigration at the centre of the public debate (Akkerman, de Lange and Rooduijn 2016). Banning populist radical right parties would probably signal that there is no space to debate the possibility of reducing the number of immigrants and demanding improved assimilation into society. Instead of proscribing these parties, liberal democrats need to take into account the demands that populists are putting forward and better consider if the policies they propose have merit within a liberal democratic framework.

The second point refers to the boomerang effect that the use of militant democratic mechanisms can generate when dealing with populism. To understand this, it is important to bear in mind that unelected institutions are normally in charge of implementing militant democracy since this is usually considered the best way to avoid the misuse of the latter in a partisan manner (Müller 2016a: 260). Courts or electoral commissions are usually the actors that judge whether the conditions to ban a political party have been met, because they are independent institutions that seek to achieve the common good instead of defending specific interests. However, as populist forces are at odds with the liberal democratic regime, they challenge the very legitimacy of unelected institutions to make decisions. Therefore, an unintended consequence of the use of militant policies might be increased questioning of the authority and validity of the liberal democratic model as such. Populists will claim that actors who are neither elected nor controlled by 'the people' have decided to censor the party which gives voice to the 'silent majority'.

In addition, by outlawing the existence of a populist party, there is fair chance that the latter not only will get more publicity, but also – and more troublingly – its populist discourse will become more persuasive for an important sector of the voting public. The reason for this is that once populist forces are declared unconstitutional, their opponents will be tempted to use moral language, whereby they present themselves as the 'good democrats' and portray the populists as 'bad autocrats'. By advancing this type of rhetoric, populist forces might become stronger, since they will have proof that the establishment acts in an arrogant manner and has no interest in considering the demands that are allegedly being raised by the people (Rovira Kaltwasser 2017). This means that treating populist followers and leaders as silly only reinforces their self-image of victimhood, which in turn can amplify the gap between the citizens and their representatives. As Kirshner (2014: 22) has pointed out, 'successfully defending democracy depends not on defeating antidemocrats, but on reincorporating them into the political community. As a result, the protection of representative democracy is by its nature a long-term political project.'

This brings me to the third and last point. Militant democracy hinges upon the assumption that there a wide consensus within society on what democracy means and who the members of the demos are. Only if both a broad majority of the population and those who possess power believe certain political behaviours should be forbidden because they put liberal democracy at risk will the use of militant mechanisms be effective. This line of reasoning has a strong relationship to the concept of political culture, according to which democracy can prosper as long as citizens have a shared understanding of the relevance of respecting democratic procedures. 'Culturalist explanations make the important point that the political viability of militant rules is linked to their broader normative legitimacy in the public sphere' (Capoccia 2013: 218). Seen from this light, militant democracy can work under the condition that there is (almost) no disagreement when it comes to determining who should be seen as an internal enemy of democracy.

Nevertheless, the very emergence of populist forces reveals that citizens have different views on how democracy should work and who should be entitled to participate in the political process. If everybody agrees that *liberal* democracy is the only game in town, then there would not be space for the rise of populist actors. This means that the proliferation of populist parties around the world challenges the often implicit assumption present in the work of many scholars and practitioners that most citizens support the existence of unelected institutions that have the right to constrain popular sovereignty and if necessary ban political forces that are seen as illegitimate. Thus, as Jan-Werner Müller (2016a: 253) has provocatively formulated, countries that really need militant democracy probably are not in the posi-tion of sustaining it:

> in highly polarized and unstable polities, characterized by deep moral disagreement, militant democracy might make some sense, but the very facts of polarization and disagreement probably prevent the creation of a militant democracy. Everyone might be too concerned about the abuse of party bans for partisan purposes, for instance, to have such measures available.

Instead of taking for granted that the whole society supports liberal democ-racy, scholars and practitioners should empirically assess the extent to which different and conflicting models of democracy are present at both mass level and the elite level.[7] This is not a minor point, because it has an important consequence for the study of how to deal with populism: it shifts the analysis from the policies one needs to develop to forbid the populist supply to the policies one should try to curtail the demand for and supply of populism. To paraphrase the terminology of Robert Dahl (2003: 142), no institutional setting can ensure militant democracy in a country where the conditions favourable to militant democracy are absent. If this is true, the question about the *prerequisites* for the consolidation of liberal democ-racy is particularly pressing when thinking about the best ways to cope with populism.

Concluding Remarks

Almost a century ago, a Jewish legal scholar called Karl Loewenstein migrated from Nazi Germany to the US, where he coined the concept of 'militant democracy' to refer to the necessity of taking a combative approach towards the internal enemies of the democratic regime. According to him, to preserve democracy sometimes it is indispensable to restrict the rights of certain political forces and the example that he had in mind was none other than the rise of Hitler in Germany. Loewenstein's argument sparked an open debate about the mechanisms at hand for democratic self-preservation, and the recent rise of populist forces across the world has brought his argument to the forefront. In effect, populist actors of very different political colour are putting liberal democracies under stress and in some cases we have even seen how the coming into power of populist leaders via democratic means can lead to the formation competitive authoritarian regimes (Mainwaring 2012; Hawkins 2016).

Therefore, one could argue that militant democracy is the right approach when it comes to dealing with populism. By outlawing populist forces, democracy will act pre-emptively to secure its own preservation. Instead of allowing the election of Chávez in Venezuela, Orbán in Hungary or Trump in the US, autonomous institutions in those countries should have forbidden the appearance of these populist leaders on the ballot. Does this approach represent the best way to cope with populism? This chapter has sought to show that it is not. Militant democracy should be thought of as a last resort whose application against populist forces produces more harm than good. This is particularly true if the populist forces one must deal with are well organised and have significant levels of public support. Under these circumstances, the adoption of militant policies will be seen as illegitimate by a section of the electorate, which in turn will strengthen its confidence in the populist forces under attack. Part of problem lies in the fact that populists are not against democracy per se but rather at odds with the *liberal* democratic regime. Therefore, claiming that populist forces are authoritarian actors, who should be outlawed to prevent the collapse of democracy, is anything but straightforward.

Whether populists represent a threat or a corrective to liberal democracy is an empirical question that cannot be answered a priori (Mudde and Rovira Kaltwasser 2012, 2017; Rovira Kaltwasser 2012, 2013). Nevertheless, there are cases in which populist actors in government have produced an erosion of the liberal democratic regime and even its collapse. However, banning populists as a safety measure is not the best way to proceed because once a majority of the electorate is ready to support populist forces it is clear that there is no societal consensus on either the meaning of democracy or on who should be entitled to participate in the political process. Under these circumstances, militant democracy is of little help, since its application will spark an unsolvable dispute over the partisan (mis)use of party bans. To prevent a significant part of the electorate from voting for populist forces, one must shift focus from banning populism to avoiding its very emergence. How can this be achieved? My impression is that the solution lies in educating the voting public on the rules of liberal democracy. This is probably the only long-term strategy for escaping the democratic rise to power of populist actors. As Malkopoulou and Norman (2018) have recently argued, it is crucial to bring in social democratic and republican democratic theory as they help us to recognise that the avoidance of extremist political forces depends on the political and economic equality of existing societies.

Notes

1. For helpful comments on previous versions of this chapter, I would like to thank Alexander Kirshner, Anthoula Malkopoulu, Sofia Näsström and Paulina Ochoa Espejo. Moreover, the author acknowledges support from the Chilean National Fund for Scientific and Technological Development (FONDECYT project 1180020) and the Center for Social Conflict and Cohesion Studies (COES, CONICYT/FONDAP/15130009).
2. For instance, Article 20 provides that '(1) the Federal Republic of Germany is a democratic and social federal state. (2) All state authority is derived from the people. It shall be exercised by the people through elections and other votes and through specific legislative, executive, and judicial bodies. (3) The legislature shall be bound by the constitutional order, the executive and the judiciary by law and justice. (4) All Germans shall have the right to resist any person seeking to abolish this constitutional order, if no other remedy is available' (Schwartzberg 2007: 155).
3. Part of this section draws on Rovira Kaltwasser (2017).
4. For a detailed discussion of the conceptualisation advanced here, see Mudde and Rovira Kaltwasser (2013, 2017). Although it is true that there are some differences between those who understand populism as a set of ideas, my impression is that this is an inside-baseball discussion. Given that populism is just one instance of a particular level or kind of ideas, it makes relatively little difference if the genus of the populist phenomenon is seen as a discourse, an ideology, a frame or a worldview (Hawkins and Rovira Kaltwasser 2017a).
5. Take, for instance, the following statement by Donald Trump, in his inaugural speech in Washington DC: 'The establishment protected itself, but not the citizens of our country [. . .] Their triumphs have not been your triumphs and while they celebrated in our nation's capital, there was little to celebrate for struggling families all across our land. That all changes – starting right here, and right now, because this moment is your moment: it belongs to you [. . .] This is your day. This is your celebration [. . .] What truly matters is not which party controls our government, but whether our government is controlled by the people. January 20, 2017, will be remembered as the day the people became the rulers of this nation again. The forgotten men and women of our country will be forgotten no longer.'
6. Of course, when the preferred policies involve the promotion of the use of violence and/or the destruction of democracy, it is relatively easy to argue in favour of banning the political forces supporting these policies. Nevertheless, it is not self-evident that populist actors necessarily promote de use of violence and/ or the destruction of democracy, since they are at odds with liberal democracy rather than with democracy per se (see below). Not by chance, the populist radical right party Alternative für Deutschland obtained 12.6 per cent of the vote in the 2017 German general elections and the Constitutional Court has not banned the party in question. It is not a coincidence that the country which it is normally

seen as the paradigmatic example of a militant democracy (Germany) has not declared unconstitutional the populist radical right party that has entered into the parliament recently (Alternative für Deutschland).

7. As Mainwaring and Pérez-Liñán (2013) have empirically shown for Latin America, the rise and fall of democracy is directly connected to the normative preferences of elites; that is, when they value democracy intrinsically its chances of survival are much better than when they adopt an instrumental attitude towards democracy and endorse policy radicalism by any means necessary. For a similar argument, related to the role that elites play in strengthening or weakening institutions (such as the judiciary and the press) as well as long-standing democratic norms, see the work of Levitsky and Ziblatt (2018).

FIVE

Three Models of Democratic Self-Defence*

Anthoula Malkopoulou and Ludvig Norman

Democratic self-defence refers to the idea that democracy cannot survive without a well-articulated line of defence against those who seek its demise. When threatened at its core by political movements aimed to dismantle democratic institutions, democracy may need to assert itself through various defensive measures. Recently, this notion has gained renewed salience in light of political developments across Europe and the US, where extremist political movements are on the rise. Yet, the method for responding to such popular threats takes a variety of forms which rely on different conceptual and normative assumptions, for example regarding the role of the people or that of the rule of law in creating and accommodating such movements. While these differences are widely acknowledged, insufficient scholarly attention has been devoted to how they are tied to broader conceptions of democratic politics and contrasting conceptions of freedom. Our aim is to disentangle these assumptions and highlight how they lead to different variants of democratic self-defence. In addition to offering a conceptual critique of existing perspectives, we provide the basis for shifting the contemporary debate on democratic self-defence, which is currently centred on various degrees of repression, to a more nuanced discussion on how to make democratic polities more resilient.

We distinguish three overarching approaches to democratic self-defence: militant, procedural and social. First, we turn to critically discussing the concept of 'militant democracy' (Loewenstein 1937a). Developed in response to the rise of totalitarian ideologies in Europe in the 1930s, it has received new traction among many who see analogies with this period in the resurgence of contemporary political extremism. While not without its critics, the idea of militant democracy has come to serve as a dominant point of departure in recent public and scholarly discussions on democratic self-defence (Sajó 2004; Müller 2012a; Capoccia 2013; Kirshner 2014).[1] Despite the broadly liberal outlook of many 'neo-militant' theorists, the discourse on militant democracy reproduces a largely exclusionary elitist notion of democratic government built on a deep-rooted mistrust in the people to govern themselves. As such, it is a model of democratic self-defence that, rather than being delimited to the specific problem of extremism, has negative implications for democratic politics more generally. Our critique highlights these ideological aspects of militant democracy and aims, thus, at unlocking the debate on democratic self-defence from the focus on militancy and repression.

To move the discussion further in this direction, the chapter engages with two main competitors to the militant model, both of which have received less attention in recent debates. The 'procedural' approach, mainly associated with Hans Kelsen's ideas (1955, 2013 [1929]), is often treated as the polar opposite of militancy. It rejects the constitutionalisation of repressive and exclusionary measures and stresses openness and pluralism as democracy's unconditional principles. The third variant, which we call the 'social' model of democratic self-defence, has garnered even less attention in recent scholarly debates. Developed by thinkers, such as Alf Ross (1952) and Hermann Heller (2000 [1928]), it posits that fascism emerges due to social disintegration and that any attempt to counter it should include efforts to rehabilitate social justice and to strengthen the democratic ethos. We argue that, while the social model is also in part based on questionable assumptions, it identifies new conceptual and operational dimensions of democratic self-defence. Specifically, we demonstrate how basing such a model on a principle of political and social non-domination helps alleviate its most problematic aspects and serves to further highlight the shortcomings of competing models.

In the following, we first provide a critical overview of Karl Loewenstein's understanding of militant democracy, as well as the ideas of 'neo-militant' democratic theorists who draw on his work. Next, we proceed by discussing militant democracy's main competing school, that of Hans Kelsen and contemporary adherents of his paradigm of inclusive proceduralism. Third, we turn to the hitherto largely neglected 'social' model of democratic self-defence and provide a critical presentation of the ideas developed by Ross and Heller. Finally, we offer a brief synthesis of these three paradigms pointing to their similarities and differences, and we explain our preference for an updated variant of the social model.

The Elitist Assumptions of Militant Democracy

The concept of 'militant democracy' emerged in response to the rise of the authoritarian ideologies of fascism and communism in the 1930s. In this respect, the German constitutional lawyer Karl Loewenstein (1937a, 1937b) was among the first thinkers to formulate a strong defence of democracy. The conclusions drawn from the experience of fascism were crucially that democracy needed to be re-conceptualised in order to protect its institutions from internal assaults. Yet, central to this re-conceptualisation was a turn away from a politics of mass participation, which was taken as the signature identity of totalitarian regimes, and a conviction that the masses needed to be kept at arm's length from political decision making (Loewenstein 1937a). Loewenstein's 'militant democracy' thus instated a fundamentally anti-participatory and elitist logic at the centre of anti-extremist politics, one that identified political participation of the masses as an intrinsic part of the problem.

The necessity of elitist militancy was derived from a distinct understanding of the causes and nature of fascism. Fascism, Loewenstein argued, came simply from a thirst for power. Its cynical motives were commensurate to its nature: not a political ideology, 'not even a realistic constructive program' (Loewenstein 1937a: 423), but simply a technique to rule, through crude emotionalism, open propaganda and military symbolism, bolstered by pretend legality. The most characteristic identifier of the fascist technique was the use of emotional devices to control the masses, such as agitation of national sentiment and intimidation.[2] The 'emotional government' put forward by fascists was the exact opposite of 'constitutional government' for Loewenstein. But precisely because democracy was founded on reason rather than emotion it had no way of dealing effectively with the emotionalism of fascism (Loewenstein 1937b).

In charging anti-democrats with emotionally manipulating the masses, Loewenstein relied on an elitist understanding of the people's role in a democracy. The people from this perspective are relieved of agency, swayed to one direction or another by their emotional impulses and uncritical reflexes, and thus exemplifying their unfitness for democratic politics. In Loewenstein's (1937b: 657) own words, 'liberal democracy is suitable, in the last analysis, only for the political aristocrats among the nations'. Thus, it is impossible to grasp militant democracy in Loewenstein's rendition without also acknowledging his deep-seated mistrust of the people's ability to govern themselves.[3] This is a recognisable pattern in older elitist theories, where political exclusion and the opposition to broad political participation is based on the notion that the masses are too easily affected by demagoguery and nurture passions that could be exploited for authoritarian ends (e.g. Burke 1999 [1774]). It also bears striking similarity to postwar theories of elite competition, such as Schumpeter's published shortly after Loewenstein's; in them, democracy is a matter of competition between elites for votes from the people *qua* masses, who have 'a reduced power of discerning facts, a reduced preparedness to act upon them, a reduced sense of responsibility' (Schumpeter 2003: 260).

From this elitist conception of democracy follows the conclusion that defending democracy requires cutting the communication lines between the opportunistic political elites and the volatile citizenry. To be sure, Loewenstein's militant recipe of 'anti-extremist legislation' included political and legal measures addressed at elites, such as the prohibition of anti-democratic parties and party militias. But it also involved restrictions on citizens, concerning basic civil rights, such as the freedom of assembly, the freedom of speech and the establishment of a political police (Loewenstein 1937b). To the extent that Loewenstein was concerned with freedom at all, his militant democratic model allows for a temporary suspension of basic freedoms and a significant degree of domination for the sake of protecting constitutional democracy. Few contemporary democratic militants subscribe to all or even most of these measures. Furthermore, they differ from each other on important points. Yet, they coalesce around the notion that safekeeping democratic institutions will often require militant measures, most of which are aimed towards curbing political participation of undesirable political actors.

Neo-Militant Democracy

In the last few years, militant democracy has re-emerged as the dominant normative framework on which liberal democracies can rely for pushing back extremist political movements that are on the rise.[4] As Capoccia (2013: 219) notes, 'scholars largely agree that limitations on basic rights of expression and participation, enacted to safeguard democracy, are compatible with the principle of liberal constitutional democracy'. However, compared to Loewenstein, the deep mistrust of the people's ability to govern themselves is far less pronounced among contemporary advocates of militant democracy. For instance, Issacharoff (2007) argues that militant measures must be neutral – and should primarily regulate activity in the electoral arena – to prevent their arbitrary use against political dissidents. Care is also taken in distinguishing between anti-democratic *actions* and anti-democratic *ideas* (Capoccia 2005: 57; Bourne 2012: 209) so that prohibitions concern only the former and not the latter, thus avoiding interference with the freedom of thought. Because it addresses these concerns, we call this new and softer version of militant democracy 'neo-militant democracy' (Backes 1998; Sajó 2004; Thiel 2009a; Müller 2012b, 2016a; Kirshner 2014).

Among these scholars, there has indeed been a turn away from the most draconian measures suggested by Loewenstein. As Müller (2016a: 258) states, few (if any) militant democrats today would support far-reaching constitutional provisions approving, for instance, the permanent disenfranchisement of particular individuals. Kirshner (2014: 40–41) argues similarly that even vehement anti-democrats are likely to have *other* legitimate interests, which such actors should be able to pursue, for instance, by being able to vote in elections.[5] Targeting parties rather than individuals alleviates some of the immediate problems associated with disenfranchisement. Justifications of party bans rely on the special responsibility of parties in shaping political claims (Müller 2016a: 147) or on the potentially harmful effects such parties may have on a society's moral-political development (Niesen 2002; Frankenberg 2004).

While the focus on Lowenstein's idea that the people are susceptible to emotionalism is less pronounced in recent accounts, Sajó (2012), in particular, concludes that the state should strive to screen out political emotionalism altogether and enforce preventive rational-legal restrictions. 'Radical emotionalism', he argues, is a critical challenge to democratic constitutionalism, stating that the people 'is passionate, is easily manipulated to follow identity agendas, or is prone to fear [. . .] it is emotionally conditioned' (Sajó 2012: 571). Apart from Sajó's explicit mention, the role of emotions in agitating crowds plays a much less prominent role in contemporary discussions. Sajó himself acknowledges that a conflation of 'people' and 'masses' is arbitrary and may echo assumptions about mob rule that often betray class bias and racism; yet, this does not stop him from endorsing an infantilising conception of the masses as irrational and emotionally unreliable, which then feeds into his justification of militant democracy.

Other scholars take a more cautionary stance and delimit the scope of militant measures. For Kirshner (2014), exclusion ought to apply only to those actors who *violate the right to participate* of other individuals or groups. Even for these cases, he adds, such bans should only be temporary. For Rummens and Abts (2010), the demands on parties to conform to democratic values are increased – and justifications for exclusion of non-democrats strengthened – as they move closer to acquiring decision-making power.

Others have historicised the question, drawing on the documented experience of particular political movements of the past. This perspective, known as 'negative republicanism' (Niesen 2002), targets only parties with an undeniable anti-democratic record, such as German Nazis, Italian Fascists and their successors. Neo-militant democrats have through such theses moderated and thereby eased some of the more troubling aspects of Loewenstein's original position. However, as we will argue in the following, militant democracy, even in its neo-militant version, retains an elitist and illiberal core, and represents a model of democratic self-defence with potentially damaging implications for the broader arena of democratic politics.

A Critique of Neo-Militant Democracy

In spite of neo-militant theorists' recent attempts to update and refine the normative underpinnings of democratic militancy, their main aim has remained to fine-tune its scope of application, rather than to question the assumptions on which democratic militancy relies. Indeed, the main question discussed among these scholars is *how* to best circumscribe militant measures, limit their side effects and prevent them from backfiring, and not *if* it is legitimate to use militant measures in the first place. This excessive focus on the conditions under which militant democracy could be used has obscured the more fundamental question of whether militant democracy is justified at all and to what extent we should accept the assumptions underlying these justifications.

As mentioned, Loewenstein entertained little respect for the capacity of the people to resist the fascist menace. Relatedly, many comparative scholars' engagement with militant democracy places strong emphasis on the choices made by democratic *elites*, heads of states, prime ministers and party leaders, when anti-system parties challenge democracy (Pfersmann 2004; Capoccia 2005; Tyulkina 2015a). From this outlook on democratic government, the people seem to be more or less absent. Instead, their role is reduced to mere spectatorship and, by way of omission, they legitimise elite actors as the sole protectors of democracy. Thus, neo-militant democrats recast Loewenstein's anti-participatory elitism and the passive role of citizens in democratic government. Through this endorsement, a more constrained understanding of democracy is reproduced.

A fundamental assumption underlying justifications for militancy is that it is justified by the 'special' circumstances in which it is enacted. Or, the value of militant democracy lies in its capacity to quickly react and effectively contain extremists in the short term (Capoccia 2005; Kirshner 2014). Its normative costs are offset by the temporary character of militant measures and the specificity of the situations, where states may apply them. Militant democracy, from this perspective, is not a recipe for democracy more generally. Rather, removing undisciplined players from the democratic 'game' is required to preserve the game itself. Unless all players accept the constitutional rules of democratic politics, democracy – like a game – will be discontinued (Jovanovic 2016; see also the discussion in Kirshner 2014: 91–105). The idea that democrats have a right to defend themselves echoes Rawls's assertion that people 'need not stand idly by while others destroy the basis for their existence' (quoted in Kirshner 2014: 3). We do not disagree with this approach inasmuch as it serves to justify the more general need for a policy of democratic self-defence. Rather, we do so out of a concern that a strategy of militant exclusion – as opposed to other types of democratic self-defence – will have negative repercussions for democratic politics more broadly for the reasons we outline below.

Our critique relies on the notion that militant democracy fails to respect the principle of non-domination, due to the arbitrariness that militancy introduces in democracy. Invernizzi Accetti and Zuckerman's (2016) engagement with Carl Schmitt, in this context, is enlightening. Their argument brings to the surface militant democracy's indebtedness to Schmitt's notion of sovereignty and state of exception (Invernizzi Accetti and Zuckerman 2016: 5). Briefly put, the sovereign can exceptionally suspend constitutional law when the constitution's political 'core' – that is, the belief system that animates it – is violated. Important here is that such exceptional powers, as in the case of militant democracy, introduce a fundamental element of discretionary power in democracy. What constitutes a threat to the political 'core' of the constitution is always based, to some extent, on an arbitrary decision: therefore, it is impossible to delimit and isolate militant measures to the specific situations for which they are intended.[6] Yet, unlike Invernizzi Accetti and Zuckerman (2016: 5), we do not consider that militant measures are necessarily tantamount to 'an exclusion from the political entity itself': for us, the main problem is that they lead to a general situation characterised by domination. An important point here is that freedom in liberal republican terms captures structural relationships. Irrespective of whether militant measures are rarely or perhaps even never applied, the constitutionalisation of militant measures establishes a structural relationship characterised by a subjection to the sovereign's arbitrary will. That is, 'the possibility of interference' (Pettit 2012: 62) is enough to establish a state of domination. The purported delimitation of militant measures to specific circumstances does not alleviate this problem.

What is more, domination is not simply a casual consequence of militancy but is linked to fundamental assumptions underlying its justification: deep-seated exclusionary *elitism* and suspicion towards popular participation are assumptions that are directly opposed to the principle of non-domination. And since non-domination is the fundamental value of liberal constitutional democracy (Pettit 1997), democracies cannot legitimately restrict the right of participation of certain groups without causing their domination. This is further elucidated by the Schmittean notion of border concept, that is, *Grenzbegriff* (Schmitt 2005). While the aim of such a concept is to deal with the *limits* of political orders, at the same time it defines the fundamental logic of such an order as a whole. From this perspective, the suggestion that militancy could be isolated to the specific situations for which it is intended without affecting the system as a whole is an illusion. Rather, both through its normative assumptions and its practical consequences, it compromises fundamental principles of democracy and liberty.

However, as neo-militants tend to argue, militancy deals with the thorny problem of anti-democrats actually exploiting democratic procedures to dismantle democracy from within. The ubiquitous reference to Goebbels's quote, in which he scorns democracy for providing its enemies with the means to destroy it, is illustrative of this position (see Fox and Nolte 1995: 208; Müller 2012a, 2016a; Capoccia 2013; Kirshner 2014; Tyulkina 2015a). Militancy, however unpalatable, may thus be justified as the lesser of two evils. Yet, to what extent is it accurate to claim that democracies can dismantle themselves from within? As an increasing number of scholars have noted, rather than exploitation of democratic procedures, the rise of the Nazi Party in Weimar Germany, which militant democrats use as legitimation, depended on widespread intimidation and political violence (Mommsen 1996; Müller 2016a: 252). This poses a problem of both historical and conceptual accuracy. Assuming the Weimar 'accident' as a backdrop for militant arguments may indeed reflect a selective reading of events, overemphasising the risk of democracies abolishing themselves through democratic means.

While we share the concerns articulated by militant democrats, we underline that conventional justifications for party bans and other restrictions of civil freedoms rely on a set of questionable assumptions which contradict the fundamental value of non-domination. Contrary to what theorists of militant democracy often assume, these measures insert a fundamentally elitist logic at the heart of democracy. It is a logic that cannot be confined to the specific domain of guarding the limits of democracy but carries with it implications for the democratic polity as a whole.

Open Democracies: Liberal-Procedural Self-Defence

Militant democracy's elitist elements come into sharper light when considering Hans Kelsen's ideas on democracy. Kelsen emerged as Loewenstein's chief challenger in the interwar years and onwards. His position is based first and foremost on a strictly procedural conception of democracy based on freedom and more specifically freedom as individual autonomy (Kelsen 2013 [1929]; Urbinati and Invernizzi Accetti 2013: 5). It is seen as a fundamental principle of democratic government that a state must allow even those political movements to participate that promote views that are widely deemed unacceptable, even overtly anti-democratic and illiberal. Conversely, the militant defence of liberal democracy through illiberal means incorporates unmanageable tensions at its very foundations, tensions that threaten the fundamental value of negative freedom (Kelsen 2006 [1932]). Kelsen (2006: 237) argued that a democracy which seeks to assert itself against the will of the majority by force ceases to be a democracy, no matter what the consequences of the majority might be. The commitment to value relativism was part of Kelsen's (1948, 2013: 103) understanding that its opposite, value absolutism, was more likely to lead to authoritarian politics. His (2013: 103) unconditionally inclusive, pluralist stance and unyielding loyalty to the democratic flag 'even when the ship is sinking' earned him Loewenstein's (1937a: 424, 431) scorn for demonstrating 'democratic fundamentalism' and 'legalistic self-complacency'.

Today, few democratic theorists seem to subscribe to the far-reaching pluralism proposed by Kelsen. Cappoccia (2013: 211) states in this regard that 'Hans Kelsen's value neutral model of pluralist democracy [. . .] according to which all political positions should be given equal rights of expression and participation [. . .] has virtually no supporters today'. Nevertheless, this binary and almost opposite type of model to that of Loewenstein does have some advocates. A moderate support for Kelsen's views is expressed in the idea that the state should be, if not passive, at least 'tolerant' towards extreme voices, renouncing extensive use of repressive instruments (Fox and Nolte 1995; Bourne 2012). In this framework, countries do not pose any restrictions on parliamentary activity or constitutional reform and deem the outlawing of parties unconstitutional.[7]

Commitment to proceduralism can also be found in countries that belong to the common law tradition. The main difference with militant democracy is that, instead of *constitutionally* condoned party bans and restrictions justified by the preservation of a 'free democratic order' (Article 21 of the German Constitution), here responses are always filtered through the *criminal code*. Hence, legal actions are subject to the demands for proof of evidence in line with regular penal law. More specifically, US jurisprudence has established the requirement of 'imminent danger of direct harm' in order to take legal action. This involves a heavy presumption in favour of free speech and association (Issacharoff 2007: 1416) and a systematic avoidance of restricting it unless it incites criminal conduct.[8]

More recently, Rosenblum has added a post-Kelsenian twist to the liberal democratic paradigm by arguing that political inclusion will temper extremism and gradually socialise its proponents into democrats, as they are increasingly prompted to play according to the rules of the democratic game. Participating in regulated rivalry will force once-radical political actors to become more moderate. The core idea is that 'electoral political competition, like any strong institutional practice, is formative' (Rosenblum 2008: 452). This will prevent dissidents from going underground and will facilitate their political integration and democratic acculturation. 'Faith in politics' per Rosenblum is thus a direct opposite to Loewenstein's call 'to fight fire with fire'. Similar views are held by other scholars (Invernizzi Accetti and Zuckerman 2016) and confirmed in empirical studies on the positive effects of integrating extremist parties, like the Spanish communists in the post–Franco transition years (Linz and Stepan 1996: 96–98), or anti-immigration parties today (van Spanje and van der Brug 2007). While we do not challenge its plausibility, the empirical argument regarding the socialising effects of democratic inclusion does not answer to an important challenge: that participation of extremists in mainstream politics might actually backfire and grant them additional resources to further their political goals – for example, a platform and a chance to normalise their claims.

Indeed, it could be argued that Kelsen's highly tolerant approach is built on an idealised conception of democracy and paid little attention to the empirical realities of interwar Europe, as charged to him by Loewenstein. Or, it may have carried a pessimistic undercurrent that, when people are set to an undemocratic course, there is little that can be done to save them from themselves (Issacharoff 2007: 1412). Still, for us, the principal problem with Kelsen's procedural approach is neither its over-optimism nor its alleged over-pessimism; rather, it is the reductive notion of democratic government as a state run by the rule of law. Indeed, his opposition to militant democracy could be read as first and foremost an argument about the need to guarantee the internal integrity of *formal* democracy and law, that is, the validity of codified procedures. As Kelsen (1955) argues, a democracy *by* the people always takes precedence to a government *for* the people. Its content, whether liberal or social democratic, cannot be made part of the definition of democracy itself (Kelsen 1955: 4). Coercive orders can only be legitimate if individuals have had a role, however marginal, in instituting the rules of such an order. In this sense, Kelsen's concern about militancy overlaps with our own critique, as his insistence on participation could be interpreted as a commitment to non-domination.

However, Kelsen's view of democratic government is based on a concept of freedom that is defined in purely negative, formal terms. For him, freedom is to draw a boundary on what one can and cannot do on others, which means that private life must remain independent of social control (Berlin 2002 [1969]). That Kelsen, in terms of personal political orienta-tions, sympathised with Austrian social democracy did not change the fact that he understood democracy in narrow procedural terms:[9]

> There is [. . .] no better means to [. . .] pave the way for autocracy, to dis-suade the people from their desire for participation in government, than to depreciate the definition of democracy as a procedure by the argument that it is 'formalistic', to make the people believe [. . .] that they have achieved the longed for democracy if they have a government for the people. (Kelsen 1955: 5)

While we are largely sympathetic to a thin definition of democracy, a demo-cratic system based exclusively on negative freedom as formal rights does not grant space for exploring social and structural preconditions of free-dom. In other words, the stress on individual autonomy reduces citizens to individual carriers of formal rights, regardless of whether they can actually use such rights to associate and collectively mobilise for common goals. Conversely, it also excludes a discussion on the non-legal conditions that may facilitate or hinder their engagement in democratic politics.

Nevertheless, Kelsenian and post-Kelsenian proceduralism have so far offered the only challenge to militant democracy in the contemporary debate on how to address the problem of extremism in democratic politics. It has inspired alternative tools to deal with extremists, such as the state's duty to promote democratic values among civil society (Brettschneider 2012; Niesen 2002) or the mobilisation of citizens as defenders of constitu-tional values (Malkopoulou 2016). Indeed, the role of democratic society, rather than the more narrowly construed constitutional questions that are conventionally preoccupying theorists of militant democracy, should be at the forefront of debates on democratic self-defence. Therefore, we now turn to discussing a third approach that has received far less attention and stresses not only political inclusion but also social integration as a response to the rise of extremism.

Immunising the People: A Model of Social Democratic Self-Defence

What we call the social democratic defence against extremism places the broader social dynamics of extremism front and centre. Compared to mili-tant and liberal approaches to popular threats, social democratic thinking engages, more broadly, with social stability as a basis for the reproduction of democratic institutions, recognising how social and political integration are central elements for democratic self-defence. While such ideas have fundamentally informed post-war thinking on how to build strong democracies (Jackson 2013), they have rarely been discussed in relation to political extremism. Here, constitutional checks and balances play less of a role, emphasis is instead placed on forging social cohesion. From this point of view, extremism results from the perceived impossibility of certain groups of the population to channel their socio-economic demands through the political system. The antidote is an inclusive organisation of democratic politics, along with an emphasis on social justice and equality.

Social democratic ideology 'prescribes the use of democratic collective action to extend the principles of freedom and equality valued by democrats in the political sphere to the organisation of the economy and society' (Jackson 2013: 348). Democratic institutions have a key instrumental value for the promotion of social justice and stand in a reciprocal relation to it. In the words of Karl Mannheim (1943: 6): 'as the working of democracy is essentially based upon democratic consent, the principle of social justice is not only a question of ethics but also a precondition of the functioning of the democratic system itself'. However, rather than exclusively built around centralised socio-economic planning and consensus, some social democratic thinkers saw the need to retain conflict as an intrinsic part of democratic politics. Here, contrary to militant democracy, democracy is built on a fundamental trust in the people to collectively shape the organisation of politics. Political and social integration is a means, not an obstacle, in the fight against extremism. Yet, in the contemporary debate on democratic self-defence, the arguments of social democratic thinkers, like Heller (2000 [1928]), Mannheim (1943) and Ross (1952), who all distanced themselves from both Loewenstein and Kelsen, have been largely overlooked.[10]

Alf Ross and the Social Basis of Democracy and Freedom

In the immediate post-war period, Danish constitutional lawyer Alf Ross examined which social conditions need to be in place for democracy to function. His work, *Why Democracy?* (Ross 1952),[11] was fundamentally informed by the Nazi occupation of his country and focused, in particular, on what could be done to avoid backsliding into authoritarianism and dictatorship after the war. First, he argued, there are certain social-psychological conditions that are necessary for democracy, conditions that are best realised through the very struggle for democracy (see also Lerner 1938). Indeed, Ross (1952: 4) argued, the attraction of fascism, in particular among the youth, in the 1930s was undergirded by how democracy had become viewed as 'banal and commonplace, no longer capable of inspiring'. It is in the process of working towards democratic rights that citizens become aware of the true value of such rights, the notion of democracy should be seen as 'a boon which every day must be fought for anew'. Thus, Ross's (1952: 169) arguments for a strong democracy, able to withstand the future onslaught of extremism, focus on its social-psychological prerequisites 'without which it will be condemned to failure and decay'.

Ross (1952: 175) was, like Loewenstein, wary of the emotional appeal of propaganda on the masses but held higher hopes regarding the possibility to make the population 'propaganda-proof'. This could be achieved through a democratic education, which must, Ross (1952: 176) argues, occupy the middle ground between all-out liberalism, on one hand, and the collectivism of communism, on the other. Contrary to many of his liberal contemporaries, he saw fascism as a greater threat to democracy than that posed by communism. Thus, apart from fascism, Ross also turned against liberal thinkers, and, in particular, Hayek's (1944) arguments as developed in *The Road to Serfdom*. Both Hayek and Kelsen argued for the incompatibility of democracy and socialism, seeing in the socialist state an inevitable turn towards dictatorship (Kelsen 1955, 2013: 97–99). Ross's discussion on this matter was partly an effort to counter that assertion, but also, more crucially, to demonstrate that the society outlined by Hayek would be unable to mount a defence against extremist pressures. Ross criticised Hayek not only for his reliance on overly abstract arguments but also for his lack of understanding of the differences between communism – which Ross also opposed – and a more moderate and democratically driven social democracy. He also saw in this all-out liberalism not respect for the individual – as Hayek did – but an expression of 'indifference and ruthlessness' (Ross 1952: 176). For social democrats, a society based on liberal and individualistic premises, rather than enhancing freedom, provides both the material and ideational conditions for deep social tensions and extremism. The organisation of society and politics exclusively around a negative and transcendental conception of freedom would, from this perspective, not be able to mount a strong defence of democracy.

Ross thus departs sharply from Kelsen's commitment to negative freedom and instead becomes a rather raw supporter of its positive variant. For him, freedom did not consist of being unconstrained by other persons from doing as one pleases, but of being a full master of one's actions, to paraphrase Berlin (2002 [1969]). In that sense, being free contains a specific direction of self-realisation. This direction is based on the idea of belonging to a greater social 'whole' of which the individual is just a part; a person's true and rational will is then identical with the collective will. It is in this light that Ross imagines the end of conflict and the emergence of a social democratic order.

In addition, Ross shared Kelsen's great optimism in science and saw scientific progress as one of the key factors in making many political conflicts obsolete, not least by short-circuiting the selfish strife for power, which was at the heart of fascism:

> Many political conflicts arise out of existing inequality, particularly the clash between capital and labor. Once these are removed, many matters will appear as technical common concerns, and there will not arise the definite clashes of interests which may lead to a struggle for power and the misuse of it at the expense of liberty and fellowship. (Ross 1952: 189)

This variety of social democratic self-defence, thus, relies on science as a way to circumvent political conflict. It does so through social levelling, which removes power from the equation. Since everyone's needs are assumed to be taken care of, the impulse to strive for power is weakened, along with the inclination to abuse authority for selfish ends.

The prerequisites for Ross's epistemic social democracy to work are a general agreement on the broad strokes of politics and the shaping of political institutions on the basis of such agreement. Thus, unlike Loewenstein, who conceptualised democratic self-defence in elitist terms, the social democratic position *per* Ross opens up for the possibility of defending democracy by expanding popular participation rather than constraining it. While, for Ross, science would in many cases displace political conflict, his view on democracy also builds on the continued involvement of the people to decide on the way forward. Nonetheless, once the epistemic production of consensus is removed, it is not immediately obvious how democracy would deal with situations characterised by fundamental antagonism and conflict. Ross's conviction that common ground on most political problems could be found through scientific and democratic means de-emphasises not only the role of conflict in democracy but also the need to appreciate its positive constructive role in a democracy.

Hermann Heller and the Central Role of Conflict in Social Democracy

In contrast to Ross, Hermann Heller, a German constitutional lawyer and social democrat working in the first decades of the twentieth century, struggled much more to preserve a space for conflict within the bounds

of democracy.[12] Heller shared with Ross the notion that democratic society was conditioned by a degree of consensus on fundamental democratic
tenets. However, he saw this as a means to retain a necessary element of
conflict in the democratic process, rather than as an intrinsic goal. To this
end, Heller stated that:

> [. . .] social homogeneity can never mean the abolition of the necessarily
> antagonistic social structure [. . .] Social homogeneity is always a social psy-
> chological sphere in which the inevitably present oppositions and conflicts
> of interest appear constrained by a consciousness and sense of the 'we', by a
> community will that actualizes itself. This relative equalization of the social
> consciousness has the resources to work through antithetical tensions, and
> to digest huge religious, political, economic, and other antagonisms. (Heller
> 2000 [1928]: 261)

Hence, rather than taking the position of Ross, who thought that many, if
not most, political conflicts would dissolve through the advances of science,
Heller retains antagonism as a central and indeed constitutive element of
democratic politics. Consensus from this perspective is not the end point,
but only supplies the platform on which political conflict can be played out
without regressing into violence. In that, he also differs from Kelsen, who
saw democratic institutions as a pressure valve that dissolves (rather than
retains) conflict (see Kelsen 2013).

Important here, for the issue of defending democracy, is the highly
process-specific character of democratic practices, including those that have
as their aim to push back extremism. Here, the non-utopian configuration
of social democracy by its key figure Eduard Bernstein lies close at hand:
'what is usually termed "the final goal of socialism" . . . is nothing to me,
the *movement* is everything' (1993 [1899]: 168–169, emphasis added). This
points to a more radically inclusive kind of politics, where reform as an
ongoing process, rather than utopian revolution, is the fundament. While
Ross's unabashed optimism in the ability of science to solve social conflict
has waned considerably since the 1950s, the preservation of conflict and
dissensus is quite discernible in contemporary post-Marxist discourse (e.g.
Mouffe 2000).

However, social and economic equalisation as a political goal furthered
by the social state is itself conditional upon strongly delineated political
identities and values. An important aspect of both Heller's and Ross's work
is the assumption that the necessary consensus that needs to be in place for
democracy to work depends on a series of shared values that generate social
homogeneity via trust, empathy and solidarity. So, while democracy, in

terms of its procedures, is conceptualised as 'thin', it relies on 'thick' shared socio-cultural values on top of which such a democracy can be built. At its extreme, this 'national *Kultursozialismus*' (Wolf 1993) can lead in a circular fashion to radical right-wing ideas, such as welfare chauvinism, according to which only deserving natives should be eligible for solidarity transfers. A strong community built around a well-defined set of values can also work to exclude, create social hierarchies and be used to fuel precisely the types of political programmes often pursued by the radical right. In spite of these problems, there are, as will be outlined in the following, more general reasons why we should pay attention to this approach to democratic self-defence.

Towards a Social Democratic Self-Defence Today

Unlike militant democrats, the social democratic theorists do not confine themselves to discussing a narrow legalistic framework of democratic self-defence. They take a broader perspective that recognises an active role for citizens in the pursuit of a resilient democracy. Here, the notion of freedom in terms of non-domination becomes a crucial component. A social model of democratic self-defence cannot rely on a negative conception of freedom as non-interference (Berlin 2002 [1969]), whereby democracy equals the establishment of a set of formal rights. Rather than reverting to the entirely positive notion of freedom, perhaps most clearly expressed in Ross's social scientific determinism, the social model drawing on Heller is closer to the negative, republican concept of freedom as non-dependence or non-domination. In a nutshell, domination occurs when an agent has a power of interference on an arbitrary basis over another person (Pettit 1997: 52; Skinner 1998). Conversely, non-domination is a sort of immunity against such possibility. The notion of non-domination, thus, serves as a safeguard against an overly substantive definition of democracy. It also, crucially, guards against attempts to implement militant measures that lead to the domination of particular groups.

Republican democratic theory holds that in order for people to avoid domination by others or by the state, they must enjoy a significant and equal degree of power over the laws that shape their lives (Pettit 2012: 4). Popular control of public institutions is a *sine qua non* of republican freedom, as is a constitutional order that grants equal power to each citizen. A social democratic self-defence which seeks to avoid the problematic aspects of positive freedom will then, like Heller, give priority to popular powers of contestation and mutual interdependence. The latter is especially important, as it suggests that the state must secure the equal enjoyment of basic liberties by all citizens 'on the basis of a guarantee of public resources and protections' (Pettit 2012: 77). This implies a range of infrastructural programmes that provide equal access to education, the legal system and the natural environment, and a system of protection of social, medical and judicial security that extends beyond formal, legal rights (Pettit 2012: 110–122). In short, the state must protect the needy from relying on relations of dependency (such as the goodwill of an employer) and guard them against private domination. Importantly, the provision of such goods is justified with reference to *political* rather than *social* non-domination. In other words, this approach does not assume that democracy is instrumental for satisfying the objective needs of citizens, but rather the opposite – that securing social non-domination is a precondition for citizens to be able to exercise their liberties. In other words, social justice is not an end in itself but rather a precondition for political participation and for stabilising democracy.

A social democratic defence against extremism built on the notion of non-domination is thus justified for two interrelated reasons. First, removing some of the burdens associated with severe social inequality enables broad political participation, not merely confined to general elections and referendums. Redistribution of public resources on the basis of a principle of non-domination will free up time and energy among the citizenry, and as a result enable them to engage more actively in social and political life. Ensuring broad and regular participation in democratic processes is surely not a guarantee against extremism. However, democratic systems should, as far as possible, spread the stakes in the democratic system broadly across the citizenry to avoid extremism. This emphasis on pluralism resembles the one championed by Kelsen. However, the social democratic model also recognises the need to create the conditions for such a pluralism to be enacted in practice. As Heller argued, Kelsen's proceduralism would award the title *Rechtstaat* to any legal regime regardless of how it fared in reality (Dyzenhaus 2000: 251); worse yet, without social homogeneity, formal democracy becomes a dictatorship of the ruling class (Heller 2015 [1933]; and Wolf 1993: 504). By contrast, the *Sozialer Rechtstaat* is crafted with an eye on social and economic reality and is based on socio-economic rights and democratic decision-making procedures; it not only involves provisions on taxation and public spending but also 'the actual capacity to shape the socio-economic order through collective decisions' (Menéndez 2015).

The second justification of a social democratic defence against extremism relies on Heller's (2007 [1929]; 2015) idea that political stability needs to be grounded in political and economic equality; conversely, political crises – such as the rise of extremism – are symptoms of the structural weakness of the socio-economic order. While there is no definite link between social inequality and extremism, we would agree with Heller (2015) that such inequalities make societies less resilient to different types of crises and thus more susceptible to political radicalisation and instability. By implication, the discussion of how best to defend democracy must move beyond whether or not extremist actors should be targeted by repressive measures, towards a more comprehensive strategy for constructing stable democratic polities.

The social democratic emphasis on political participation and its social preconditions stand in contrast to militant democracy, which reduces the *liberal* aspect of democracy into a set of exclusionary elitist principles. That is, while militant democracy aims at protecting liberal rights, its underlying assumptions reveal a deep-seated distrust of the people's ability to make decisions that would bolster and protect a democratic polity. On the other hand, the Kelsenian liberal position views trust in the people as a corollary of their formal, legal rights. In contrast to both, the social model of democratic self-defence places the people at the forefront of any effort to safeguard democratic institutions, making democratic self-defence part of an ongoing *process* of realising democracy.

Conclusion

By engaging with the assumptions underlying contemporary debates on militant democracy, we have sought to broaden the perspectives on democratic self-defence. The dichotomy between militancy and all-out pluralism has made militancy the given point of departure for debates on these issues. While advocates for militancy have, in most cases, taken significant strides away from Loewenstein's original call for militant democracy, we argued that his elitist legacy still informs many of the contemporary arguments of neo-militant democrats.

The apparent allure of militancy seems to have pushed aside alternative ways of thinking about how democracies can defend themselves from those who oppose it. The procedural and social approaches to democratic self-defence presented in this chapter supply a slightly different take on the issue of extremism in politics. More specifically, these two approaches see citizens, rather than elites, as the driving force of democracy and its defence. By contrast, militant democrats inherit from Loewenstein an elitist distrust of the people.

The social democratic model, similar to post-Kelsenian liberal proceduralism, nourishes a 'faith in politics' that requires unconditional democratic inclusion. However, for the proceduralist position, this stance relies on an individualised conception of democracy as a set of formal rights and says little about the conditions under which such rights could be exercised in practice. Instead, the social model of democratic self-defence informed by the notion of freedom as non-domination highlights the social conditions that enable political participation as the *sine qua non* of a journey towards democracy. A central aim of this chapter has been to show the relevance of the social democratic model of self-defence for contemporary democracies as an alternative to the elitism of militant democracy, on one hand, and the atomistic individualism of liberal proceduralism, on the other hand. While there are of course no fail-safe ways to protect democracy, our chapter provides the basis for moving towards a model that is aligned with democratic, liberal and social values.

Acknowledgements

We would like to thank warmly all commentators, particularly Uwe Backes, Christian Fernandez, Giuseppe Martinico, Cesare Pinelli and Giovanni Orsina. We are also very grateful to the editors and three anonymous reviewers for their very constructive feedback. Any remaining errors are fully our own. This chapter has been presented in earlier form at the ECPR General Conference (2016), the Swedish Political Science Conference (2016) and LUISS University Rome (2016).

Funding

The author(s) received no financial support for the research, authorship and/or publication of this chapter.

Notes

*   This chapter is republished from Malkopoulou and Norman (2018). We would like to thank the publishers for the permission to republish the article in the current volume.

1. Several efforts to ban extremist parties were underway during 2016 in countries such as Germany, the UK and Finland.

2. In view of this diagnosis, Loewenstein (1937a: 421–422) discarded several competing attempts to explain the rise of fascism, such as a lack of democratic traditions, national humiliation following military defeat, economic depression or capitalist anxiety.

3. For a discussion of how this general mistrust in the people was reproduced in Loewenstein's post-war work, in particular his views on European political cooperation, see Norman (2016).

4. Here, we refer mainly to the electoral victories of ultra-right parties, such as Golden Dawn and Jobbik.

5. Invernizzi Accetti and Zuckerman's (2016: 5, 8) insistence on the point that militant democratic measures work to exclude members of the political community seems, from this point of view, slightly misdirected.

6. Ancient Athenians recognised this inherent political bias in identifying democracy's enemies and, therefore, used political rather than legal means to identify and expel them (see Malkopoulou 2017).

7. Bourne (2012: 210) calls these 'abstentionist' states – in the sense that they abstain from militancy – and further divides them to 'permissive' ones, that have no rules for party proscriptions, and 'passive' ones, that have rules, but refrain from using them.

8. To be sure, there is no clear consensus whether countries belonging to this tradition – such as the US – can indeed be termed non-militant. One objection is that not disposing of a constitutional principle of militancy does not automatically make them less hostile to extremist movements, McCarthyism being a case in point.

9. It is illustrative that, as Jabloner (1998) notes, Kelsen declined membership to the party on the grounds that it collided with his scientific ethos.

10. This being said, Mannheim did not exclude the possibility of democracy resorting to militant measures.

11. The volume was originally published in Danish in 1946.

12. Heller's argument was in important parts an intervention in the debate between Hans Kelsen and Carl Schmitt and did not revolve explicitly around the issue of militant democracy, especially since it preceded Loewenstein's theory by a decade or so. However, it is relevant here, as it serves to highlight precisely the antagonistic elements of politics largely absent in Ross (cf. Dyzenhaus 2000: 253).

SIX

Resolving the Paradox of Tolerance

Stefan Rummens

At the heart of the debate on militant democracy lies the paradox of toler-ance. This well-known conundrum points to the difficulties we encounter when we are faced with opponents who do not share our commitment to the value of tolerance. On the one hand, this commitment suggests that we should accept that others who do not share our values are equally free to voice and promote their own beliefs even when they are preaching intol-erance. On the other hand, tolerating the intolerant might turn out to be unwise and even self-destructive as giving free rein to political forces that promote inequality and discrimination might lead to the subversion of our open and tolerant society.

The main purpose of this chapter is to re-examine the paradox of toler-ance and to show that the associated dilemma is easily resolved when we properly reconstruct the normative and political commitments that con-stitute liberal democracy as a political regime. A consistent commitment to the practice of tolerance by democrats is best realised on the basis of a model of *defending democracy* which I have previously developed together with Koen Abts and Stefan Sottiaux and which focuses on the *concentric containment* of extremist political actors in the democratic system (Rummens and Abts 2010; Sottiaux and Rummens 2012).

The argument for resolving the paradox of tolerance proceeds in three steps. In the first section I make use of the distinction introduced by Chan-tal Mouffe between *agonistic adversaries* and *antagonistic enemies* to show that our relationship with democratic opponents is qualitatively different from our relationship with the extremist enemies of democracy. Importantly, this distinction should not merely be understood in terms of an underlying difference in value commitments. The distinction is essentially *political* in nature and therefore explains why a different political treatment of the intolerant does not commit democrats to a form of self-contradiction. A proper appreciation of the political antagonism between the tolerant and the intolerant makes clear, on the contrary, that a more militant approach towards the intolerant is not only justifiable but actually an integral part of a consistent commitment to tolerance and democracy.

Whereas the first section of this chapter aims to show *that* a different political treatment of the enemies of democracy is legitimate, the second section focuses on *how* they should be treated differently. Here, the model of defending democracy makes use of the concentric structure of our democratic system to propose a *guideline of decreasing tolerance*. This guideline stipulates that there should be significant leeway for extremist actors at the periphery of the system in the informal public sphere but that this tolerance for the intolerant should decrease as they come closer to the centres of actual decision-making power in parliament and government.

This concentric approach to defending democracy is capable of countering a number of criticisms which have been raised against militant models of democracy more generally. In the third section (entitled 'Dealing with Some Objections') I reject, in consecutive order, the charges that defending democracy leads to a *moralisation* of politics in which the extremist runs the risk of being dehumanised (see subsection 'A Moralisation of Politics'); that the distinction between adversaries and enemies is *arbitrary* and therefore introduces an element of authoritarianism (see subsection 'Inherent Arbitrariness'); that the concentric model represents a form of *elitism* which fails to take seriously large sections of the citizenry (see subsection 'Elitism') or that it leads to a *neglect of the underlying causes* of the rise of extremist movements (see subsection 'Neglecting Deeper Causes').

Tolerance as a Political Practice

In order to resolve the paradox of tolerance it is useful to keep two different distinctions in mind. First, I propose to distinguish between the scope and the extension of tolerance. The *scope* of tolerance refers to the community of people to whom we are willing to apply our commitment to tolerance, whereas the *extension* of tolerance refers to the types of action that we are willing to tolerate of those people. I believe that the concept of tolerance is best understood as a concept that is always *universal in scope* but, at the same time, also always *limited in its extension*.

The nature of these limitations can be understood on the basis of the second distinction I wish to highlight between tolerance as a moral value and tolerance as a political practice. Tolerance as a *moral value* has, as suggested, a universal scope in the sense that it commits us to the idea that *all* people should be maximally free to say and do the things they want even if we disagree with their ideas or disapprove of their actions. The value of tolerance can, however, only be given a coherent meaning if its extension is limited. Even if we believe that people should be free to say and do as they please, this freedom can only be universally granted to all people indiscriminately on the condition that it is limited by the equal freedom of all others to do the same. And indeed, it is common practice in our open societies that we do not allow people to do or say things that infringe upon the liberty rights of other citizens and that we implement these constraints by means of criminal law provisions. Importantly, these constraints on the extension of tolerance should not be seen as contingent or external constraints. They represent, rather, a *conceptual condition of possibility* inherent in the idea of tolerance as a universal value.

The idea of tolerance as a *political practice* adds another layer to our conceptual analysis. It refers to the fact that the value of tolerance is never automatically realised but always needs to be politically implemented. In our modern societies the primary locus of implementation has been the liberal democratic regime with its core commitment to the values of freedom and equality. Importantly, however, just like any other regime, liberal democracy itself always remains vulnerable in the sense that it might always face challengers who aim to supplant it by a different political regime based on incompatible political principles. The need to deter the political enemies who aim to subvert or overthrow our political practice of tolerance adds a *pragmatic condition of possibility* for the realisation of tolerance to the conceptual condition mentioned before. To the extent that the need to preserve the practice of tolerance implies a need to further limit the extension of the acts we are willing to tolerate from our political enemies, these additional limitations can be justified without self-contradiction. Indeed, they once again fail to represent an external or arbitrary constraint on tolerance but amount, rather, as before, to an integral and constitutive part of the practice of tolerance itself. With regards to the charge of self-contradiction, the tables should be turned. Liberal democrats who fail to take the measures needed to deal with the threat posed by intolerant opponents are the ones who run the risk of committing a performative contradiction undermining the very practice they are engaged in.

The idea that the charge of self-contradiction fails to apply to those who are prepared to take a militant stance has already been presented in a characteristically colourful way by András Sajó (2004: 211, 2006: 2268):

> This charge of self-contradiction is erroneous, and the paradox is only illusory or, in fact, hypocritical. There is a clear difference between those who disagree regarding permissible democratic policies and those who simply deny the reliance on democracy as a primary process of decision-making and the legitimacy of democratic life forms in civil society.

The important idea that I wish to draw from Sajó's remark is that the need to impose additional restrictions on the extension of the tolerance we owe the intolerant is both generated and justified by the fact that our *political relationship* with the enemies of tolerance is *qualitatively different* from our relationship with ordinary political opponents. I believe, furthermore, that this distinction is best analysed in terms of the difference between *agonism* and *antagonism* which Chantal Mouffe (2000, 2005a) has introduced in developing her agonistic model of democracy.

As is well known, Mouffe starts from the idea defended by Carl Schmitt (1996) that the opposition between friends and enemies provides the defining criterion of the sphere of the political. The antagonism between friends and enemies is thereby existential in nature, which means that the enemy is seen as a threat to our collective identity and that the aim of the political struggle is therefore to eliminate him. For Schmitt, political antagonism primarily takes the shape of an opposition between the people and its internal or external enemies, whereby the people itself is conceptualised as a homogeneous collective with a singular will. Mouffe (2000: 49–57, 98–105, 2005a: 14–21), however, strongly disagrees with this conception of the people and argues 'with Schmitt against Schmitt' that the political struggle should be internalised within the people. She therefore advocates a form of *agonistic pluralism* which recognises the pluralistic nature of the democratic people and which emphasises that the will of the people is subject to an ongoing and open-ended democratic struggle.

In order to internalise the political struggle within the people it is necessary, however, to *relativise* the antagonistic opposition between enemies into an *agonistic* opposition between *adversaries*. This means, according to Mouffe, that agonistic adversaries are no longer out to eliminate one another but recognise each other as legitimate opponents. This mutual recognition requires a common symbolic framework constituted by the commitment of all parties involved to *the ethico-political values of liberty and equality for all* (Mouffe 2000: 102–104, 2005a: 31–32, 121–122). Although the opposition between adversaries thus presupposes a consensus about the basic principles of liberal democracy, this consensus remains, at the same time, a *conflictual consensus*. The democratic struggle should therefore be understood as an ongoing agonistic struggle about the proper meaning and implementation of these shared ethico-political principles.

Importantly, this distinction between adversaries and enemies should not be reduced to a mere *moral* disagreement regarding the 'ethico-political values of liberty and equality for all'. The distinction also implies that our *political relationship* with adversaries is qualitatively different from our relationship with the enemies of democracy. As I have argued more fully elsewhere, I believe that this difference is best captured by saying that the struggle between democratic adversaries is a *non-hegemonic struggle*, whereas the struggle between democrats and the enemies of democracy is a *hegemonic* one (Rummens 2009).

The concept of *hegemony* is extensively used in the work of Mouffe as well as in the work of the co-author of some of her earlier work, Ernesto Laclau. It implies that every particular political regime is constituted by a specific pattern of power relations that shapes society and that thereby necessarily excludes alternative patterns (Mouffe 2000: 21–22, 98–101, 2005a: 17–19). In this sense, liberal democracy itself is an example of a hegemonic political regime. It constitutes a specific ordering of power relations which is incompatible with competing orderings such as fascism, communism or theocracy. As Laclau and Mouffe emphasise, the struggle between competing hegemonic conceptions of society is always an antagonistic struggle between conceptions that are 'strictly incommensurable' (Laclau 2005: 94) and which do 'not admit *tertium quid*' (Laclau and Mouffe 1985: 129). A hegemonic struggle is therefore always an all or nothing affair whereby one conception can only prevail on condition of the total exclusion of the other.

The mutually exclusive nature of the hegemonic struggle between democracy and its enemies marks a sharp contrast with the democratic struggle between adversaries who share a common symbolic space. Liberal democracy is a highly original political regime with the unique ability to open up a space for a *non-hegemonic* struggle in which political opponents can legitimately co-exist and whereby the victory of the one does *not* lead to the political elimination or delegitimisation of the other.[1] It is true of course that in a democracy not everybody can govern at the same time and that the opposition will not see its own policy proposals realised as long as the majority remains in power. In that sense, the government of the majority in a way also 'excludes' the minority and the policy proposals it stands for. The crucial difference is, however, that this exclusion is limited because it takes place within a wider and more inclusive common framework constituted by a shared commitment to the liberal democratic values of freedom and equality. This shared commitment implies that the exercise of power by the majority over the minority remains strictly limited in several ways. The majority cannot impose laws or policies that would undermine the basic constitutional rights of minority groups. The majority has to recognise the ongoing democratic legitimacy of the opposition as a legitimate representative of the people. The majority has, crucially, to recognise that it can only hold power on a temporary basis and that the next elections will decide whether or not they get another turn.

The distinction between adversaries and enemies now explains why the concept of toleration does not lead to self-contradiction and why a case in favour of militant democracy can be made. With regards to our democratic adversaries, with whom we are engaged in a *non-hegemonic* struggle over the proper interpretation of the values of liberty and equality, the restriction of the extension of tolerance remains limited to what we have called the conceptual condition of possibility of tolerance and which refers to the need to limit the freedom of citizens by the equal freedom of all others.

With regard to the enemies of the liberal democratic regime, however, the situation is different. Our relationship towards them is one in which a *hegemonic* power struggle is at stake between two incompatible views about the basic power structures of society. It is a struggle in which only one of the opponents can prevail and which therefore poses a potential existential threat to the political practice of tolerance we are committed to. Taking a stance in favour of liberal democracy implies that we also take seriously its pragmatic conditions of possibility and that we therefore cannot consistently recognise the legitimacy of extremist views that aim to subvert this regime in favour of an antagonistic alternative. The symmetry that exists between me and my democratic adversary in view of our common symbolic framework simply does not extend to my relationship with the extremist. With regard to the supposed paradox of tolerance, the inconsistency or self-contradiction therefore lies with those who mistakenly suppose that they have to treat unlike opponents in a like manner. The only consistent commitment to tolerance, in contrast, rightfully accepts that adversaries and enemies pose different challenges and should therefore also be dealt with differently.

The Concentric Containment of Extremism

Since tolerance has been politically institutionalised in our societies in the form of a liberal democratic regime, it makes sense to use this regime as a normative yardstick and to define *extremism* as referring to any type of ideology which fails to endorse its core values and principles. This implies that the intolerant can be identified as the extremist enemies of liberal democracy who fail to share our commitment to the normative ideals of liberty and equality. To the extent that these intolerant opponents effectively advocate or endorse political attempts to implement policies, legislation or constitutional changes at odds with these core values, they pose a political threat to the preservation of our practice of tolerance and should, therefore, be politically contained.[2]

Although the argument in the preceding section has already shown *that* there is an a priori justification for taking a different and defensive political stance towards the intolerant, it has not yet explained *how* we should deal with these extremist challengers when they confront us. Here, we should be cautious and not be tempted by the Schmittian rhetoric about the need to eliminate the enemy. As we have argued, tolerance is a value with a *universal scope* which therefore also covers the intolerant opponents themselves. Consequently, all we have shown is that it might be legitimate to further restrict the *extension* of tolerance we owe the intolerant on condition that such an intervention is needed to preserve the existence of the political practice of tolerance itself. A legitimate militant model of democracy can only aim to remove the *threat to the integrity of the political system* posed by the enemies of democracy, not the enemies themselves. The underlying commitment to tolerance implies, rather, that the militant strategies deployed should always strive to minimise the impact upon the basic rights and liberties of the extremist actors affected.

Before explaining how a concentric containment model for defending democracy can fulfil this promise, a more preliminary remark is in order. It should be noted that, in my view, the regime we aim to protect is *liberal democracy*, this is a democratic regime committed to the protection of the individual liberty rights of its citizens. This approach therefore differs from more proceduralistic models which define democracy more narrowly in terms of a set of democratic decision-making procedures and which consequently tend to limit the threat to be dealt with to extremist opponents intent on thwarting these procedures (Fennema and Maussen 2000; Kirshner 2014). Although the proceduralistic conception of democracy has a reputable pedigree in the works of, among others, Hans Kelsen, Joseph Schumpeter and Robert Dahl, I believe that a commitment to democratic procedures cannot be coherently dissociated from a commitment to individual liberty rights (Rummens 2006).

Although an argument for this claim is beyond present purposes, it should be pointed out that some of the most prominent political theorists of recent times, including John Rawls, Jürgen Habermas and Claude Lefort, have all argued – be it in different ways – for the 'co-originality' of liberalism and democracy. All of these authors conceive of democracy in terms of a *democratic project* engaged in by a community of free and equal citizens. This democratic project combines substantive and procedural aspects in an inextricable manner. Freedom and equality provide the *substantive core* of the project in the sense that law and policy-making processes are essentially geared towards the realisation of the basic liberty rights of all citizens. At the same time, the realisation of these liberal democratic values essentially relies on democratic *procedures* in the sense that only the citizens themselves can determine which laws and which policies are best suited for the promotion of their own freedom.

The concentric containment model for defending democracy which I advocate attempts to make full use of the fact that the democratic processes at the heart of this democratic project are complex and constitute an extended democratic system. In this regard, Bernhard Peters (1993: 327–352) has argued, more specifically, that representative democracy has a *concentric two-track structure*. At the centre, we find the track of the formal decision-making institutions of parliament and government in which laws and policies are made. This core, however, is encircled by a second essential track, constituted by the informal public sphere in which ordinary citizens and civil society organisations participate in a wider public debate. If the democratic system is to be properly responsive to the needs and concerns of citizens, the borders between the two tracks should be permeable. This means that the debates in the wider public sphere, in which the concerns of citizens are picked up and processed, should be able to effectively influence the decision makers operating in the core of the system.

Recognising the complexity of the democratic system as an extended system is important because it naturally suggests a comprehensive approach to the protection of democracy against its antagonistic challengers. In this regard, our concentric model sides with authors advocating a form of *defending democracy* which goes beyond a more narrowly construed militant model (Capoccia 2005; Pedahzur 2004). Militant democracy traditionally tends to focus on legal measures, such as banning parties or restricting free speech, or on forms of administrative and intelligence controls by means of special police forces or security services. Defending democracy now argues that such harder measures should indeed be part of the toolbox, but that they should also be complemented by a series of more inclusive measures aimed to actively strengthen the democratic system. Here, we should think, for instance, of educational tools, of measures strengthening civil society or the quality of the media, or – most importantly – of the need to deal with the underlying cultural, socio-economic or other problems that might explain or trigger the success of extremist actors.

As will be clear, the concentric model assumes that the task of dealing with extremists is a responsibility that is shared by a plethora of different actors at different locations in the democratic system and includes a role for politicians, judges, journalists, educators, civil society organisations as well as ordinary citizens. The main organising principle which provides guidance in assessing which techniques should be used when and by whom is what we have called the *guideline of decreasing tolerance*. This guideline aims to make use of a suggestion made by Maleiha Malik that the distance between the core and the periphery of the democratic system allows for a policy in which 'the process of engagement with extremists can be "slowed down" and "expanded"' (Malik 2008: 93). In line with this suggestion our guideline stipulates that extremist actors should be given a lot of leeway in expressing their extremist views at the periphery of the democratic system but that our tolerance towards their political activities should decrease as they succeed in coming closer to the centres of actual decision making in the core.

The guideline of decreasing tolerance aims to achieve the two goals we set out at the beginning, i.e. to be as inclusive as possible towards the intolerant while at the same time protecting the integrity of the democratic project. The leeway we grant to extremists in the periphery of the system is in line with the procedural dimension of democracy in the sense that it helps us in *tracking* all the possible relevant concerns that live among the citizenry. If we were to use legislation to curtail the free expression of extremist ideas by individuals or smaller organisations in the wider public sphere, we would force these views to go underground and we would thereby undermine the signalling function of the public debate as well as hamper political efforts to deal with the potential causes of political resentment on the side of voters.

Although we should take the signalling function of the public debate very seriously, we should, at the same time, also make sure that extremist views, which are at odds with the core principles of our liberal democratic regime, are never translated into actual legislation or policies. Although we should try to meet the underlying concerns of extremist citizens as much as possible, we can only do so on the basis of laws and policies that are squarely in line with the core values of freedom and equality. In line with the substantive dimension of democracy, we should therefore make use of the distance between periphery and core to *filter out* these extremist ideas. This means that we should take a firmer stance towards extremist actors as they organise with the aim of gaining the political power needed to influence or make actual decisions.

Here, certain restrictions could already be contemplated with regards to civil society organisations, for instance concerning the conditions under which they can be publicly funded or concerning the conditions under which they are allowed to assemble or operate. With regards to political parties, our demands should become stricter still. Here again, certain conditions – for instance, a clear commitment to the protection of human rights – could be imposed on parties applying to obtain public funding or even, more generally, as a condition for entering elections. With regard to extremist parties which actually gain access to parliament, a so-called *cordon sanitaire* – an agreement by the other parties not to form a coalition with the extremist party – might be in order. Although the possibility of a party ban should also be part of the militant toolkit, this measure should always remain a measure of last resort. As with all of the possible measures under consideration, we should always make sure that their impact is proportional to the threat that the targeted extremist actors effectively pose to either the democratic procedure itself or the maintenance of the core values of freedom and equality.

As this latter remark makes clear, it is important to keep in mind that the ultimate rationale behind the concentric containment model is the preservation of the integrity of the liberal democratic regime. In this sense, the relevance of the distance separating the extremist actor from the centres of power – the parameter that marks the originality of the concentric approach – should be properly understood. Since the *threat to the system* provides the ultimate criterion, the guideline of decreasing tolerance is, in fact, a two-parameter guideline, whereby the threat to the system is determined by a combination of the *extremity* of the extremist ideology and the *distance* of the extremist actor to the core of the system. This means, for instance, that a vicious neo-Nazi organisation might require a firmer response compared to a more 'ordinary' radical right organisation operating at the same distance to the core. A possible justification for this different treatment could refer to the fact, explained by Peter Niesen (2004: 104), that neo-Nazi organisations tend to use tactics of intimidation that undermine the openness of the public debate and that could even generate silencing effects that severely distort the democratic process.[3]

Although the guideline of decreasing tolerance only provides a first general orientation regarding matters of defending democracy, I believe that it can be fruitfully used as a starting point for more detailed analyses of the appropriateness of certain measures. Here, I would like to briefly mention two issues which I have elaborated more fully elsewhere in collaboration with others. A first example is the case study Stefan Sottiaux and I have made of the European Court of Human Rights case law on freedom of expression and freedom of association as protected, respectively, by Articles 10 and 11 of the European Convention on Human Rights (Sottiaux and Rummens 2012). Here, we concluded that the Court is adequately protective of the freedom of association as is exemplified by the famous *Refah*-test. This test, which the Court developed to assess whether the ban of a political party can be justified under Article 11, rightly focuses on the 'sufficiently imminent' risk to democracy an organisation or party must pose in order to warrant its dissolution. This protective stance contrasts sharply, however, with the case law regarding freedom of speech. Here the Court fails to provide adequate protection in the sense that it is often tempted to uphold free speech convictions merely on the basis of the content of the contested speech acts even when the threat to the democratic system was negligible. According to the concentric containment model the Court's jurisprudence is wrong-headed in the sense that it provides stronger protection to associations already close to the core of the democratic system compared to individual citizens or politicians uttering extremist claims in the periphery of the public sphere. A more consistent approach would retain the strict reference to the 'sufficiently imminent' risk in the context of the freedom of association but would have to apply the same criterion also in the context of the freedom of speech. Since individual speech acts rarely generate more risk than the actions of organised groups of people, such a similar standard would, in practice, lead to a very wide protection of the freedom of speech and this is, according to the concentric containment model, exactly as it should be.

As a second example, Koen Abts and I have analysed the use of the often-maligned *cordon sanitaire* as an appropriate measure of containing extremist parties (Rummens and Abts 2010). Here, we have concluded that such a measure can be both normatively adequate and empirically successful on the condition that it is properly executed. This means that a cordon should never stand on its own but should always be part of a twofold strategy which is *exclusive* towards the extremist party that is targeted but which remains, at the same time, *inclusive* vis-à-vis its voters. The latter means that democrats should always be very concerned about the underlying causes that give rise to the electoral success of extremist parties and should therefore listen very carefully to the concerns of these extremist voters. Democrats should never simply dismiss these concerns as the whining coming from a 'basket of deplorables' but should consequently try to come up with alternative policy proposals that might provide different and democratically acceptable solutions to these underlying concerns. If this twofold strategy of maintaining a cordon while simultaneously providing voters with a democratic alternative is pursued consistently, it will help serve the realisation of the twofold aim promoted by the concentric model of protecting the democratic system against potential threats while remaining as inclusive as possible towards extremist opponents.

Dealing with Some Objections

A Moralisation of Politics

One of the objections raised against militant approaches to democracy is that they supposedly lead to a 'moralization of politics' (Mouffe 2005a: 64–89, 2005b; de Lange and Akkerman 2012: 40–41; Mudde and Rovira Kaltwasser 2012: 213). Although this criticism is most often raised against the implementation of a 'cordon sanitaire', its thrust is more general and usually involves a plea not to treat extremist actors any different than we would ordinary political opponents.

Let me say first that I object to the suggestion lurking behind this critique that politics and morality should be strictly kept apart. It is true, of course, that Carl Schmitt (1996) has argued that political struggles are necessarily existential in nature and should not be fought in the name of moral convictions. But, surely, this is a fine opportunity to disagree with Schmitt. Although politics cannot and should not be reduced to morality, it is also true that tolerance as a political practice is based on a prior commitment to tolerance as a moral value. When we confront the enemies of democracy, we are engaged in an antagonistic *political* struggle in which only one of the parties can prevail, but we are waging this battle because we prefer to live in a liberal democratic society in which the *values* of liberty, equality and tolerance are properly respected.

The concern behind the charge of moralisation is, however, more specific than this. Mouffe, for instance, believes that the idea of framing the struggle in terms of an 'us, democrats' versus 'them, the enemies' might make us complacent and hamper a self-critical analysis on the side of democrats with regards to the true causes of the rise of extremism. This concern, however, clearly does not apply to the concentric containment model as presented here. With regards to the cordon sanitaire, we advocate, as explained, a twofold strategy which combines the cordon with an active attempt by democrats to provide alternative but democratically acceptable solutions for the underlying concerns of voters. More generally, the need for the widest possible protection of the freedom of speech of extremists is based on an appreciation of the potential political relevance of their contributions to the democratic process.

This leaves us with the final, and perhaps the most pressing, concern behind the critique of moralisation. As Matthias Lievens (2010) explains,

Carl Schmitt's reputation as a belligerent philosopher has somewhat obscured the fact that his critique of a moralisation of politics is based on a concern to try and limit the violence of politics as much as possible. Schmitt makes a distinction between what we could call a 'relative' and an 'absolute' enemy, whereby our struggle with the former ends when we have safeguarded our own existence but the latter only ends with the annihilation of our opponent. According to Schmitt, a war waged in the name of moral ideals necessarily leads to the type of absolute struggle he dreads, a struggle which '[. . .] is necessarily unusually intense and inhuman because by transcending the limits of the political framework, it simultaneously degrades the enemy into moral and other categories and is forced to make of him a monster that must not only be defeated but also utterly destroyed' (Schmitt 1996: 36).

The problem of moralisation raised here is probably well illustrated by some of the aspects of the war on terror that has been waged against the so-called 'axis of evil' and which has, indeed, failed to respect some of the moral and political constraints we would normally expect to be upheld. The fact that the risk of a dehumanisation of the opponent is real in some circumstances, does not mean, however, that this risk also applies to the concentric containment model. In this context, Mouffe (2005b: 58) makes the surprising remark that a moralisation of the struggle against the extremist leads us to treat him as a 'moral enemy' whereas we should treat him, in fact, as a 'political adversary'. This claim is, however, deeply problematic because it is manifestly inconsistent with her own characterisation of the category of the 'adversary' in terms of a shared commitment to the ethico-political principles of liberty and equality. Since extremists by definition do *not* share this common symbolic framework, they do *not* fall into the category of ordinary political adversaries.

The deeper problem here is that Mouffe confronts us with a false dilemma. Extremists are neither political adversaries nor moral enemies. They are, in fact, political enemies. To be more precise, they are political enemies in the sense that they force us into an antagonistic struggle in which the preservation of the political practice of tolerance is at stake. The threat they pose warrants a temporary limitation on the extension of the acts we are willing to tolerate from these extremists, but is does *not*, as emphasised before, mean that we are out to 'eliminate' them – neither in the relative nor in the absolute Schmittian sense of that word. In this regard, the concentric containment model is very much in line with Alexander Kirshner's plea for a 'self-limiting theory of militant democracy'. Kirshner rightly points out that democrats engaged in defending democracy have a democratic responsibility to try always to minimise the impact of their interventions on the legitimate interests of all citizens, including the extremists, as well as a responsibility to 'treat antidemocrats as future partners in democracy and to rapidly secure the conditions that will allow all of a polity's members to participate safely' (2014: 7). The aim of defending democracy is not to turn antagonism into a war of annihilation but rather to restore the normal agonistic relationship with *all* members of the citizenry as soon as possible.

Inherent Arbitrariness

In a recent article, Carlo Invernizzi Accetti and Ian Zuckerman (2017) launched a direct attack on the idea of militant democracy. Also drawing on the work of Carl Schmitt, they argue that it is conceptually impossible to identify the enemies of democracy in an objective manner and that, as a result, militant democracy is marred by a form of arbitrariness which inevitably opens up the possibility of authoritarian abuse.

In response, it should be conceded, first of all, that in matters of militant democracy – as in all matters of politics – a certain amount of contingency cannot be avoided. Although the distinction between adversaries and enemies is clear in theory, it is true that it is not always possible in practice to draw a sharp line between ideas and proposals that are still compatible with the core values and practices of liberal democracy and those for which that is no longer the case.

Two general remarks can help explain why this ineliminable contingency undermines neither the necessity nor the feasibility of a militant model of democracy. It should be emphasised, first of all, that the vagueness of a certain boundary does not in any way affect its reality or its relevance. It's not because there is a grey zone in which matters are not fully clear that the distinction between black and white no longer makes sense or that we should no longer worry about the dark forces opposing us. As Carl Schmitt (2004 [1932]: 82) himself remarks in a different context, the inference from the vagueness of a boundary to its irrelevance or even its non-existence is a logical fallacy which is widespread but which remains a fallacy nonetheless.

Second, it should also be pointed out that the concentric containment model presented here is particularly well suited to deal with the vagueness of the boundary between adversaries and enemies. By making full use of the extended nature of the democratic system, this decision is no longer an all or nothing affair but one which allows for a more gradual approach whereby the room for manoeuvre for extremist actors is increasingly restrained as they near the core of the system. This incremental approach fits nicely with the existence of a grey zone and although, of course, it will never eliminate all elements of contingency in the identification of the enemy or in the choice of strategies for dealing with her, it will strongly reduce the political impact of questionable or 'mistaken' decisions. The concentric approach at the same time also strongly diminishes the risk for authoritarian abuse precisely because the comprehensive nature of defending democracy implies that it involves an extensive division of labour between many different actors (citizens, civil society organisations, politicians, courts . . .) who all have a limited power to intervene and who can mutually check each other's assessments and decisions.

Although these general remarks should suffice to explain why the critique of arbitrariness does not really stick, it is worthwhile also to have a brief look at the two more specific arguments provided by Invernizzi Accetti and Zuckerman (2017: 186). Their first argument refers to a passage in Schmitt (2008 [1928]: 75–82) in which he indicates that constitutional norms cannot by themselves answer the question of how to deal with emergency situations in which the core of the constitution is threatened. Here, authoritarian decisions by a sovereign political actor are needed to safeguard the constitution. In response, several remarks are in order. It should be noted, first, that Schmitt is explicitly dealing with state of emergency-type situations which require extraordinary powers and the temporary suspension of constitutional rights. Although effective political decision making in these circumstances will undoubtedly require an additional dose of authoritarianism, it is unclear how this observation generates a relevant critique for a model of defending democracy that is explicitly meant to apply to ordinary circumstances where *pre-emptive* measures aim to deal with the extremist threat before it gets out of control. It should be noted, second, that Schmitt indeed emphasises the need for authoritarianism and even dictatorship in times of crises, but that he would never agree that this also leads to arbitrariness. The role of the sovereign is precisely to safeguard the core constitutional choices originally made by the people and his interventions are only legitimate to the extent that they serve that purpose (Schmitt 2008: 80). It should also be pointed out, finally, that there are no conceptual reasons why a model of militant democracy designed for ordinary circumstances could not operate in full agreement with the rule of law. Probably the most intrusive legal measure belonging to the militant armoury is the party ban. But even here, there are no a priori reasons why the conditions under which such a ban can be legitimately imposed could not be regulated by law and why the ultimate decisions in this regard could not be left in the hands of (constitutional) courts (Issacharoff 2007: 1453–1458; Müller 2016a: 260–261). Although these courts indeed will have to make tough decisions about the effective threat posed by extremist ideologies and actions, Invernizzi Accetti and Zuckerman fail to show why these kinds of decisions necessarily go beyond other types of judicial or constitutional review in which courts have to interpret, weigh and assess constitutional norms in view of the constitution's underlying core values.

The second argument made by Invernizzi Accetti and Zuckerman (2017: 186) refers to the fact that the identification of the enemy of democracy amounts, in their view, to a repoliticisation of the boundaries of the demos. Since democratic decision making presupposes that the boundaries of the demos are already fixed, so they argue, this identification itself can never be democratically legitimate but is necessarily done in an arbitrary and authoritarian manner. Again, several remarks are in order. Although they present this argument once more as a Schmittian argument, it is doubtful that Schmitt would agree that democracy presupposes that the boundaries of the people are already fixed. It seems more plausible, instead, to suggest that, for Schmitt, the people actually constitutes itself through the existential choices in which it defines its enemies. Second, it is obvious that democracies in fact repoliticise the boundaries of the demos on many occasions. This is the case, for instance, when we discuss the possibility of lowering the voting age or when we consider giving (local) voting rights to non-citizen residents. This is also the case when countries – for instance within the EU – decide to grant certain decision-making powers to supranational political institutions accountable to a much larger supranational constituency. In all of these cases, the charge that these decisions are 'undemocratic', 'arbitrary' or 'authoritarian' would seem highly questionable and is, in fact, hardly ever raised. It is, in any case, unclear why the charge as raised here against militant democracy would not also, and more forcefully, apply to these other types of political decisions. Third, and most fundamentally, it is in fact misleading to characterise militant measures as measures that repoliticise the boundary of the demos, as Invernizzi Accetti and Zuckerman do. As emphasised before, the aim of militant interventions is precisely *not* to exclude extremists from the demos but to make sure that their rights as citizens are guaranteed as much as the preservation of the practice of tolerance allows for. Again, militant measures only limit the extension of tolerance, not its scope.

Elitism

Another charge sometimes raised against militant democracy is that it is characterised by an *elitist distrust of the people* and that it therefore assigns a passive rather than an active role to ordinary citizens (Müller 2016a; Malkopoulou and Norman 2018). By way of a general response, it should be pointed out, once again, that this criticism simply fails to apply to the concentric containment model because this model assumes that defending democracy is a task for the democratic system as a whole. Although political leaders and judges thereby play important roles, the same also holds for ordinary citizens and civil society organisations. They too have to remain vigilant with regard to the possible rise of extremist views and they too are responsible for the maintenance of a democratic culture in society. More generally, their active participation in the wider public sphere is an essential precondition for the proper functioning and the preservation of the democratic regime.

The charge of elitism has been made more specific in two different ways. One version of the charge targets the ground-breaking work of Karl Loewenstein (1937) as well as a more recent contribution by András Sajó (2012) in which extremism is associated with *emotionalism*, which is a form of politics shaped by the emotional manipulation of the masses. This emotionalism supposedly contrasts sharply with the institutional design of constitutional democracy which 'by its very nature, can appeal only to reason' (Loewenstein 1937a: 428). Here, I concur with the gist of the critique in the sense that I agree that the fear of the masses and the fear of emotions displayed by these authors is unwarranted. It is unclear to me, however, how this critique could be generalised into a critique of militant democracy as such. There is no obvious reason why militant models of democracy would necessarily have to rule out a more constructive role for emotions or for the mobilisation of the masses in politics. Personally, I believe that Chantal Mouffe makes a very important point when she emphasises the constitutive function of affect and emotion in a democratic regime. In fact, I believe that she rightly attributes the rise of populism and extremism in recent decades to the fact that traditional parties – in our post-political era – fail to present real political alternatives and genuinely inspiring narratives regarding the future of society (Mouffe 2005a: 64–89). This failure to inspire leads to a loss of political identification on the part of voters who seek rescue with extremist challengers who do understand the inelinimable need for more emotional forms of politics. And although the sharp opposition between rationalism and emotionalism, which is drawn on both sides of this debate, is, in my view, a false opposition, I do believe that emotions are part of the solution rather than part of the problem when it comes to defending democracy.

Another version of the charge of elitism has specifically targetted the concentric containment model by claiming that its focus on the signalling function of extremism is supposedly *deeply patronising* because it treats both the extremist party and extremist speech as 'a kind of political probe to better understand society, rather than as a way for citizens to express values and advance interests' (Müller 2016a: 259). Here, I would like to respond that this argument really turns things upside down and fundamentally misrepresents the militant stance which is part of the concentric containment model. It is precisely because we take the extremists' claims *very seriously* that we advocate the need to protect society from their anti-democratic intentions.

Let me turn the tables and suppose, a contrario, that in order to avoid paternalism we would have to engage in a normal political debate with extremist parties and treat their views and proposals as legitimate contributions that should be seriously considered as the potential basis for future policy making. This approach would be deeply problematic in one of two ways. It would either constitute a form of *inconsistent relativism* on the part of democrats who fail to recognise that democracy is a hegemonic regime which is based on a specific set of values that could be undermined by allowing incompatible views to influence actual policy making. Or, it would, alternatively, amount to a form of *democratic complacency* which unduly minimises the threat posed by extremists and assumes that it will all blow over quickly if we make no fuss and just treat them as we would any other opponents.[4] Both attitudes, in different ways, fail to take seriously the position of the extremist and therefore amount to a form of paternalism of their own.

Of course, all of this is not meant to imply that we should not engage in debate with extremists at all. It simply means that we should remember that this is an antagonistic type of debate in which we should stand firm. Though we should enquire openly about the concerns that motivate their extremist views, we should, at the same time, make it unambiguously clear that when we are discussing possible solutions the core values of freedom and equality always constitute the non-negotiable constraints of the debate.

Neglecting Deeper Causes

A final objection against militant approaches claims that militancy leads to a neglect of the underlying causes of the rise of extremism in society. We have already encountered this critique in Mouffe who submits that the antagonism between 'us, democrats' and 'they, the enemies' leads to complacency on the side of democrats with regards to their own failure to inspire extremist voters. A related argument can be found in the work of Malkopoulou and Norman who propose a model of 'social democratic self-defence' which focuses on the broader social and democratic preconditions needed to preserve the social and political integration of society and, thus, to prevent the rise of extremism.

Although Malkopoulou and Norman (2018: 454–455) present their model as an 'alternative' approach which 'stands in contrast' with militant democracy, I again fail to see where this alleged opposition between militancy on the one hand and the strengthening of political and social cohesion on the other comes from. As explained before, a more comprehensive model of defending democracy pursues a twofold strategy. An *exclusionary* stance towards extremist actors coming close to the centres of power is essential in order to prevent damage to the democratic regime. But this militant stance needs to be complemented by an *inclusionary* openness towards the citizenry at large for the purpose of picking up and taking seriously all the possibly relevant concerns they might have.

Malkopoulou and Norman (2018: 450) submit that '(. . .) extremism results from the perceived impossibility of certain groups of the population to channel their socio-economic demands through the political system. The antidote is an inclusive organisation of democratic politics, along with an emphasis on social justice and equality.' Although I am very sympathetic to the gist of this observation, two remarks are in order. First, the concentric containment model aims to take seriously the underlying causes of the rise of extremism but is not wedded to the social democratic ideology in the same way that Malkopoulou and Norman's model seems to be. This means, for instance, that there are, in my view, no a priori reasons to restrict our attention exclusively to the 'social-economic' demands of citizens. Here, the traditional opposition between a more left-wing approach which focuses exclusively on socio-economic issues and a more right-wing approach which focuses exclusively on cultural issues does not seem very fruitful. A more comprehensive approach should make sure that *all* possibly relevant concerns are heeded.

When trying to understand the difficulties citizens encounter in channelling through their demands, it is also important, second, to look into the deeper damage our democratic infrastructure has suffered in recent decades. Here, I side with authors such as Colin Crouch (2004), Peter Mair (2013) and Chantal Mouffe (2013) who all point the finger at the depoliticisation of politics as one of the main causes of the current problems our democratic institutions are facing. It seems to me that the *globalisation* of politics, the rise of technocratic *governance* institutions and the hegemonic dominance of the *neoliberal ideology* have all contributed to the emergence of a *postpolitical regime* in which the traditional political institutions of parliament and government have lost much of their power. This loss of power undermines the faith of voters in these institutions and leads to forms of political disaffection which are, as Mouffe rightly explains, grist to the mill of extremist challengers.

We should be aware of the scale of the threat the post-political regime poses to our democratic institutions. In terms of the conceptual framework used in this chapter, it is fair to say that this regime in fact also presents an *antagonistic challenge*. Its power structures have already significantly corroded and replaced the power structures needed to preserve a liberal democratic regime in which free and equal citizens are capable of shaping their own lives and their own societies on their own terms. The post-political regime poses, moreover, a *very elusive threat* in the sense that its dynamics and its proponents operate in much more intractable ways compared to the vociferous extremist challengers the militant model of democracy is designed to deal with. Coming to grips with this threat will therefore require a different kind of analysis and different types of strategies than the ones developed here.

Conclusion

This essay resolves the paradox of tolerance on the basis of an analysis of the conceptual and pragmatic presuppositions of tolerance as a political practice. In view of the hegemonic nature of this practice, our political relationship with ordinary agonistic adversaries, who share our commitment to tolerance, is qualitatively different from our political relationship with the antagonistic enemies of tolerance, who aim to impose incompatible values and practices. This difference explains why it is both necessary and justified to impose additional limitations on the extension – not the scope – of tolerance in our dealings with these antagonistic challengers.

The guideline of decreasing tolerance provides more specific instructions about *how* these challengers should be handled by proposing to give much leeway to extremist actors at the periphery of the system but to also impose increasingly severe restrictions as they approach the centre of decision making. This model of concentric containment allows the rebuttal of a series of criticisms that have been raised against militant models of democracy. These rebuttals generally refer to the distance between the periphery and the centre of the democratic system as providing us with a lot of leeway and a lot of flexibility in our dealings with extremist actors. It allows us to manage the fact that the distinction between adversaries and enemies is not always very sharp in practice. It also allows us to stretch our commitment to tolerance to the limit by being as inclusive and as accommodating as possible towards extremist actors and the concerns they represent without thereby endangering the basic fabric and the basic values of our liberal democratic regime.

Notes

1. Mouffe herself assumes that the struggle between democratic adversaries within the context of a liberal democratic regime also remains hegemonic in nature. I believe that this assumption reflects an untenable inconsistency within her own work which leads her to underestimate the qualitative difference between agonism and antagonism (Rummens 2009).

2. Of course, extremists often have an interest in hiding their true intentions by posing as democrats. In this sense their identification is not always unproblematic and often requires a comprehensive assessment of their words, their actions and their (hidden) intentions. As will be explained below, I believe that the concentric containment model is well suited to deal with this problem in the sense that it promotes a wide and gradual array of measures taken by a wide variety of actors in a way that limits the political impact of questionable or 'mistaken' assessments (see section 'Inherent Arbitrariness').

3. I would like to thank Anthoula Malkopoulou and Alexander Kirshner for encouraging me to clarify this point.

4. This minimising attitude regarding the risk of extremism is reflected in the surprising claim 'that there are very few historical examples of democracies that were destroyed from within through entirely legal means' (Müller 2016a: 252; compare Malkopoulou and Norman 2018: 447–448). I believe that, in this regard, the recent history of countries such as Venezuela, Russia, Turkey or Hungary – to name but a few – should give us reason for pause. The same minimising attitude also underlies the plea for more 'faith in politics' which suggests that an inclusive approach towards extremist parties will, in the end, have a civilising effect upon them (Rosenblum 2007; Invernizzi Accetti and Zuckerman 2017). This optimistic assumption is increasingly belied by empirical research showing that extremists who come to power effectively aim to implement their extremist views (Albertazzi and Mueller 2013; Akkerman and Rooduijn 2015).

SEVEN

Militant Democracy and the Study of Political Tolerance

Giovanni Capoccia

Introduction

The 'democratic dilemma' of 'how much freedom for the enemies of freedom' has traditionally been an important theme of debate for political and legal theorists (e.g. Müller 2012c). By contrast, political scientists have paid much less attention to how different democratic regimes navigate this dilemma in practical terms – namely, how and why democracies actually vary in their response to the actions of anti-democratic groups. The absence of a robust comparative empirical research agenda on 'militant democracy' (Loewenstein 1937a, 1937b), defined as the set of policies that a democratic state enacts and implements to limit the rights of expression and participation of (real or perceived) anti-democratic actors (Capoccia 2018c), constitutes a substantial lacuna in our knowledge and, at the same time, a puzzle. A lacuna because the boundaries that democratic decision makers set to distinguish legitimate from illegitimate political dissent is a crucial aspect of democratic rule, as cases ranging from 1930s Germany to 1990s Algeria show. A puzzle because the issue of how to respond to the destabilising action of anti-democratic political actors has been persistently salient in the politics of many democracies. In his seminal writings on militant democracy from the 1930s, Karl Loewenstein mapped the policy and institutional responses of many West European democracies to the rise of fascism and Nazism. The problem of responding to extremism in democracies, however, did not disappear with the defeat of the Axis in the Second World War. Since then, democratic regimes have continued to face anti-democratic challenges, including, for example, communist parties during the peak of the Cold War, extra-parliamentary extremism in the 1960s and

1970s, and the recent rise of Islamic fundamentalism. And yet, in post-war comparative politics, there were no successors to Loewenstein: political scientists have studied the rules and institutions of militant democracy mostly in descriptive studies, and this topic has been absent, broadly speaking, in mainstream political science (Capoccia 2013).

One important reason for this absence is that 'mainstream' political science is largely defined by the rise (and decline) of rival approaches to the study of politics that provide scholars with theoretical lenses, research programmes, conceptual vocabularies and normative assumptions (e.g. Almond 1990).[1] And all such approaches, even those that potentially yield important insights, have blind spots. The issues raised by the restriction, by democratic governments, of the rights of political participation and expression of some subset of their citizens for political reasons have been of continuous interest to comparativists. Typically, though, political science's dominant theoretical and normative lenses have led to the analysis of rights-restricting policies in democracies not per se, but in the context of research programmes focused on related phenomena – such as, for example, state repression, human rights violations, or the policing of social movements (Capoccia 2018b). In particular, the long eclipse of institutional analysis between the 1940s and the 1990s (Hall and Taylor 1996) left little space for the systematic comparative analysis of the policies of militant democracy as an independent object of study. These circumstances have not just been detrimental to our knowledge of this aspect of democratic rule but, as I argue below, the lack of such knowledge has also had negative repercussions on the results of the above-mentioned research programmes themselves. In this chapter, I illustrate these points by discussing the most important of the research programmes in comparative politics that address problems that are relevant to militant democracy: the analysis of political tolerance.

The empirical study of political tolerance constitutes an established subfield of comparative politics. Started in the US during the 1950s, research on political tolerance has now gained a strong comparative dimension: questions on tolerance, for example, have become a stable part of important comparative surveys such as the World Values Surveys and the Eurobarometer (for reviews, see Gibson 2006, 2011). As an important example of the behaviouralist approach to the study of politics, tolerance research focuses on individual attitudes, typically via the analysis of mass surveys. Demonstrating the continuing political salience of the policies and institutions that regulate dissent in democracies, this literature typically measures tolerance by asking survey respondents about their support for or opposition to policies that restrict the rights of expression and participation of 'unpopular' groups. These are obviously the policies that, when targeted at political extremists,

In later years, however, a number of studies have convincingly pointed out that the way in which rights-restricting policies come to be enacted does not respond to a simple demand-output model.[4] Gibson, for example, points out that the data available are insufficient for researchers to establish a clear causal nexus – let alone a linear, unidirectional one – between mass opinion and public policies. In his analysis of anti-communist repression in the US states, he argues that it is by no means evident that mass opinion drives public policy, and that the opposite causal arrow is at least as plausible – although the available evidence prevents any conclusive interpretation (Gibson 1988). In his analysis of the repression of campus protests against the Vietnam War, Gibson finds that mass opinion and repressive policies were *negatively* correlated across the US states: states where mass opinion was more tolerant had more repressive legislation (Gibson 1989). He speculates that the relationship between mass tolerance and repressive policies might take a quadratic functional form: more tolerance encourages more dissent, but when the disruption that comes with dissent surpasses a certain level, states are more likely to pass repressive legislation to quell it. Again, however, Gibson is careful to specify that existing data do not allow for testing this hypothesis. Other studies have maintained that courts and law enforcement institutions may have an independent effect on which policies are enacted and implemented (e.g. Gibson 1992a: 570, 1996; and Barnum and Sullivan 1989). However, these insights into the causes of variation of rights-restricting policies towards specific groups have not been systematically developed.

The Study of Political Tolerance and Democracy as a 'Marketplace of Ideas'

The predominance of intolerant attitudes among the US mass public made scholars pessimistic about Tocqueville's classic argument on the importance, in a democracy, of a civil society that supports civil rights and freedoms (e.g. Griffith, Plamenatz and Pennock 1956; see discussion in Prothro and Grigg 1960: 281, 291–294). Indeed, Stouffer's findings mentioned above spurred the debate on the so-called 'elitist theory of democracy' and set the agenda of research on political tolerance for several decades (Gibson 2006). Variously supported or criticised (e.g. Dahl 1961: 320; Key 1961: 197–199; Nunn, Crockett and Williams 1978: 148; McCloskey and Brill 1983; see Bachrach 1967 for a synthesis of the normative debate), the elitist theory of democracy essentially restricted the scope of Tocqueville's original proposition by arguing that democratic masses were not necessary to a thriving democracy, but democratic elites were. Many later studies of political tolerance focused on proving (e.g. Prothro and Grigg 1960; McCloskey 1964; Sullivan, Piereson and Marcus 1979; Sullivan et al. 1981; Barnum and Sullivan 1989, 1990) or disproving (e.g. Gibson 1988; Gibson and Duch 1991; Duch and Gibson 1992) the elitist theory of democracy, at times highlighting its lack of specification (Gibson and Bingham 1984; Gibson 1992b: 338). Others pointed out that the difference between 'elites' (often defined differently in different studies) and 'masses' was either not significant or driven by third factors such as education (e.g. Jackman 1972).[5]

Even though it very soon became clear *empirically* that a democratic regime did not require a tolerant population (or even a tolerant majority), most scholars of tolerance continued to identify *conceptually* and *normatively* 'tolerance' and 'support for democratic norms' (e.g. Gibson 2011; see Gibson 2006: 23 for some nuancing of that view). Stouffer had pointed out that political tolerance embodied 'two of the more delicate elements of the democratic creed', namely 'specific support for civil liberties' and the 'principle of minority rights' (Stouffer 1955: 221). Such equation of political tolerance with 'support for democratic norms' (e.g. Barnum 1982) is essentially based on the age-old conception of democracy as a political system based on a 'marketplace of ideas':[6] liberal democracy can only flourish if competition among ideas is unconstrained, because this is the only way in which 'superior ideas are found to be superior . . . almost if as guided by an invisible hand' (Gibson 2011: 412). This notion has noble ancestors including, among others, John Stuart Mill and Oliver Wendell Holmes. Reference in the political tolerance literature is also made to Robert Dahl's influential concept of 'polyarchy' – i.e. real-existing rather than ideal democracy – which is based on the same view (e.g. Gibson and Bingham 1985: 2–17; Gibson 1988: 513, 1992b, 1996: 5–6; Gibson and Duch 1991; Peffley and Rohrschneider 2003: 248).[7] Analysts of tolerance have certainly not been exceptions in holding such views. Indeed, as some have argued, this conception of democracy was part and parcel of the behaviouralist research programme itself. The pluralistic system of individuals and groups which constituted the model of the political system for most behaviouralist political scientists rested on a general consensus on the values of liberalism, and it reflected, at least in the early phase of the programme, an idealised image of American society (e.g. Farr 1995: 205).

Whatever its intellectual origins, the logical corollary of conceiving democracy as an unrestricted marketplace of ideas is that all policies that restrict the rights of (non-violent) groups are *anti-democratic*, including policies targeted at groups that advocate the demise of democracy (e.g. Stouffer 1955: 13; 221; Barnum 1982: 497–498; Gibson 2006: 23).[8] Hence, important studies of political tolerance frequently take the view that in a democracy speech in support of violence and suicide bombing should be tolerated (Gibson 2011: 411–412), not least because 'the threat of violence, especially from outside agitators and other anti-system elements, is an intimate part of struggle over civil liberties' (Gibson and Bingham 1982: 618). This position is of course normatively legitimate but fails to consider that the threat of violence has historically been functional to both pro- and anti-democratic agendas, and that in some cases anti-democratic forces have come to power (or threatened to do so) through constitutional channels. Different historical experiences may lead to the predominance of different views of democracy.

The *normative* definition of democracy as an unrestricted 'marketplace of ideas' and the consequent consideration of all rights-restricting policies as inherently anti-democratic, even when targeted at actors who advocate openly anti-democratic ideologies, influenced the *conceptual* and *theoretical* apparatus of most scholars of tolerance. In particular, it was perfectly logical to consider all public support for rights-restricting policies (i.e. intolerant attitudes) as equally detrimental for democracy, irrespective of: (1) whether such support is expressed in the context of a fully consolidated democratic regime or in transitional, illiberal or otherwise precarious democracies (see e.g. Gibson 1996, 2002; Gibson and Gouws 2001; Marquart-Pyatt and Paxton 2007); and (2) whether in democratic regimes rights-restricting policies are targeted at anti- or pro-democratic groups.

The first of these two analytical moves de facto lumps 'militant democracies' in the same category as hybrid regimes or illiberal democracies.[9] This move implicitly reduces the conceptual space for studying policies that restrict the rights of anti-democratic opponents as a separate phenomenon in full-fledged democracies – or, more precisely, across regimes that are normally considered as full democracies in other debates within comparative politics, as well as in common parlance. In other words, the conceptual categories of the tolerance literature lump together rights-restricting policies in, say, the Federal Republic of Germany and the Netherlands with those in, say, Putin's Russia or other hybrid regimes. Yet, in the latter regimes, such policies may be used as one of many ways to frustrate *any* opposition to the incumbents (e.g. Levitsky and Way 2010), while in the former (democratic) systems such policies have historically been targeted mostly at fringe and openly anti-democratic groups, while maintaining political pluralism and the rights of democratic oppositions.

The second analytical moves mentioned above treat groups such as atheists or homosexuals (two categories often studied in this literature as potential targets of intolerance – e.g. Stouffer 1955; Gibson 1987; Gibson and Duch 1993; Bahry, Boaz and Gordon 1997) on the same footing as groups that advocate the demise of democracy. Support for limiting the freedoms of either type of groups is considered to be indicative of intolerance and weak democratic norms. As a result, it is not possible to conceptualise and study separately *militant* democracy. Militant democracy is comprised of policies that address the 'democratic dilemma' mentioned at the beginning of this chapter. As such, it only consists of policies that are aimed at *anti-democratic* actors – that is, actors that pursue the goal of subverting democracy. The concept of militant democracy certainly does not extend to rights-restricting policies that are aimed at other types of political opposition and, even less so, at social minorities.

Even more importantly, this second analytical move neglects the possibility that, in some contexts, policies specifically directed at anti-democratic groups may be considered by elites and masses to be *supportive* of, rather than antithetical to, democracy, precisely because of the purpose of the policies in question of protecting democracy from internal attacks. In these contexts, democracy may not be conceived as an *unrestricted* marketplace of ideas. This possible variation in the commonplace conceptualisation of democracy might, in turn, render problematic the interpretation of some findings of tolerance research itself. I discuss this problem in the next section.

Comparative Analyses of Political Tolerance and Militant Democracy – a Missing Variable

Even though democracy as an unrestricted marketplace of ideas is a time-honoured normative position, it is not the only plausible one, as the long-standing debate in legal and political philosophy about the 'democratic dilemma' shows.[10] Therefore, an approach that assesses tolerance exclusively on the basis of the 'unrestricted marketplace' concept risks understating the associated support for democracy, depending on the political context. In the US, which has been the main empirical terrain for agenda-setting tolerance studies (e.g. Stouffer 1955; Prothro and Grigg 1960; McCloskey 1964), the unrestricted marketplace definition of democracy reflects what most observers would perceive, temporary aberrations aside, as the 'normality' of the constitutional and legal system: all (non-violent) dissent is allowed irrespective of its ideological content, and courts have set a rather high bar for government prohibitions on speech (e.g. Gibson 1988: 511; Barnum and Sullivan 1990: 719; on the historical roots of the legal treatment of free speech in the US, see e.g. Whitman 2000).[11] The same considerations broadly apply also to the UK, Canada and New Zealand, empirical cases that also figure prominently in the tolerance literature (see e.g. Sullivan et al. 1985; Barnum and Sullivan 1989, 1990; Sniderman et al. 1989a).

In other contexts, however, the historical trajectory of democratisation has sometimes given rise to rules restricting the political rights of anti-democratic actors not as temporary or exceptional measures but as rather stable elements of the constitutional order. Importantly, this may apply to regimes that, no less than the Anglo-Saxon countries just mentioned, are considered to be full democracies, and that are often taken as models of stability and effectiveness both by specialists and the general public. Indeed, democratic regimes do not emerge from a common blueprint, but historically, as collages of superimposed institutional arrangements that are often introduced to address the problems of specific political contingencies (Capoccia and Ziblatt 2010). In democracies which have emerged from the collapse of an authoritarian regime, for example, it is possible that the new democratic political elites, intent on preventing the resurgence of anti-democratic forces, include safeguards in the country's constitution and statute books that legally restrict the possibilities for political proselytisation by anti-democratic organisations, first and foremost by the supporters of the previous authoritarian regime. The country's legal and political scholars, mainstream political organisations and the courts may over time come to view these legal restrictions not as a breach of some abstract normative view of democracy, but as supportive of democracy given their declared aim of protecting democracy. The above is even more likely to occur in countries that have a history of democratic breakdown at the hands of authoritarian forces that grabbed power – or endangered democratic survival (Capoccia 2005) – by exploiting *unrestricted* democratic rights of expression and participation. Goebbels's oft-cited dictum 'It will always be one of the best jokes about democracy, that it provides its mortal enemies with the means to destroy it' (cited in Fox and Nolte 1995: 1), and the 'democratic dilemma' that it evokes, resonate much more forcefully in the politics of some democracies than others.

In these contexts, a view of democracy as a *restricted* marketplace of ideas – restricted not in general but specifically with respect to the participation and expression rights of anti-democratic forces may constitute a more plausible term of reference to assess elites' and masses' support of democracy on the basis of their political tolerance.[12] If, due to a country's historical trajectory, restrictions on certain actors come to be seen widely as part and parcel of democracy, intolerance for such actors is more likely to indicate support for democracy (in the sense of protecting it from internal enemies) than opposition to it. Take the example of the Federal Republic of Germany, in which the possibility of restricting several fundamental political rights of anti-democratic individuals and groups was included in the Basic Law and several federal statutes (e.g. Kirchhof and Kommers 1993). As several scholars have pointed out, West German constitution makers introduced these rules as a corrective to the excessive leeway for anti-democratic forces built into the Weimar constitutional and legal system, which was blamed for ultimately facilitating Hitler's rise to power (e.g. Schäfer 2002). Even though these protective rules have periodically come under criticism for various reasons in the German scholarly and public debate, a large majority of legal and constitutional scholars, as well as political analysts, continue to see these rules as an integral element of the Federal Republic's postwar *democratic* constitutional order; their democratic legitimacy has been affirmed by all mainstream democratic parties; and most of the relevant prohibitions have been endorsed by courts, with a remarkable degree of consistency over time. It is therefore plausible to consider these restrictions on political extremism as describing the 'normality' of the German democratic system, no less than the model of an unrestricted marketplace of ideas describes the 'normality' of democracy in the US.[13] Hence, when German elites and masses are surveyed on whether they support the restrictions on rights of participation of anti-democratic groups, their affirmative answer is more likely to indicate abidance by democratic norms than opposition or indifference to such norms.

These contextual factors have been taken into account only partially, if at all, in the comparative literature on political tolerance. For example, Gibson and Duch study tolerance towards 'fascists' in Western European countries by analysing mass and elite support for policies that restricted their rights of political expression, free demonstration and association (Gibson and Duch 1991; see also Duch and Gibson 1992). Taking their lead from the view of democracy as an unrestricted marketplace of ideas, the authors consider support for such policies (i.e. intolerance towards 'fascists') as revealing opposition to democratic norms. Yet the 'unrestricted marketplace' normative yardstick might lead to misinterpretation of the survey results. Even though most of the results of Gibson and Duch's analysis do not attain conventional levels of statistical significance, it is striking that in the case of Germany (probably the most developed, and certainly the best-studied, system of 'militant democracy' in Europe) 'opinion leaders' (i.e. 'elites') are found to be broadly *less* tolerant towards fascists than the mass public. I concur with the authors' interpretation that, for historical reasons, German elites are likely to have internalised 'systemic norms' that include intolerance towards neo-fascists. It is less clear, however, that the German case should be viewed as an exception to a rule that older democracies develop clearer and more pervasive 'democratic norms', as the authors also maintain (Gibson and Duch 1991: 199–202).[14] In fact, with respect to whether 'fascists' should be tolerated or not in a democracy, Germany is less likely to be an isolated exception than a case to be placed at the end of a continuum. In several Western European democracies – in particular those that were created or re-established after the demise of fascist regimes (either autochthonous or collaborationist regimes during wartime) – legislation or even constitutional norms against the public expression of neo-fascist ideology have existed in various forms since at least the end of the Second World War, with varying levels of support across the political spectrum and the judiciary (Capoccia 2018a). Depending on this variation, survey respondents may associate the legal exclusion of fascists with protecting democracy, not with the violation of democratic norms.[15]

In a broad comparative study, Peffley and Rohrschneider acknowledge the potential importance that the illegalisation of certain groups and ideologies may have on the nexus between intolerance and support for democracy in some countries, but they are not fully consistent in drawing the logical consequences of this insight. Criticising the presence of criminals among the potential targets of tolerance included in the World Values Survey (1995–1997) they rightly argue that:

> . . . *political intolerance represents a threat to democracy only if the targets of intolerance are entitled to the same political rights and privileges as everyone else in the polity.* Unfortunately including criminals among unpopular groups and organizations makes little sense *from the standpoint of democratic theory* . . . In most countries, criminals do not enjoy the same citizenship rights as not criminals (e.g. they might lose the right to vote in elections). Thus, *refusing to extend to criminals the rights to run to office may be more a reflection of our countries' legal framework than of political intolerance.* (Peffley and Rohrschneider 2003: 247, emphasis added)

In some of the Western and Eastern European countries included in this study, however, political groups such as the Nazis, fascists and communists – all mentioned as potential targets of intolerance in the survey questions analysed by the authors – are also treated differently from ordinary citizens for purposes of 'political rights and privileges' (e.g. Niesen 2012). Therefore, support for policies which restrict the right to run for office of members of one or more of these groups may also be interpreted as 'the reflection of that country's legal framework' rather than as a sign of lack of belief in democracy. Yet, the authors consider supporting policies that deny such groups the right to freely demonstrate and the right to hold public office to be 'the hallmark of an intolerant citizen' and therefore to be opposed to democratic norms (Peffley and Rohrschneider 2003: 248).[16]

Of course, the point here is less to show the limits of specific studies than to bring into relief how the lack of systematic knowledge of variation in rights-restricting policies across democratic regimes may have negative consequences for the correct interpretation of comparative findings on political tolerance. Adding this 'missing variable' to comparative analyses of political tolerance would not only improve the validity of these interpretations but also theoretically ground the views of those who have argued that intolerance for anti-democratic dissenters in survey responses does not necessarily indicate opposition to democratic norms. This is the view, for example, of Sullivan, Piereson and Marcus, who argue that tolerance should not be identified with support for democratic norms but be seen in trade-off with other democratic values, which opens the possibility that in some cases being intolerant might actually support, rather than undermine, the cause of democracy (Sullivan, Piereson and Marcus 1982).[17] Similarly, Sniderman and co-authors maintain that '. . . it is by no means intolerant – indeed, it may reflect an effort to defend tolerance – to refuse to accept as legitimate a group because its conduct is ambivalent and illegal. To refuse to tolerate socialists is to be intolerant; but to refuse to tolerate terrorists is to be tolerant' (Sniderman et al. 1989b: 42). Marquart-Pyatt and Paxton explicitly argue that models of tolerance that have been developed for the US may not apply to Western or Eastern European democracies, in which people have dire memories of the harmful effect for democracy of 'least-liked groups', which in some cases may have led to their illegalisation (Marquart-Pyatt and Paxton 2007: 104). Lacking a clear metric of the legal and judicial boundaries of legitimate dissent across different democracies, however, these authors are ultimately unable to clarify *where* certain types of intolerance (i.e. the support for rights-restricting policies of a given intensity and directed to given targets) are more likely to signify support for democratic norms rather than opposition to them. Finally, in their study of Denmark, Petersen et al. (2011) find that, with some exceptions, tolerance is high towards groups that observe democratic rights, while groups that are associated with violence and disrespect for the rules of democracy are tolerated much less. The authors attribute this pattern to 'norms of reciprocity': democratic rights are accorded by respondents to groups that, even though disliked, themselves observe and acknowledge democratic rights, and vice versa. However, it is likely that the very meaning of 'reciprocity'

will be different depending on what is generally seen to constitute obser-
vance and acknowledgements of democratic rights in different countries.
In countries in which, say, *any* neo-Nazi activities are strictly forbidden,
non-violent expression by a small neo-Nazi group might be seen by many
as disrespecting the rules of democracy. Countries with more permissive
policy regimes may instead set a more capacious boundary for 'respect for
democratic rights'.

Conclusion

This chapter makes a twofold point. First, the absence of an empirical
research programme in post-war mainstream comparative politics on the
variation in the rights-restricting policies associated with 'militant democracy' is not due to the political unimportance of the issues underlying the
policies in question but to the theoretical, conceptual and normative lenses
characterising the approaches that have successively dominated the subdis-
cipline. These approaches have led analysts to consider rights-restricting
policies targetted at anti-democratic actors in the context of broader or
narrower objects of study, typically reducing the conceptual and theoretical space available for the comparative analysis of militant democracy per
se. Second, the lack of systematic comparative knowledge from a robust
research programme on militant democracy has been detrimental not
only to our understanding of democratic rule but also to the research programmes that have focused on phenomena related to rights-restricting
policies in democracies.

This chapter illustrates these points through a discussion of the empirical research on political tolerance. The discussion focuses on how the identification of democracy with a model of an unrestricted marketplace of
ideas, which underlies many analyses of tolerance, has led to conceptual
and analytical moves that have restricted the theoretical and conceptual
space for the study of 'militant democracy' as an independent phenomenon that happens in, and varies across, full-fledged democratic regimes.
The chapter furthermore shows how a more reliable empirical knowledge of variation in rights-restricting policies across different democracies
would be likely to improve our interpretation of comparative findings on
political tolerance. As explained, the historical trajectories and the political circumstances of different countries may entrench politically, judicially
and culturally the democratic legitimacy of specific legal restrictions of
the political rights of one or more anti-democratic groups, thus leading the
normative concept of democracy to depart from the version based on the

unrestricted marketplace of ideas. In these contexts, elite and mass support for such restrictions would be more likely to signify support for democratic norms rather than opposition to them.

What is needed, and what was missing for much of the post-war period in mainstream comparative politics, is an analytical focus on institutions per se, in particular their causal strength, their dynamics of development over time and their social underpinnings. The resurgence of interest in institutional analysis since the late 1980s and early 1990s has brought important advances in the comparative politics field, and to useful theoretical and conceptual bridges with the literatures in public policy and history (e.g. Pierson 2006; Capoccia 2016). So far, longitudinal analysis of institutional development has mainly – although not exclusively – concentrated on social and economic policies. We now have the instruments to extend the findings and concepts to other policy sectors, including, importantly, rights-restricting policies – or, put another way, how 'militant' democracies are, against whom, and why.

Notes

1. I use the more generic term 'approach' rather than the more contested term 'paradigm' (e.g. Ball 1976; Eckberg and Hill 1979).

2. A discussion of whether the actions by McCarthy and the US Senate Permanent Subcommittee on Investigations (and the parallel ones by the House Un-American Activities Committee) should be considered normatively legitimate exceeds the scope of this chapter. Most supporters of militant democracy would *not* consider normatively legitimate restrictions of rights that are marred by procedural abuse, lack of effective judicial review, or disproportionality – which have been documented in the case of McCarthyism – even if these actions were targeted at unquestionably anti-democratic actors. As discussed below, the conception of democracy at the basis of much empirical research on tolerance was such that would instead consider *the very possibility* of restricting rights of the enemies of democracy as democratically illegitimate.

3. The definition of political tolerance evolved somewhat in this literature, and discussions on measurement have been robust but never questioned the strategy of measuring political tolerance towards a certain group by asking individuals whether they supported or opposed policies aimed at restricting basic rights of members of that group.

4. Gibson (1992b) raises doubts on whether mass (in-)tolerance has *any* influence on public policy and argues that the most likely principal consequence of diffuse intolerant attitudes is to encourage a climate of social conformism and to stifle social criticism and opposition.

5. Furthermore, scholars disagreed on exactly *what aspect* of democratic rule would be negatively affected by the predominance of intolerant views among the population (see discussion in e.g. Jackman 1972: 758; Barnum 1982: 485) – whether democratic stability (Prothro and Grigg 1960), government effectiveness (Gibson and Bingham 1985: 9) or the application of tolerant norms to specific controversies regarding civil and political rights (e.g. Barnum 1982; Gibson and Bingham 1985; Gibson 1987).

6. This is the core of the so-called 'classical theory of democracy', typically evoked in this literature in opposition to the above-mentioned 'elitist theory of democracy'. According to this view (for which 'classical' is somewhat of a misnomer: in the US it is mainly based on Oliver Wendell Holmes's views on free speech; see Sullivan, Piereson and Marcus 1979) democratic outcomes depend on whether citizens hold dear the respect for civil liberties.

7. Dahl considered that the definitional traits of polyarchies were the equality of opportunity for *all* political actors to formulate their preferences and signify them to the government and to their fellow citizens for individual and collective action; and to have the government weigh their preferences equally, that is, weigh them with no discrimination due to the content or the source of the preference (Dahl 1971: 1–2).

8. This view considers as equally anti-democratic the beliefs, say, of a Nazi group, and of those in favour of curtailing the political rights of that Nazi group in order to protect democracy (e.g. Stouffer 1955: 221).

9. The analysis of mass tolerance in these contexts is often invoked to substantiate the ongoing importance of this literature. Gibson puts this point perhaps most explicitly of all: 'The topic is today no less important than it was in the days of Joseph McCarthy . . . since intolerance in one form or another fuels the conflict in Northern Ireland, the Middle East, Rwanda, and many other areas of the world. And even where intolerance does not directly produce political violence, the failure of democratizing regimes to embrace political freedoms for all, even those in the opposition, has become one of the most important impediments to the consolidation of democratic reform throughout the world (as in the so-called illiberal democracies)' (Gibson 2011: 410).

10. This debate is too extensive to review here. For recent contributions, see e.g. Brettschneider (2012), Kirshner (2014) and Issacharoff (2015).

11. Scholars of political tolerance are of course aware of the several circumstances in the history of the US in which the government has exerted harsh preventive repression on real or supposed enemies (e.g. Goldstein 1978). These, however, are typically considered as transient deviations from a default rule of generalised tolerance for non-violent extremism, as reflected in the vast legal literature on free speech in the US (e.g. Tribe 2000).

12. Some scholars of tolerance have expressed scepticism about the possibility of establishing objective bases for whether a group can be considered to be anti-democratic before it achieves its political goals (e.g. Gibson 2013: 62; see

also Gibson and Bingham 1985: 11–12, 25, 41; Gibson 1988: 516). The difficulties inherent in such *ex ante* classification are apparent, but the task is not impossible (see Capoccia 2002 for a broader discussion). On the other hand, maintaining that *any* classification of opposition groups *ex ante* as pro- or anti-democratic is necessarily arbitrary leads to paradoxical conclusions, such as the impossibility of classifying as anti-democratic, say, the German Nazi Party in 1932, or the Czechoslovak Communist Party in 1947 – i.e. just in advance of the realisation of their anti-democratic political objectives.

13. Acknowledging that different historical conditions may legitimise a model of democracy in which the 'marketplace of ideas' may be variously restricted vis-à-vis anti-democratic actors does *not* mean adopting a relativist position in which the majority's mere labelling as 'anti-democratic' of any opposition would bestow democratic legitimacy by *fiat* onto any legal restriction of their political rights. Apart from any other consideration, such a position would incur the same conceptual fallacy of lumping together 'militant democracies' and illiberal or semi-authoritarian regimes, which was criticised earlier in the chapter. Rather, the position defended here is the empirical enactment of many scholars' (including among others Karl Popper and Carl Joachim Friedrich) normative view that democratic constitutions are not 'suicide pacts'. Hence, the restriction of anti-democratic dissent in a democratic regime for preventive and defensive reasons – at a minimum to stave off a realistic prospect of democratic breakdown – should not by itself lead scholars to consider the regime in question as hybrid or authoritarian. Whether the extent of the restrictions and their proportionality to the threat, the presence of partisanship or procedural abuse, or even doubts concerning the anti-democratic nature of the target of restrictions are such as to justify reclassifying the regime from democratic to non-democratic will be a matter of scholarly debate and of classificatory and empirical analysis.

14. Gibson and Duch (1991: 209) accept that restricting the rights and liberties of certain groups may be considered 'desirable in certain circumstances', but supporting such restrictions remains intolerant and therefore undemocratic.

15. I refer here to the legal possibility of restricting the rights of anti-democratic actors *in principle* – that is, avoiding partisanship, abuse, disproportionality and other distortions *in the practice* of applying such restrictions, practices that are considered incompatible with democracy among those who see militant democracy as legitimate (see discussion e.g. in Kirshner 2014).

16. The authors acknowledge that in post-authoritarian democracies such as Germany, some rights, such as the right to teach in a school, may be legally restricted for individuals who hold anti-democratic views. This is one reason why they drop that specific indicator of intolerance from their analysis (Peffley and Rohrschneider 2003: 248). However, they do not extend this view to the rights to free demonstration and to hold public office, which may be subject to similar restrictions in Germany as well as in other post-authoritarian democracies.

17. It should be noted that Sullivan, Piereson and Marcus's 'content-controlled' measurement of tolerance – i.e. measuring tolerance of the 'least-liked group' rather than named groups (Sullivan, Piereson and Marcus 1979) – is at odds with this insight, since in some democracies the 'least-liked' groups might actually be illegal (e.g. Marquart-Pyatt and Paxton 2007: 104).

EIGHT

Liberal Democratic Sanctions in the EU

Tore Vincents Olsen

Introduction

Hungary and Poland are currently being criticised for violating the liberal democratic values on which membership of the EU is based. In those countries, political majorities are using their powers to undermine conditions and institutions which are central in liberal democracies, such as independent public media, the freedom of civil society organisations, academic freedom and the independence of the judiciary. In Hungary, Viktor Orbán's government, in power since 2010, has used its large majority to make its social policies part of the constitution so that it would require a two-thirds majority to change them again.[1] This arguably goes against the notion that constitutions should establish a level playing field between competing political programmes and it puts future alternative majorities at a serious disadvantage. Orbán has explicitly stated that he wants to create an 'illiberal state' where the national interest is given priority over liberal values (Orbán, in Tóth 2014).

The developments in Hungary and Poland have raised concerns because they represent a backlash against the values and tenets of liberal democracy, which in the European context are based on the experience of the interwar period and the horrors of the Second World War. That experience is central to their introduction into the EU's value base. However, as we shall argue, these values can also be defended on the basis of democratic theory. In the European context, they are important because they ensure the status of all European citizens as co-rulers in their efforts to decide their common concerns together democratically. Value violations undermine the status and full protection of citizens as co-rulers not only at the national level, but also at the European level. They imply (a partial) exclusion of citizens from democracy.

The problem with the (partial) exclusion of citizens also points to why EU sanctions against governments that violate EU values might be problematic. As sanctions are currently discussed and stipulated in the treaties, some of them imply the (partial) exclusion of citizens from democratic government. They thus touch upon the paradox of a militant democracy defending itself by excluding some citizens and political parties from full political rights and participation in democratic procedures (Müller 2016a: 252–253). Critics of militant democracy claim that it is undemocratic to exclude people from democracy. We think that this is only partly true, especially when considering the situation in Hungary and Poland where people with little regard for the democratic rights of others hold power over key political institutions. Critics overlook that democracy is not only a procedure but also a substantive set of values, and therefore democracy cannot be neutral towards itself. However, the problem in the EU is that the exclusion that is envisioned in the treaties and much of the current discussion includes those who are not in violation of EU values. From a normative point of view, more proportionate sanctions should be considered.

This chapter will discuss why and how the EU should respond to the violations of EU values from a principled liberal democratic point of view. This means that the chapter does not aim to predict whether it is realistic to introduce the sanctions it proposes into the EU legal framework or predict which sanctions would be effective in bringing member states to conform to EU's liberal democratic values. Finally, it does not extensively discuss whether and how Poland and Hungary are in fact violating EU values.

The chapter will proceed in the following manner. The next section looks at European values and how they are justified from a normative point of view. The third section discusses why a violation of those values is a problem in the EU beyond the fact that they are EU values: is it a bigger problem for EU citizens that they are violated in the EU than if they were violated anywhere else in the world? The fourth section looks at the sanctions and the sanctioning mechanisms in the EU and how they are discussed in the literature. It demonstrates that most of them rely on a problematic notion of collective responsibility and include too many citizens who should not be held responsible for EU value breaches. The fifth section suggests alternative targeted sanctions. Section six concludes.

Why European Values?

The values of the EU are stipulated in Article 2 of the Treaty of the European Union (TEU) as 'the values of respect for human dignity, freedom, democracy, equality, the rule of law and respect for human rights'. They are commonly interpreted as the values of liberal democracy and as having their basis in European history. The historical lesson from the interwar period, especially the Weimar Republic, and the horrors of the Second World War and the Holocaust led to the rejection of unconstrained parliamentary democracy and the embrace of constitutional constraints on politics, not least in the form of individual rights.[2] The European Community (now EU) itself was also based on the idea that national parliamentary democracy and politics of mass mobilisation should be constrained. It represented depoliti-cisation and technocratic governance allowing policy makers to avoid the constraints of popular democracy and accountability (Norman 2017: 542; Müller 2011b: 146–150). Thus, while there is no singular model of liberal democracy that all member states should emulate, and while the EU officially respects the constitutional orders of member states as part of their 'national identity' (TEU Article 4.2), the expectation is nonetheless that member states represent some form of liberal democracy. EU membership can only be con-ferred on states that respect EU values (TEU Article 49).

For many, the historical lessons may be sufficient to justify liberal democracy as limited government. And the EU's original purpose might not have been democracy, but to promote 'peace and prosperity (Weiler 1999). Nonetheless, not all limitations on democracy can be justified on the basis of the previous excesses of unconstrained national democracy. Moreover, 'history is not destiny and its purported lessons do not automatically con-vey legitimacy' (Müller 2013a: 143). If people are to abide by the rules and principles of a specific type of government, then it is required that they are presented with good reasons for accepting them. What is needed is thus a theory that can integrate and defend both the democratic and the liberal aspects of liberal democracy.

Brettschneider (2007) presents us with such a theory. He criticises pure procedural accounts of democracy for not being able to respond adequately to situations in which democratic procedures lead to outcomes such as the violation of important individual rights or even destruction of democracy itself due to their lack of any standards for legitimate democratic decisions beyond the democratic procedure itself (Brettschneider 2007: 11–17). Con-versely, he also criticises the most common defences of liberal democracy based on notions of external procedure-independent standards of justice, in particular human rights, that must not be violated by democratic pro-cedures. Democracy is here seen as the on-average best available means to realising external standards of justice. The problem is that this defence pre-sumes the ready availability of relatively uncontested conceptions of justice, and that this is paternalistic: it underestimates the value of self-rule by the people (Brettschneider 2007: 17–23).

In Brettschneider's alternative 'value-based' conception of democracy the democratic ideal is based on three values – the equality of interests, political autonomy and reciprocity – which aim to protect citizens as 'rulers' in both public and private life. These values underlie both the democratic procedures and the constraints on democratic outcomes constituted by the rule of law and basic individual rights. This means that constraints on democratic procedure do not refer to some external pre- or non-democratic standard for justice, but to the values of democracy itself (Brettshneider 2007: 26). It also means that the theory can recognise that there is a 'democratic loss' in instances where democratic procedures have led to outcomes which violate the status of citizens as rulers – that is, the violation of the values of equality of interest, political autonomy and reciprocity – and therefore have to be overridden. Furthermore, it implies that this democratic loss must be balanced up against the gravity of the violation of the values and that in some cases the democratic procedure and its results would have to be given priority regardless of their prima facie conflict with the rule of law and key individual rights (Brettschneider 2007: 137–138, 142–148).

But how is it possible to tell when decisions are in conflict with democratic values? Brettschneider's two principles of *democratic contractualism* provide the answer. The *principle of democracy's public reason* asks which reasons for coercion could be accepted by citizens in their capacity as rulers. Reasons that explicitly or implicitly go against the three values of democracy will be ruled out. Examples are arguments for slavery, apartheid (separate but equal) and interpretations of equality as 'equality before God' (Brettschneider 2007: 63–64). The *principle of democratic inclusion* asks what state coercion each individual citizen, accepting the values of democracy and aiming to reach universal agreement with all, could reasonably accept or reject, taking into consideration his or her particular social context (Brettschneider 2007: 64–69). This principle yields that some forms of coercion are reasonable and necessary to protect people's freedom while other forms are not, for example prohibitions against sodomy. The inclusion principle, emphasising the individual citizen's point of view and not just the general point of view, also tells us why breaches of rule of law principles, such as retroactivity and bills of attainder, are unacceptable. Retroactivity, for example, makes it impossible for individuals to predict what the laws require of them, even if the content of retroactive laws could be justified with reference to the three core values of democracy (Brettschneider 2007: 65).

The value theory of democracy integrates the main insights from both the procedural and the substantive conceptions of democracy and demonstrates how both the democratic (participation, procedure) and the liberal (individual rights, rule of law) aspects of liberal democracy relate to the status of citizens as equal co-rulers. This explains why violations of liberal democratic values like those in Hungary and Poland are problematic. But why would it matter more to EU members, states and citizens that liberal democratic values are violated in other member states than if/when they are violated anywhere else in the world outside the EU. The next section looks at this question.

Why is Value Violation in Individual Member States a Problem?

One answer is that the EU needs to ensure consistency with its own values to remain credible in its external relations, including with prospective member states (Closa 2016: 19–22). Another similar answer is that in order for the mechanism of mutual recognition of legal decisions in civil and commercial matters to work, states and citizens need to be able to trust that individual rights and the rule of law are protected in all member states (European Commission 2014; Closa 2016: 16–18). The third answer emphasises that European states and citizens cannot be indifferent to non-liberal democratic government representatives participating in EU decision making via membership of the Council. Through this and other channels, the non-observance of liberal democratic values might spread, undermining citizens' liberal democratic rights (Müller 2015: 144; Closa 2016: 18–19). These three answers all in some way refer to the 'all affected principle' stating that all affected by decisions should have a say in those decisions (see Goodin 2007). Since all other member states and citizens are likely to be negatively affected by a member state violating EU values, they should have a say in what happens there.

We are sympathetic to these answers but would like to introduce a more comprehensive view that integrates them while it underlines the problematic democratic aspect of value violation in a member state. The central argument here is that European citizens, due to the way in which they are connected economically, socially, legally and politically, stand in relations of potential domination with each other. Additionally, on average, they are more closely connected to each other than they are to other people. Domination takes place when decisions are made that affect the choices you are able to make without tracking your interest (Pettit 1997: 51). That is, they are arbitrary. Domination is not only based on the actual decisions of others that may interfere with your choices but also on the knowledge that others could interfere with your choice options. This implies that when people are tied together in relations of potential domination – as they are within the EU – they should structure their interactions by establishing common political institutions that ensure them all a status of equal democratic membership. Only equal democratic membership can offer securities against domination (Bohman 2010; Olsen and Rostbøll 2017).

With common European institutions which integrate national legal and political institutions and with the creation of EU citizenship, the EU has approximated a condition in which European citizens are able to rule together with regard to their common concerns. Obviously, what their common concerns are is a relatively open question and the democratic credentials of EU institutions are not perfect.[3] Nonetheless, the problem with non-liberal democratic governments and policies in the EU is that they undermine or endanger the status of citizens as equal democratic co-rulers in common European concerns.

Most fundamentally, when a member state government pursues non-liberal democratic policies, it undermines the rights and the status of European citizens, both those who live in the member state in question (including other EU citizens) and those who have the right to move to it (that is, more or less all EU citizens). Note that national politics and national political institutions are part of the overall European political and legal structure. European institutions expressly give an institutional role to national governments, parliaments, courts and administrations. When equal political rights are violated at the national level, they affect the equal rights of EU citizens. When rights are violated on the input side, it affects the democratic credentials and representativeness of governments and national parliaments. Violation of equal rights and rule of law guarantees in the administration and application of the law creates an unequal and insecure membership status for some citizens.

Recall also that national institutions and rights play an important part in European politics. The latter not only takes place via European institutions and European media but is rooted in the political and legal infrastructure of all the individual member states. It is for example not only with regard to national issues that, say, Polish and Hungarian government control over the media is problematic. The political opposition with regard to European issues is also treated unequally, for example with regard to their appeals to other European citizens outside the country. This points to a further reverse problem with the rights violation, namely that it excludes other citizens from interacting in a democratic manner with those citizens whose rights are being violated. The former cannot rely on the latter having the full and secure freedom to interact with them.

These considerations show why it is appropriate for citizens to equip European institutions with the ability to intervene and sanction. Breaches in values lead to the partial or complete exclusion of some citizens. The dilemma is that sanctions themselves might also entail the partial or complete exclusion of some citizens. As mentioned, this is the paradox of a militant democracy defending itself against anti-democratic political forces.

Brettschneider's value theory of liberal democracy is in line with a moderate theory of militant democracy. Brettschneider (2007: chapter 7) prefers judicial review and thus court-backed constitutional restraints on the democratic procedure as a way of defending liberal democratic rights.[4] Such measures can be seen as a first line of defence against anti-democratic forces. Militant democracy theory entertains further possible defences against anti-democratic forces, in particular the restriction of their participation in politics and political institutions. As Kirshner (2014: 9–18) emphasises, once the stage has been reached where a majority wants to pass legislation that infringes the democratic rights of others, it might actually be too late (for courts) to save democracy. This points to the problem of how to defend democracy under varying conditions. The general logic of a moderate militant democracy would be that when there is democratic stability and the number of anti-democrats is small, then constraints on anti-democrats' political participation needs to be very modest or perhaps avoided altogether (Kirshner 2014: chapter 3). When anti-democrats are a credible political force who have shown themselves willing to remove or weaken the democratic rights of other citizens, then anti-democrats' participation might be curbed by party bans and/or limitations on the use of political propaganda, etc. (Kirshner 2014: chapter 5). This might stop anti-democrats from ever seizing the government and taking control over central democratic institutions (see also Rummens, Chapter 6 this volume).

The case we are discussing here is one in which political actors with a problematic attitude towards the full democratic rights of all citizens have gained control over the government in a member state and have been able to change key policies and the constitution in their favour. We still have a majority of member states and EU institutions which presumably are willing and able to defend liberal democratic values. This raises the question of what to do in this case.[5] The desideratum would be that measures or sanctions against anti-democrats and anti-democratic policies are designed in such a way that they harm citizens with no responsibility in undermining democracy the least, including in terms of exclusion from political participation. If they do not, the sanctions would seem to violate the very same values that they are supposed to protect. This brings us to the sanctions and sanction mechanisms that are envisioned within the treaties as well as within the political and scholarly debate.

Collective Sanctions in the EU

TEU Article 7 describes the possible sanctions against member states that breach EU values. The procedure can be initiated by other member states (one third of them acting together), the European Parliament (EP) or the Commission. As a first step, the European Council can, on the basis of a four-fifths majority and with the consent of the EP, 'determine that there is a *clear risk of a serious breach* by a Member State' of Article 2 values. This is a preventive step that allows the EU and the member state in question to engage in a dialogue to prevent the breach from occurring and/or to allow the member state to undo political decisions that are perceived to violate values. As a second step, the Council, acting on the basis of unanimity and with the consent of the EP, can rule that there *is a serious and persistent breach* of EU values (unanimity does not include the state under consideration). Finally, as a last step, the Council, acting alone, may decide on the basis of a qualified majority to suspend certain rights 'deriving from the application of the treaties to the Member State in question, including the voting rights of the representative of the government of that Member State in the Council' (TEU Article 7.3). The rights deriving from the treaties are not closely circumscribed and may not only be rights that result from the treaties themselves, but also any right resulting from secondary EU law (Besselink 2017: 131). This includes money from regional development funds. The only sanction that is explicitly excluded is the termination of membership (TEU Article 7.3; Besselink 2017: 130).

It has been debated whether these sanctions are effective. The first issue is whether they will ever be triggered. Some perceive the mechanism as a 'nuclear option' that member states will be very reluctant to use out of fear that it could be used against themselves at a later point. With regard to the second step, the unanimity requirement arguably makes it very unlikely that a determination that there is a serious and persistent breach of values would be made. It only takes one 'defecting state' to veto the decision. The second issue with regard to effectiveness is whether the sanctions, if they were to be issued, would have the desired effect. With regard to pecuniary sanctions, fines or withheld funds, some commentators seem to think that they would be effective (Bárd et al. 2016: vii). EU funds, for example, make up about 4 per cent of Hungarian GNI and cohesion funds accounted for 55 per cent of public investment in 2015–2017 (Wróbel 2018). Their loss would have a large negative impact that the government would want to avoid. Others argue that it is unclear that governments which rely on illiberal practices to maintain their power would react to pecuniary sanctions (Sedelmeier 2017). It is similarly unclear whether the preventive stage, which relies on a 'naming and shaming' strategy, would have the desired effect. In Romania, criticism from the EU of unconstitutional attempts by the Ponta government to get rid of an unpopular rival party president seemed to work. On the other hand, the criticisms of Hungary and Poland expressed not least by the Commission seem to have had little or no effect. It is difficult to predict what would happen if decisions were made according to the Article 7 procedure and at least four-fifths of the member states stood behind the criticism.

The discussion about the effectiveness of Article 7 sanctions have led both scholars and European institutions to consider alternative sanction mechanisms. In response to what the EU Commission saw as a high threshold for triggering the Article 7 procedures, it developed its own pre-preventive stage by way of a Rule of Law Framework (2014). This has formed the basis of its criticism of Poland. The Council has also installed an annual dialogue to 'promote and safeguard the rule of law' (Council of the EU 2014: 20–21).[6] The Commission has also started infringement proceedings against member states for the violation of EU law in specific areas such as age discrimination (forced early retirement of judges), rules on funding of NGOs and legislation regarding higher education. As of now, it is not possible to start infringement procedures directly on the basis of Article 2 of the TEU. Scholars have discussed the extent to which it is possible to have national and European courts play a role through fundamental rights complaint procedures at the national and European level as well as through procedures of treaty infringement (Scheppele 2016; Blauberger and Kelemen 2017; Von Bogdandy, Antpöhler, C. and Ioannidis 2017). Blauberger and Kelemen (2017) argue that in order to have courts, and not least the European Court of Justice (ECJ), enrolled in the protection of liberal democracy at the national level, a new clear legal basis would have to be created, lest the law and the courts be politicised.

The EU Commission's and the Council's rule of law mechanisms are easier to trigger, but it is not clear how effective their naming and shaming strategy would be. Legal mechanisms also seem easier to trigger. If there was a clear legal basis for it, and member states would be willing without further ado to repeal laws and policies that went against European values and principles, then that would of course be preferable to the kind of more wide-ranging sanctions that are envisioned in Article 7.3. One caveat, however, is that evaluation of whether a member is in violation of EU values is a more complex problem that might easily turn political.

As a compromise between the political mechanism in Article 7 and the discussed legal mechanism of infringement, it has been proposed to create a new European body that would be perceived as less political and more impartial than the Commission. Müller (2013a, 2015, 2017a) has thus suggested a Copenhagen Commission (named after the 1993 EU accession criteria) which should carry out annual reviews of how well *all* member states are living up to the fundamental values of the EU. Similarly, Bárd et al. (2016) have proposed a European Rule of Law Commission. Müller and Bárd et al. are both concerned with the body's impartiality and professional authority in these matters. Müller thinks it should be manned with legal experts and stateswomen and -men with proven 'track records', while Bárd et al. are more in favour of staffing such a body with independent experts and academics. Both emphasise that evaluations of 'systematic breaches' should be monitored on the basis of clear criteria while at the same time avoiding a simple 'checklist' approach. The latter could not accommodate the fact that national legal and political systems are more than the sum of their parts, considering for example how checks and balances' mechanisms work differently within different systems (Rijpkema, Chapter 9 this volume).

Müller (2013a, 2015) argues that a negative report should eventually result in substantial fines being issued by the European Commission to member states. And the Commission should be *required* to issue fines without having any choice in the matter. However, he also points out that it is important that reactions are based on what governments actually do (and not on what they say or might do), that breaches are systemic and that time is given for democratic self-correction inside the member state.

The Rule of Law Commission and the Copenhagen Commission would seem to make it less difficult to trigger sanctions against member states in breach of European values. They also remedy the worry that sanctioning mechanisms are used selectively only to target 'the little guys' and that they focus too much on statements by political actors and not on what they actually do. The question is still, of course, whether they would have the desired effect. The same applies to the last discussed sanction, namely ejection of a member state. This might be the corollary of conditioning EU accession on the respect for EU values and take place in situations like military coups (Müller 2015: 150).

This brief review demonstrates how some sanction mechanisms are uncontroversial from a liberal democratic point of view, for example naming and shaming strategies, while others are not: withholding funds, suspending other rights resulting from the treaties – not least rights of political representation in the Council – and ejecting member states from the EU. The latter rest on notions of collective responsibility and also apply to citizens, notably members of democratic minorities, who cannot be ascribed responsibility for the violation of liberal democratic values in the member states.[7] They therefore seem prima facie illegitimate.

But could they not be defended on the basis of principles of collective responsibility? The latter suggest that minorities might be given part of the responsibility for a specific result if they share values and practices that create a certain environment that leads to a specific result or if they are part of a scheme of cooperation that has led to this result (Miller 2007: 120).

Miller argues that the more democratic a nation is, the easier it is to tell whether all members of a nation have shared in the production of a given outcome (Miller 2007: 130). If minorities are included in the democratic decision making, they would normally be held responsible for the result of policies even if they have voted against them. Conventional conceptions of political obligation imply that minorities are required to subject themselves to majority decisions. According to Miller, something similar applies when the minority shares the political culture of the majority, even when they disagree with the majority on singular issues, for example on whether or not to go to war (Miller 2007: 132–133).

But can minorities also be held responsible for 'outcomes' that undermine liberal democratic institutions? As argued above, the harm that is done by non-democratic governments and policies in individual member states is not only a harm done to its own citizens in the democratic minority, but one that harms all EU citizens. This raises the question of whether such EU-wide responsibility can also be ascribed to the minority in the member state in question; they might be complicit in harming people other than themselves. A further consideration is whether the minority can be assigned remedial responsibility for bringing their own 'house back in order' even if they had no causal responsibility for breaching EU values.

Miller stipulates some demanding criteria for letting minorities off the hook but emphasises that share in collective responsibility does not ensue when 'a group [. . .] is excluded from decision making altogether, or [. . .] forms a permanent and oppressed minority' (Miller 2007: 132).

From a liberal democratic perspective, it is not clear that sharing a political culture is sufficient for assigning a share of collective responsibility to minorities. It is more convincing that minorities' equal share in decision making would give them such a share. In the cases of Hungary and Poland, the majorities have changed the legal and political institutions after an election (at least the initial election) that must be deemed fair, and it is not obvious that the minority did not share their nations' political cultures. On Miller's conception of responsibility, this implies that if the minority did not criticise the majority vehemently enough it would also have some share of the responsibility for the resulting value breach. However, minorities might not have had sufficient information to mobilise against specific policy programmes and planned reforms of the rival parties which after the election formed the government. Moreover, minorities might have pro-tested more if they had known that they were to become a minority in a non-liberal state. The level of minority protest at an election is therefore not a reliable indicator of how much a minority dissents from the dominant political culture and the governing parties.

Hence, it is implausible that minorities should be held responsible for the outcome of government reforms that undermine their rights and make them permanent minorities by disadvantaging them in future political pro-cesses. A distinction must be made between the responsibility that minority members can be given for substantive policies that fall within the range of 'normal politics' and the responsibility they can be assigned for 'constitu-tional policies' that undermine their basic democratic rights.

However, a further question is whether the minority should be seen as remedially responsible for bringing their own house back in order. This remedial responsibility could be based on their special obligations *qua* shared nationality towards their co-nationals and common national insti-tutions or on their higher capacity for changing the situation compared to outsiders (Miller 2007: 103–104). These are forward-looking conceptions of collective responsibility not tied specifically to any causal responsibility for the breach of values (Smiley 2017).

We are not convinced of the cogency of the notion of special national obligations (see Caney 2009). However, the above argument about the obligation to establish equal democratic membership in relationships of potential domination points to stronger responsibility of national citizens who are more densely involved in such relations with each other than they are with outsiders' others to ensure equal democratic membership among themselves and thus to remedy the situation. The capability argument also holds some plausibility. As insiders, democratic minorities, say in Hungary or Poland, have a better starting point than other European outsiders for convincing their co-nationals to correct the bad decisions of the past. Out-siders are likely to be seen as illegitimate forces interfering with domes-tic affairs (Jenne and Mudde 2012). However, it is difficult to know who is most capable: insider minorities whose rights are infringed or outsiders who have their democratic rights preserved and the backing of national and European institutions.

Both arguments imply that democratic minorities have some remedial responsibility. However, given their lack of – or perhaps lesser – casual responsibility for the breach of liberal democratic values, the main remedial responsibility would still rest, first, with the political actors – the governing parties – that have effectuated the policies and institutional changes, and, second, the members of the majority who voted for them. Not only are they causally responsible for the violations, they also control the situation and are more able, even if unwilling, to correct it. To attribute equal responsibility to minority members, who are also victims, would not be fair (Isaacs 2014).

Hence, the EU should not issue collective sanctions against member states that equally affect the democratic minorities. That would not be in line with the values that the sanctions are supposed to protect. Generally, liberal democracies are expected to issue sanctions that are in proportion to the wrong committed and they should only apply to those who have committed wrongful acts (Bedau and Kelly 2017). In the present case, this would be, first, the governing parties and, second, members of the democratic majority who voted for them. As to the latter, it is not entirely clear that one can see ordinary citizens as actors in the relevant way (although see Malkopoulou 2016). The main purpose of representative democracy is to elect representatives who act on behalf of ordinary citizens. Moreover, the secret ballot excludes exact knowledge of which individual citizens belong to the majority. The main target of sanctions should therefore be the governing parties and their leaders.

One further objection could be, first, that in liberal democratic orders punishment is also justified on the basis of its consequences. Sanctions are supposed to deter people from carrying out wrongful acts in the first place and induce them to exercise their duties, including potentially to defend liberal democratic values to the best of their ability. These forward-looking considerations match the remedial responsibility that democratic minorities in member states violating liberal democratic values, as argued above, could be assigned. The threat of future collective sanctions is meant to make all citizens more vigilant and therefore is not unfair.

Second, although decisions based on European law can result in sanctions, or fines, against infringing states, in cases in which governments are likely not to abide by decisions, the EU due to its lack of an own law enforcement agency can only resort to sanctions in the form of exclusion of that member state from rights pertaining to EU membership. The EU cannot directly intervene in a given member state in order to sanction governments, parties and individuals. Realistically, the EU has to rely on conventional 'international sanctions' against the country and the government in question and they tend to be of a collective nature. The objection is thus that collective sanctions are not completely unjustified because of their duty-inducing nature and because they are also the only realistically available means.

In this chapter, we primarily focus on the normative question. From this viewpoint we find it unconvincing that citizens who stand to lose their democratic rights need the extra inducement of collective sanctions. That said, there are more targeted forms of sanctions which would lie within the scope of what is realistically possible within the EU of today and which may in fact have positive effects. This leads us to the question of what appropriate sanctions might look like.

Alternative Targetted Sanctions

There are different levels of sanctions. At the first level is the expression of official criticism (naming and shaming). It does not involve any exclusion from participatory rights and is an invitation to self-correction for member state governments and their supporters. However, if no self-correction takes place, this sanction leaves national democratic minorities in the lurch and becomes a de facto acceptance of value violations.

The next level is targeted economic sanctions. Again, even if political participation does presuppose sufficient and generally secure economic means, European funds and other sanctions relating to economic activity cannot be seen as exclusion from political participation as such. The EU Commission has proposed that the receipt of EU funds should be dependent upon national governments properly protecting EU values, especially the rule of law. However, if EU funds are withheld it also harms the democratic minority in the member states in question. A better idea is therefore that the EU fully takes over the administration of funds (currently the administration shared between the EU and member states), so it can channel them to actors who are supporters and promoters of EU values within the member states and exclude the government and its supporters. Another advantage of this sanction is that it could be applied within the framework of the existing treaties (Barsøe 2018). Sanctions of this kind could be combined with personal embargoes against individual government members and their supporters in parliament, relating to their ability to travel and make financial transactions outside their own country. Personal embargos would most likely require treaty changes insofar as they cannot be construed as rights that *member states* have as a result of the treaties.

This brings us closer to the type of sanctions which are usually discussed in the literature on militant democracy and which would require significant treaty changes, and perhaps as such are unrealistic to envision. The first would be the exclusion of the relevant member state's government representatives from the European institutions, notably the Council. Again, to avoid cutting off democratic minorities at this level, the general set-up of national representation in the Council would have to be changed so that both government and opposition have representation in the Council. When a government is in breach of EU values, the opposition representative(s) remain(s) in place. This type of sanction remains within the remit of access to European institutions. The next level of sanctions would entail direct intervention into member states.

At a preventive level one could imagine that the EU would be able to issue party bans against parties that are a credible threat towards continued support for common EU values in the individual member states. Here close attention should be given to whether parties have explicit intentions to act in ways that contravene liberal democratic values, for example concrete electoral promises or legislative bills (Kirshner 2014: chapter 5; Müller 2016a). Should parties of this kind have already gained government power and control over key national institutions, as is arguably the case in Hungary and Poland, the EU could be authorised to dissolve the government, ban parties and call new elections that would allow the majorities in the member states to 'correct themselves'. If this does not occur, EU envoys would be able to take over the administration of the country (see Kirshner 2014: chapter 6). Obviously, all of this is very far from what can realistically be obtained in the EU of today, not just because of countries like Hungary and Poland, which are unlikely ever to agree to treaty changes that would give the EU such powers, but also because it would conflict with prevailing notions of what it means for member states to be sovereign and 'Masters of the Treaties'.

With regard to the latter type of sanctions we should consider their costs. First, there is the charge of hypocrisy: how can democracy defend suspending participation in democratic procedures? In the context of the EU, the hypocrisy charge is likely de facto to be even stronger due the EU's democratic deficit (Weiler 2016). The cost lies in the possibly impaired trust among segments of the citizenry that institutions do work on the basis of democratic procedures. To minimise it, it is therefore important to clearly communicate why participation is reduced (Kirshner 2014: 56).

Second, the more important loss from a normative point of view is connected with the consideration that anti-democrats also have moral and political interests not related to the nature of the political regime that need to be included and taken into account (Kirshner 2014: 44–45). Moreover, as Brettschneider (2007) points out, there is a democratic loss in overriding democratic outcomes that follow or – in this case – could have followed from democratic procedures, even when they go against democratic values (Barsøe 2018).

Hence, militant measures should not be used to pursue 'ideal democracy'. Kirshner (2014: 5) cites Robert Dahl's concept of polyarchy as a modest and reasonable goal. As long as the key features of polyarchy are secure, there is no need for democracy to turn militant against its opponents. Furthermore, the long-term goal must be the reintegration of anti-democrats into democracy, not their permanent exclusion. Given the moral and political interests of all citizens and the limited ability of some citizens to rule without the input of others (including their ability to detect and defend their interest), militant democrats should not rely too much on their ability to rule alone (Dahl 1989: chapter 7; Kirshner 2014: 148–152). The purpose of ensuring the reintegration of anti-democrats also shows why ejecting a value-violating member state from the EU is not a normatively plausible option. Being a collective sanction, not only would it exclude democratic minorities, it would also seriously (and perhaps permanently) impair the ability of European citizens to rule together democratically in the future.

In order to prevent abuse of militant democratic measures, a clearer basis should be created for judging whether a given political actor is pursuing policies that go against liberal democracy. The definition of the values is ideally the task of the European legislator and should not be left to other non-democratic bodies. The European legislators have neglected this task. There is no elaborate description of EU values, although commentators point to the Charter of Fundamental Rights as a possible interpretation of what they are in terms of principles and rights (Jakab 2016; Scheinin 2016; Toggenburg and Grimheden 2016).

Without a clear basis, decisions as to whether liberal democratic values are being breached will become – or at least appear to be – arbitrary and thus suffer in terms of legitimacy (Rijpkema, Chapter 9 this volume). Indeed, critics of militant democracy claim that any decision regarding whether there is a breach of values and the principles and norms that follow from them would be arbitrary and therefore represent an act of domination (Invernizzi Accetti and Zuckermann 2017; Malkopoulou and Norman 2018). This objection overlooks that (within a legal order) no norm automatically applies itself. There is always a designated body entitled to decide whether norms are followed or not. All things being equal, a more precise specification of what liberal democratic values entail will reduce arbitrariness, but it cannot fully remove it. In addition, as Kirshner (2014: 56) points out, militant democratic measures should come with the right of alleged anti-democrats to challenge them. This partially but not fully compensates for the arbitrariness since it allows for tracking the interests of alleged anti-democrats. Moreover, the objections to the (partial) exclusion from political participation of anti-democrats tend to relate to the situation where anti-democrats have not yet seized power. They fail to consider the exclusion of democratically minded citizens and minorities who are put in a situation in which they are being dominated.

Critics of militant democratic measures point to other ways of defending democracy. One of them is the widely shared idea that citizens should be taught liberal democratic virtues through various forms of civic education. Another is making sure that all citizens have the social and economic preconditions for participating in politics on an equal footing with all other citizens. Social justice improves the stakes of all citizens in democratic systems and shields them from the bad socio-economic situations which provide fertile ground for political extremism (Malkopoulou and Norman, Chapter 5 this volume). It seems right to argue, as many democratic theorists have done, that political participation presupposes equal socio-economic preconditions for all. And there is no doubt that bad economic conditions further extremism: developments after the post-2008 economic crisis in Europe testify to this. The social democratic strategy combining civic education and social justice thus has great merit. But the strategy is, first of all, long term. It does not tell us what to do here and now, when institutions are (likely to be) overtaken by anti-democrats. Why would anti-democrats pursue policies to create good independent-minded democratic citizens when they have control of government? Second, the strategy has an element of manipulation and social engineering to it. Citizens are actively induced to accept existing political institutions (see Brighouse 1998) and social rights distributed in order to avoid the development and diffusion of certain political views. The social democratic strategy wants to make ordinary citizens safe for democracy by indirect means rather than by addressing anti-democratic views directly and thereby falls short of democracy's publicity requirement.

Given the complex nature of the question of whether parties and governments in the EU are living up to liberal democratic values, we think that that judgement is better left to a politically representative body that is forced to take liberal democratic values seriously and one that is not seen as a party to its own cause (see Waldron 2006). One such EU institution could be the EP. However, concerns about the de facto legitimacy of such judgements might point in the direction of constructions like the Copenhagen Commission proposed by Müller. In all cases, reviews of member states should include all member states and should be systematic, following a much more elaborate definition of the EU's liberal democratic values than the one currently available. The latter would contravene concerns about discrimination and arbitrariness.

Conclusion

In this chapter we have argued that the EU can legitimately respond to member states' violations of the EU's liberal democratic values. Protecting the values of liberal democracy is important because they ensure the status of all citizens as democratic co-rulers. Value violations undermine the ability of citizens in Europe to rule together democratically in their common concerns. However, sanctions against value violations need to be as consistent as possible with the values themselves. They should not unnecessarily harm or exclude citizens with no responsibility for the value violation from full democratic rights. We have argued that the collective sanctions envisioned in the treaty and in much of the academic debate are problematic since they also harm innocent democratic minorities. Instead, more targeted sanctions which differentiate between actors according to their responsibility for value violation should be considered. In addition, they should be issued on the basis of a more comprehensive description of the EU's liberal democratic values so that decisions to sanction do not become arbitrary.

Acknowledgement

Some of the ideas in this article have been inspired by the supervision of Anne Barsøe's MA thesis in the *Fall* 2017. Please see Barsøe (2018).

Notes

1. Technically speaking, these policies were introduced via cardinal laws, which are not strictly part of the constitution, but which still require a two-thirds majorities to be changed. Constitutional changes under Orbán's government opened up the passing of cardinal laws.
2. It should be stressed that the Weimar Republic was in fact not a fair and well-functioning democracy that abrogated itself (Müller 2016a: 252).
3. Space does not allow us to discuss the democratic deficit of the EU itself. From the viewpoint of democratic theory, both the constitutionalisation of a specific economic policy within the Economic and Monetary Union and the weak ability of European institutions to track the preferences of the electorate are problematic (compare Follesdal and Hix 2006 with Moravcsik 2004).
4. Brettschneider (2012) argues that the democratic state in its expressive capacity should protect democracy through democratic persuasion of citizens to become and remain committed to the equal democratic rights of all citizens.
5. Other possible cases are those in which anti-democrats have the majority and have taken over the majority of member state governments/institutions as well as the European institutions. Then a theory of militant democracy turns into a

theory about how to (re)establish democracy through means other than democratic procedures (Kirshner 2014: 4).

6. Critics suggest that the Council's aim with the dialogue has been to pre-empt the Commission's Rule of Law Framework from being activated (Kochenov and Pech 2015: 534, 536; Sedelmeier 2017: 348).

7. TEU Article 7.3 in fact points to this problem, stating that the Council, in deciding on sanctions, should 'take into account the possible consequences of such a suspension [of rights] on the rights and obligations of natural and legal persons'.

NINE

Militant Democracy and the Detection Problem

Bastiaan Rijpkema[1]

Introduction

When George van den Bergh gave his inaugural lecture as professor of constitutional law at the University of Amsterdam in 1936 (Van den Bergh 2014 [1936]), democracy was on the defensive across the European continent. Van den Bergh argued that, under certain circumstances, it must be possible to ban anti-democratic parties. He justified this position by pointing to, among other things, democracy's ability to self-correct – a unique feature; no other political system contains similar safeguards to ensure decisions can be corrected (Van den Bergh 2014: 128–129). A democracy, understood in this way, may resist one particular decision: the abolition of democracy itself. In *Militant Democracy: The Limits of Democratic Tolerance* (Rijpkema 2015),[2] I try to develop Van den Bergh's idea into a full-fledged theory of militant democracy called 'democracy as self-correction'.[3] In this, I follow a track that Van den Bergh himself eventually abandons – he opts for a different justification: a set of fundamental principles that function as the 'entry gate' to the democratic arena (Rijpkema 2015: 60–66, 70–71).

In this chapter, I try to further elucidate the theory of democracy as self-correction by addressing what I would like to call the 'detection problem' of militant democracy. May we expect that democracy as self-correction, as a theory of militant democracy, will actually succeed in detecting anti-democratic parties *in time*? When it comes to comparative law and politics, this detection problem is identified by several scholars: how can we identify deteriorations of liberal democracy in very different national contexts (Scheppele 2013; Greskovits 2015; Kornai 2015: 41; Uitz 2015)? These difficulties are also sometimes mentioned in the context of militant democracy (e.g. Müller 2013b: 18). In the present chapter, I aim to explicitly transpose the detection problem from comparative law and politics to the realm of militant democracy to examine and address its implications for militant democracytheory.

After briefly summarising the main characteristics of the theory of democracyas self-correction (§2), the detection problem is introduced and subsequently divided in two variants (§3). First, I will discuss whether a theory of militant democracy, and democracy as self-correction in particular, can be expected to actually detect anti-democratic parties *before* they are in a position to damage democracy (§4). Second, I discuss the related question of whether the 'democratic vs. anti-democratic parties' framework is still relevant. Some authors suggest that currently, 'anti-liberal' (or 'anti-rule of law'), and not so much 'anti-democratic' forces, constitute the foremost threat to liberal democracy. If correct, it would mean that even *if* detection of anti-democrats is possible, it would only be of very limited value, since the 'real' threats lie elsewhere and remain *undetected* (§5). The conclusion summarises the main arguments (§6).

The Theory of Democracy as Self-Correction

In the theory of democracy as self-correction, the justification for intervening against anti-democrats is sought in democracy's unique ability to self-correct. Van den Bergh writes:

> One of the most powerful characteristics of democracy is its 'self-correction'. Every democrat will admit that democracy often leads to wrong decisions. Yet, democracy offers many safeguards – more than any other system – to make sure that these decisions, as soon as their wrongness has been proven in practice, will be revised. (Van den Bergh 2014: 129)

For Van den Bergh, democracy is citizens governing themselves through self-correction. If we then imagine all the possible decisions a democracy could take, there is one that quickly comes to the fore as fundamentally different from *all* others: the decision to abolish democracy itself. Van den Bergh argues that this is the only decision that is not amenable to correction, rendering it the only *truly* irrevocable decision a democracy can make. Of course, if a monument is demolished, it can never return in the exact same way, so it is 'irrevocable' in a very practical sense – but the decision itself is not irrevocable, and citizens can decide to restore it as much as possible (Rijpkema 2015: 65). When it comes to abolishing democracy, however, the decision *itself* is irrevocable, the framework that made it possible in the first place is lost; citizens are not able to peacefully, democratically undo it (Van den Bergh 2014: 129). If democracy is understood this way, it becomes clear that this *one* decision can be characterised as truly undemocratic. As such, a democracy does not betray its own principles in resisting this decision (Rijpkema 2015: 63–66, 104).

In *Militant Democracy: The Limits of Democratic Tolerance* I developed this idea further along the following lines.[4] What does it mean to say that the essence of democracy is not majority rule alone, but rather self-correction? Democracy as self-correction shifts the focus from *making* decisions to being able to *revoke* decisions. There are connections to the work of the philosopher of science and politics Karl Popper when it comes to the *learning* aspect of democracy as self-correction. Unlike any other political system, a democracy is able to learn from mistakes; in this, it approaches science, though imperfectly of course. Democratic leaders are exposed to the most far-reaching criticism from citizens, potentially, causing them to make fewer mistakes and to persist in past mistakes for a shorter time than their autocratic counterparts. In addition, democracy as self-correction emphasises the *impermanence* of majority decisions: majorities rule, but they are expected to allow for the possibility that their decisions will eventually be reversed and replaced by other majorities.

Next, I try to translate this idea into workable legal grounds for banning anti-democratic parties. Just concluding that a democracy may resist those who seek to end democratic self-correction will not do. We have to know which proposals and measures *exactly* endanger democracy's self-correcting mechanism. In other words: we have to flesh out *self-correction* – what does it take for us to speak of genuine democratic self-correction? To do this, I analyse the way in which two prominent and influential legal institutions in Europe, the European Court of Human Rights and the German *Bundesverfassungsgericht* (BVerfG), define and use the term *democracy*. On the basis of this, I arrive at three principles that are essential for democratic self-correction.

First, there is the principle of *evaluation*. In order to safeguard self-correction, every so often there has to be a moment at which a forced evaluation of policy takes place, or, in other words: regular elections. Ideally, of course, evaluation of policy happens all the time by elected representatives and office-holders throughout their terms, but elections provide a hard 'sanction' against unresponsive officials. If they neglect to perform the needed self-correction, do not acknowledge mistakes and refuse to embrace new ideas, representatives and officials can be replaced. This ensures that democratic self-correction always continues.

However, the principle of evaluation is an empty shell if elections do not offer a genuine choice – although elections are held, there would be no real correction. This is why *political competition* should also be protected. Representatives and governments should tolerate the presence of competitors: other politicians also running for office. Competition ensures that alternatives to existing policy are thought up, a different societal ideal is imagined, or a shadow budget is drafted – in other words, that there is an actual *choice* on election day.

Finally, *free speech* ought to be ensured as well. In order to come to a meaningful evaluation of policy, uncensored discussion and criticism of existing policies and the alternatives on offer is a must.

My view is that if these principles are protected, democratic self-correction is safeguarded, so that a democracy can keep doing what makes it a democracy: self-governance by self-correction. A party that opposes one of these principles – and seeks to damage it in its essence[5] – can be banned, with an emphasis on *can*. First, the court needs to acquire an overall picture of the party in order to determine how this picture relates to the principles of democracy as self-correction – a single undemocratic turn of phrase in a debate is insufficient to characterise a party as anti-democratic. Such a 'holistic approach' is also followed by, for instance, the European Court of Human Rights in its assessment of party ban cases *(ECtHR Refah Partisi v. Turkey*, par. 101).[6] Second, the observation that a party is anti-democratic does not need automatically to lead to a ban; in an 'opportunity test' the court must explicitly weigh how the risk to democracy balances against the restriction of rights a party ban constitutes (Kirshner 2014: 55–56; Rijpkema 2015: 71–72, 198, 199, 211). An anti-democratic party with little electoral potential should therefore not be banned (see also BVerfG NPD II, par. 585–586; Ellian, Molier and Rijpkema 2017; Molier and Rijpkema 2018).[7]

The Scope of Democracy as Self-Correction

The above-mentioned principles of democracy as self-correction constitute a very *minimal* core – on purpose. It is the bare minimum at which we can still speak of democracy at all. I would not argue, therefore, that these principles alone guarantee a flourishing liberal democracy. Only that which is absolutely indispensable to democratic self-correction receives protection. In this, democracy as self-correction aims to erect the *widest possible* limits around democracy. First, because otherwise free democratic debate could become unduly limited. Second, because narrow and concrete legal grounds for prohibition protect courts. Vague legal grounds ('the verdict could be a or b, but also c to e') make judges vulnerable to allegations of politically motivated rulings, endangering their independent position, especially in these kinds of proceedings. And, third, because narrow legal grounds are an important safeguard against abuse – i.e. a judge acting in bad faith, aiming to illegitimately use militant democracy against political opponents (Rijpkema 2015: 179). The broader the legal grounds for a party ban, the easier it is to prohibit all sorts of 'disagreeable' parties.

All of this means that proposals that do *not* affect the three principles of self-correction are, in principle, part of the normal democratic debate (Rijpkema 2015: 196). That is true of, for instance, a proposal to grant women (or men) fewer rights on the work floor. Such an idea is clearly highly undesirable, shocking even – it openly violates the principle of equality, but it cannot be a reason to impose a party ban. The guarantee that democracy as self-correction offers is that, as soon as the electorate has returned to its senses, such shocking decisions can *always* be repealed. However, if such a party's next proposal would be to take away women's (or men's) active or passive suffrage (respectively the right to vote and the right to be elected), or to attach further conditions to it (e.g. Wagemans and Talib 2016; Brennan 2017: 204–230), that would be a bird of a different feather. Such proposals directly affect the essence of democracy as self-correction: both the principle of evaluation (by limiting active suffrage) and the principle of political competition (by limiting passive suffrage) are impacted. In other words: democracy as self-correction only threatens to impose a party ban over violations of the principle of equality *in a political sense*. That is not to say, of course, that a more general principle of equality should not be forcefully protected. It only means that democracy's *most powerful* instrument, a party ban, ought to be restricted to violations of political rights. The equality principle in a *non-political sense*, violated by unequal labour laws for men and women, is protected by fundamental rights in liberal democracy.

The Detection Problem in Militant Democracy

Let us now turn to the detection problem and the challenge it poses to democracy as self-correction and other theories of militant democracy. After the Second World War, many democracies drew their lessons from the catastrophic collapse of 'Weimar'. They became militant, in a 'Loewensteinian' fashion, when it came to threats against their democratic systems (Loewenstein 1937a, 1937b); between 1945 and 2015, approximately thirty-five parties – depending on the definitions used – were banned in European democracies (Bourne 2018). At the same time, lessons were drawn by the challengers of democracy, consciously or unconsciously.[8] The new challengers of democracy no longer explicitly attacked it. Doing so in the post-war constellation immediately positions a party outside of the political spectrum (Müller 2013b: 18; Rijpkema 2015: 156–157; Müller 2016b: 6; Snel 2016; Camus and Lebourg 2017: 53, 56). It is therefore not very useful to try to detect modern-day challengers of democracy with a kind of fascism detector, or by looking for openly anti-democratic statements or party programmes (Kieft 2017: 149; Te Slaa 2017: 14–15, 270). The modern challenge to democracy is more subtle.

In the context of comparative constitutional law and politics this 'detection problem' was identified, in particular regarding modern-day Hungary, by Kim Lane Scheppele as early as 2013 (Scheppele 2013) and later by, among others, Greskovits (2015) and Uitz (2015). All these authors convincingly argue, *mutatis mutandis*, that a more contextualised approach is needed to detect deteriorations of liberal democracy (Scheppele 2013: 562; Greskovits 2015: 35; Uitz 2015: 300). This detection problem also has serious implications for militant democracy theory, where the need for a subtle detection mechanism is supplemented by an arguably equally important need for legal certainty in its application.

Two variants of the detection problem in militant democracy can be distinguished. The first variant, discussed in the next section, concerns the question whether a specific theory of militant democracy may reasonably be expected to detect *anti-democratic* threats in time; or, in short: does the deployed 'antenna' *function*? This variant accepts the 'democratic vs. anti-democratic parties' framework, i.e. democracy should focus on anti-democratic threats.

The second variant, discussed in the subsequent section, however, does not. The detection problem is not caused by a malfunctioning antenna (causing anti-democratic threats to remain undetected), but rather by deploying the wrong antenna in the first place, i.e. the whole venture itself is thought to be ill-founded. The real threat to modern-day liberal democracies consists of anti-liberal parties – which remain invisible in a 'democratic vs. anti-democratic parties' framework.

The next section (§4) will start by explaining the first variant of the detection problem in more detail, and then test the theory of democracy as self-correction against it. In the section after that (§5), the same is done with the second variant.

Does the Antenna Function? Detecting Anti-Democrats

There are several indexes that try to measure democracy, the rule of law and freedom in a broader sense in various countries. Think of *The Economist*'s 'Democracy Index' (The Economist Intelligence Unit 2016), the World

Justice Project's 'Rule of Law Index' (2016), and Freedom House's 'Freedom in the World' report (2017). In these organisations' reports, Hungary still does moderately well. In the 'Democracy Index 2016', the country is in the middle range of the 'flawed democracies' category (which, at the top end, also includes the US). In the 'Rule of Law Index 2016', Hungary ranks 49 (out of 113) worldwide, just below Greece, but one place higher than Bulgaria, for instance, and far above Turkey. In 'Freedom in the World', Hungary is the only European country to appear on the list of countries that have seen the biggest *regression* in liberty in the past ten years. Nevertheless, in 2017, Freedom House still places Hungary in the category 'free'.

At the same time, constitutional jurists and Hungary experts are wondering whether it is even possible for the opposition to win elections anymore (Scheppele 2013: 561), or actually to change the country's course if the opposition *would* win (Müller 2013b: 6; Kornai 2015: 47). After winning the 2010 elections, Orbán and his Fidesz party embarked on an impressive legal restructuring (Scheppele 2013: 561; Ágh 2016: 280–281). Neutral institutions such as the Constitutional Court and the Central Bank were turned into Fidesz-dominated institutions (Rupnik 2012: 133; Müller 2013b: 6; Kornai 2015: 35), the powers of the Constitutional Court were restricted (Bugaric and Ginsburg 2016: 73; AIV [Dutch Advisory Council] 2017: 47–48), Fidesz deployed an extraordinary form of gerrymandering, resulting in a two-thirds Fidesz parliamentary majority in 2014 out of a 45 per cent Fidesz vote (Kornai 2015: 41–42; AIV 2017: 42), the party entrenched regular political issues in hard-to-change so-called 'cardinal laws' (Venice Commission 2011: 6–7, 35), and Supreme Court President (and government-critic) András Baka was removed from his position by what Fidesz presented as neutral reforms (*ECtHR Baka* v. *Hungary*, par. 151; AIV 2017: 48).[9] To János Kornai, Orbán's Hungary left the category 'democracies' as early as 2015 (Kornai 2015: 43). Others speak of a 'democradura', after the Latin-American 'democracies' of the 1970s and 1980s (György Konrád, in Rupnik 2012: 134),[10] a 'Potemkin' (façade) and 'defective democracy' (Ágh 2016: 280), a 'semi-authoritarian regime' (Bugaric and Ginsburg 2016: 70), or a 'seriously damaged democracy', in which the basic requirements for democracy have already been gravely endangered (Müller 2017b). Time to sound the alarm, one would say, but the combined indexes still classify Hungary as 'free', a 'flawed democracy' and an average achiever when it comes to the rule of law.

This is why Kim Lane Scheppele criticises the 'checklists' of international organisations as instruments by which to understand what is happening in a country like Hungary (Scheppele 2013). Such checklists operate on the basis of a number of indicators – numbers of judges, the possibilities for appeal, etc. – in order to make countries' evaluations as objective as possible (Scheppele 2013: 560; Müller 2013b: 23). The problem, however, is that such lists hardly take the *interactions* between the different indicators into account. Therefore, using *only* checklists will not do.[11] In Scheppele's words:

> When perfectly legal and reasonable constitutional components are stitched together to create a monster [. . .] I call it a Frankenstate. Victor Frankenstein's monster – nameless in Mary Shelley's novel – was assembled from various component parts of once recognizably reasonable bodies. However, he went on to look and act a monster. The Frankenstate, too, is composed of various perfectly reasonable pieces, and its monstrous quality comes from the horrible way that those pieces interact when stitched together. (Scheppele 2013: 560)

According to Scheppele, Hungary is the perfect example of such a Frankenstate. Many of Fidesz's reforms of the justice system are not indefensible in and of themselves. The point is that, when you put it all together, Scheppele says, you get a system in which it is nearly impossible for the opposition to win elections (Scheppele 2013: 561). In other words: the sum of these 'neutral' measures is more negative than its constituent parts, but you have to look at the broader context to see this. It is a dynamic which also has been observed by others with regard to Hungary (Greskovits 2015: 30), and which can also be seen elsewhere, to various degrees, from Ecuador to Zimbabwe, and the US (Mickey, Levitsky and Way 2017: 22). It leads to a system of 'competitive authoritarianism': the democratic institutions are functional, but the government uses the state's power to disadvantage opponents (Mickey, Levitsky and Way 2017: 20). The degradation of democracy, so they argue as well, mostly stems from the *combination* of factors: '. . . it would take place through a series of little-noticed, incremental steps, most of which are legal and many of which appear innocuous. Taken together, however, they would tilt the playing field in favour of the ruling party' (Mickey, Levitsky and Way 2017: 21).

It enables such changes to remain largely 'below the radar of EU institutions and international watchdogs' (Greskovits 2015: 30). That is why Scheppele pleads for a greater focus on the interaction between the different components of a constitution and, besides the checklists, proposes the undertaking of a 'forensic legal analysis' (Scheppele 2013: 562). We have to ask a number of *what if?* questions. The system ought to undergo a number of 'trial runs' with different test cases to see how different parts of the system interact. Only then would we see how, for instance, the Hungarian Budget Authority's veto, *combined* with the president's power to disband parliament, gives Fidesz the power to bring about new parliamentary elections within a year *if* it were to lose an election (Scheppele 2013: 561–562). Scheppele concludes that 'although checklist-based rule-of-law indicators may seem an advance over fuzzy definitions, only forensic legal analysis can tell how a constitutional order works in practice. And ultimately that is the rule-of-law indicator that really matters' (Scheppele 2013: 562).

What does all of this mean for militant democracy? Scheppele does not address this question specifically, but the problems are similar. Just like the checklists of international organisations such as Freedom House, a militant democracy tries to develop criteria in order to establish, with as much accuracy as possible, if a party is anti-democratic. Therefore, we would do well to take Scheppele's analysis to heart. She warns that, in the quest for objectivity, overly narrow criteria risk negative 'interactions' within a system being overlooked.

However, there is an important difference between the checklists of monitoring institutions and militant democracy. A militant democracy cannot linger in the analysis stage (is a party anti-democratic?). In the end, a judge must *decide*: will a party be banned or not? And the judge must do this on the basis of criteria that everyone can consult and understand beforehand. First, because the limits of the democratic playing field ought to be apparent: the democratic debate is hampered if it is unclear which proposals are permissible and which are not, but also because otherwise it puts the judge in a very precarious position. In party ban cases, ample room for interpretation is of no benefit to a judge – allegations of politically motivated rulings are easily made. To give an example from the Netherlands, the wording of the current Dutch provision governing party bans is no cause for optimism (Molier and Rijpkema 2017; similarly, in the EU context: Müller 2013b: 18–19). The legislator must give the judge as much legal clarity as possible. As early as 1936, George van den Bergh already criticised the lightness with which this matter was handled in the Netherlands – how is the judge supposed to find 'legal clarity' in a notion such as 'public morals' (the provision's wording at the time)? In the 1950s, similar criticism was levelled against the wording of the German party ban. In Germany, parties can be banned when they conflict with the 'freiheitliche demokratische Grundordnung' – the 'liberal democratic order' (Article 21, paragraph 2 of the German Constitution). This is all the judge has to go on: not an easy task for the Constitutional Court in the then fledgling German democracy (Schneider 1957: 533–534, 537; Kommers 1997: 218). Consequently, when it came to reside over the first party ban case in 1952, the first thing the German Court did was provide a firm legal footing by developing a list of more or less concrete criteria *itself* (BVerfG SRP: 12–13; Rijpkema 2015: 159–165).[12]

This means that a militant democracy must navigate between two extremes. On the one hand, it should not go too far in its ambition to create solid legal footing by 'over-defining' criteria (such as: 'elections will be held every four years'), thereby lapsing into legal formalism – this creates the risk that the principles are only formally honoured, while real deteriorations of democracy go unnoticed (Hungary also has regular elections, an opposition, etc.). On the other hand, the court cannot be expected to work with a purely contextual approach: concrete underpinnings are needed – i.e. criteria to apply – otherwise there is a risk of its judgement being questioned for not being based on pre-set, legislatively established norms of what is and is not democratic.[13]

I believe it is possible to find a balance between these two poles. An example can be found in the approach of the German *Bundesverfassungsgericht*. As said, the BVerfG has had to work out for itself what is meant by 'liberal democratic order', and it has done so quite well, formulating a number of essential principles such as 'the separation of powers', 'popular sovereignty' and 'the multi-party principle'. The problem, of course, is that the German Court had to formulate these principles *itself*, which left it vulnerable. The list also became quite broad – after all, there is no precise limit to the concept of a 'liberal democratic order'. As such, a relatively high number of principles were included, eight in total, and, in addition, some principles are rather loosely worded, such as 'respect for human rights' (BVerfG SRP: 12–13; Rijpkema 2015: 159–165). Still, the method of laying down a number of *principles* is a fruitful one – striking a balance between checklists and context.

In the militant democracy theory I propose – democracy as self-correction – it is emphatically the *legislator* who has to do this work. The legislator has to provide the courts with these principles (not with an abstract concept), so the judge does not have to deduce them from the wording of the banning ground, *and* these principles have to be limited to that which is indispensable to democratic self-correction (Rijpkema 2015: 175–178). Take, for instance, the principle of *political competition* – inspired by the BVerfG's multi-party principle (Rijpkema 2015: 164, 176, 210). This is supported by, among other things, passive suffrage (an individual's ability to run for office) and the freedom of establishment for political parties. Yet at the same time, it would also enable the timely recognition of *other* proposals which, on their own or in interaction with others, threaten to compromise democracy. It is not unthinkable that, for instance, one of the interactions Scheppele discusses, Orbán's electoral reforms – a combination of the abolition of the two-round election system, severe gerrymandering and the curtailment of political advertisements (Scheppele 2013: 561) – *taken together,* could be characterised as an infringement on the principle of political competition; after all, the deck is stacked substantially in favour of Fidesz.[14] In the end, the judge must decide: are we dealing with a sufficiently significant degradation, in which the essence of the principle is compromised, and is the proposal characteristic of the nature of the party? Then we can classify it as anti-democratic. And then, as argued above, the judge still has to conduct an 'opportunity test': is this the right *moment* to intervene?

However, the question here is not whether Orbán's measures should *indeed* be viewed as an infringement (sufficiently significant) of the principle of political competition, let alone if we should conclude from this that the party as a whole is anti-democratic, and whether the time is right to step in. It is only to show that, in a system such as democracy as self-correction these negative interactions that can take place within a political system – and that anti-democrats can purposefully seek to create (Scheppele 2013: 560; Mickey, Levitsky and Way 2017: 20–22) – do not have to go unnoticed. At the same time, the three principles of democracy as self-correction should offer the courts sufficient solid footing in these crucial cases in which it is exceptionally vulnerable – certainly in comparison with such broad and multi-interpretable concepts with which the German Constitutional Court had to work.[15]

The Wrong Antenna? Militant Democracy and the New Anti-Liberal Threat

The events in Hungary also raise another issue: are we not dealing with a new type of threat, namely anti-liberal, rather than anti-democratic, parties? Amsterdam professor of political science Meindert Fennema puts forward this argument in the final chapters of the updated 2016 edition of his biography of Geert Wilders. He offers an informative analysis of the Dutch Party for Freedom's (PVV) ideology (Fennema 2016: 272–274), and sees this party as part of a new trend:

> Today, we are facing a different phenomenon [than anti-democratic parties, BR]: a political party that seeks to democratically abolish the rule of law. For the Netherlands, this is a new experience. In Turkey, it is already being put into practice. In that sense, a Prime Minister Geert Wilders might become Recep Tayyip Erdoğan's counterpart. But we are not even close to that point yet. (Fennema 2016: 292)

Dutch scholars, like the political scientist Meijers (2016), political theorist Geling (2016) and historian Snel (2016) offer similar commentaries, in part in response to *Militant Democracy* (Rijpkema 2015). They represent, I believe, a specific kind of argument: the idea that democracy is being confronted by a 'new anti-liberal threat'. I will try to summarise Fennema's and these other authors' commentaries, and I hope of course not to do the individual authors an injustice.[16]

In these commentaries, the *rule of law* – or, roughly, the 'liberal' in liberal democracy – is clearly seen as conceptually different from democracy (as e.g. in Mudde 2016: 28; Müller 2017b: 549), although it is not further defined by the authors. Nevertheless, we may assume they have the common definition of the rule of law in mind: the constraint of government power by law, with *fundamental rights*, but also (supervision of the adherence to these rights by) an *independent judiciary* as two important means to realise this limitation of power (Cliteur and Ellian 2016: 59–60; Belinfante and De Reede 2015: 18; AIV 2017: 17–20). Both elements are present in the commentaries: *fundamental rights* are explicitly mentioned by Fennema and Geling, and considering the examples of the 'new anti-liberal threat' that all authors mention – Turkey and/or Hungary – they seem to identify the rule of law with *judicial independence* too (since courts are under severe pressure in these countries).[17] Following this, it seems that two distinct but closely related claims make up the 'new anti-liberal threat' argument:

1. the *modern-day* challengers of liberal democracy are not focused on democracy but on the liberal (or: rule of law) in liberal democracy (Fennema, Geling and Snel), and
2. the issue of anti-liberal parties is conceptually *different* from that of anti-democratic parties (all authors named).

I will focus on these two claims here. If they are correct, this has consequences for the theory of militant democracy. After all, these are parties that you may *try* to detect using a 'subtler detection mechanism' such as democracy as self-correction, but that you will always 'miss', and not because the antenna is not sufficiently sensitive but because this type of party does not focus on democracy at all. Therefore, we should not be speaking of *anti-democrats* but of *anti-liberals*. It is important to note here that this is not about *concealed* anti-democratic ideas – that would involve the first variant of the detection problem. But here we are dealing with a *different* variant of the detection problem, namely parties that fall outside the 'democratic vs. anti-democratic' framework because they do not oppose democracy but supposedly target the rule of law.

How are we to judge these claims? The first claim is ultimately a factual assertion – and it is one that can at least be contested. Orbán is an interesting case in this respect. He has taken measures that undoubtedly affect the liberal aspect of liberal democracy, such as his far-reaching reforms of the Constitutional Court (Bugaric and Ginsburg 2016: 73; AIV 2017: 47–48). He also speaks of building an 'illiberal' but *democratic* state (Orbán 2014). At the same time though, Orbán has certainly also affected crucial *democratic* principles, as formulated within democracy as self-correction. Consider, for instance, Fidesz's positions being laid down in 'cardinal laws' that cannot be changed by a regular majority (the principle of evaluation), the extensive gerrymandering, the curtailment of political advertising campaigns (Scheppele 2013: 561), the measures to make postal voting more difficult for a specific group of Hungarians (Wittenberg 2017: 553–554) (political competition), and the domination of the media landscape by pro-Fidesz media (AIV 2017: 43–44; Heller 2017: 543) (free speech). As suggested earlier, it is a different question whether these degradations actually impair the essence of the principles in question or if they can still be tolerated, but it is clear in any case that they predominantly affect *democracy*, not so much the rule of law. This is the case through the lens of democracy as self-correction and defining democracy even more narrowly would not change it. Insulating regular political issues from normal majority rule, 'gerrymandering on steroids', unequal postal votes, and restricting political advertising – all of it *also* affects the most minimalist, procedural definition of democracy. That conclusion is also drawn by Jan-Werner Müller regarding the Hungary of 2017:

> [. . .] it is not just what conventionally are considered the liberal elements of liberal democracy – above all, the rule of law – which have been imperilled in Hungary; it is also rights and practices central to democracy itself. Unless one wants to say that it's good enough to earn the description 'democracy', if the ruling party does not stuff ballot boxes on election day, it is clear that Hungarian democracy itself is seriously damaged (to say the least). OSCE observers went on record after the 2014 elections that the vote had been free, but not fair, given gerrymandering and the use of media for the governing party's purposes (the present volume further describes the ways in which, for instance, media pluralism has been diminished). (Müller 2017b: 549)

We should at least conclude that, as he rolls out his programme, Orbán's hand is not especially 'steady' in cutting only the *liberal* elements from liberal democracy.

But even then, one might retort that the modern challengers to liberal democracy are *mainly* concerned with the liberal element, although they sometimes also make proposals that affect democracy. This seems to be largely true of the PVV in the Netherlands. Wilders certainly makes statements that are problematic from a democratic perspective, such as, for instance, his words about a 'revolt', spoken at a meeting of his European faction: 'If I win the election and other politicians don't want to cooperate with me, the people won't accept it. It'll cause a revolt. We won't let that happen' (De Koning 2016). He later softened these words by adding that he certainly wants to prevent a 'revolt' and *that is why* other parties should have entered into negotiations with him if he had won the election in March 2017 (De Koning 2016). Wilders also hoped that any possible 'revolt' would be 'democratic and non-violent' (De Koning 2016). Still, it is not *really* a democratic answer, but more a kind of political blackmail (along the lines of 'my supporters are ready to blow: talk to me!'). Genuinely 'democratic' would have been telling possibly agitated supporters that the Netherlands has a multi-party system which does not guarantee a seat at the negotiating table when the new government is formed after elections. And in 2018, the PVV's proposals actually started to venture into the realm of democracy more explicitly with the proposal to strip all Dutch citizens with dual (or more) nationalities of their right to vote and the right to stand for elections if they retained their other nationalities alongside their Dutch one – which would effectively mean that Dutch citizens of Moroccan descent would lose these rights, as they, in practice, cannot discard their Moroccan nationality (Jonker and De Winther 2018).[18] However, until then, a large number of PVV proposals indeed primarily affected the liberal elements of liberal democracy, such as the roundly unconstitutional plan to close down all mosques and Islamic schools – both part of his party's one-page 2017 election programme (impairing Articles 1, 6 and 23 of the Dutch Constitution, respectively the principles of equality, freedom of religion and the freedom of education) (Fennema 2016: 291; Molier 2016: 2438–2439; Jessurun D'Oliveira 2017: 28–29).

Therefore, the first claim can be disputed on factual grounds, at least when it comes to Hungary's Fidesz, the oft-cited example of the 'new anti-liberal threat', and to a lesser extent regarding the Dutch PVV. The 'democratic vs. anti-democratic' framework of militant democracy seems to remain relevant.

Now for the second claim: let us indeed, for the sake of the argument, accept the first claim and posit that there are parties that turn exclusively against the liberal in liberal democracy. In that case, are we dealing with a *different* problem than if the party had been anti-democratic? A problem that falls outside of the scope of militant democracy?

I want to argue the opposite. Both types of parties pose a threat to liberal democracy, which ultimately leads us to the same political-philosophical question: where do we draw the line? And in the context of militant democracy, more specifically: can democracy's most powerful instrument, the party ban, be used? Do we draw the line at impairing the rule of law, or at the impairment of democracy? Democracy as self-correction chooses the latter option and only considers the exclusion of political parties justified when a party seeks to impair democracy's self-correcting capacity. That is, however, not the end of the story, as a militant democracy is only *one* of the lines of defence in a liberal democracy (Van der Woude 2009) – and the very *final* one.[19] For proposals which do not affect democracy's self-correcting capacity, but which *do* degrade elements of the rule of law, the party ban cannot be employed, but for those proposals we do have the 'liberal line of defence': they face a more stringent procedure that requires larger majorities and often judicial review.

As such, the theory of democracy as self-correction is not 'blind' to anti-liberal parties; it just holds that such parties should not be met with a ban. We ought to confront them in the democratic debate (the 'democratic line of defence'), knowing that a difficult procedure stands in the way of the passage of a legislative proposal that impairs fundamental rights, and that even if it passes it will still be subjected to judicial review (both part of the liberal line of defence), and, finally, that democracy as self-correction will ensure that such a proposal, *if* it should clear all those hurdles, can always be reversed (the final line of defence).[20]

From a political-philosophical perspective, therefore, the question about anti-liberal parties *is* the question about anti-democratic parties.[21] That is to say: a militant democracy has to decide at *what* stage a party ban is justified, when a party is anti-liberal or only when it is anti-democratic; the theory of democracy as self-correction reserves the party ban for the latter category of parties.

Conclusion: Militant Democracy and the Detection Problem

In modern-day democracies, blunt opposition to the idea of democracy itself is rare. In this chapter it was argued that theories of militant democracy therefore need to pay attention to the detection problem. Just as in comparative politics and law, a sufficiently subtle mechanism is needed in militant democracy to differentiate between what is 'democratic' and what is 'anti-democratic', otherwise anti-democratic threats might go undetected. At the same time, the stakes are remarkably higher here: a militant democracy has to decide on the fate of actual political parties – which brings with it demands of legal certainty.

The detection problem can be subdivided in two variants. The first variant of the detection problem is the question of whether we can expect that a militant democracy can actually succeed in detecting anti-democrats in time:

is the antenna finely tuned enough? This means that a militant democracy has to strike a balance between a highly contextual approach that would lack the necessary legal certainty and a too legalistic 'checklist' approach in which anti-democrats might remain undetected. In testing the theory of self-correction against this first variant, I argued that it can form an intermediate alternative. Democracy as self-correction – an approach grounded on the three central principles of evaluation, political competition and free speech – combines, as much as possible, the more nuanced detection of a contextual approach and the legal certainty of checklists. On the basis of the principle of political competition, for instance, it would be possible to identify clear encroachments on the right to vote, such as restricting suffrage to certain groups, while it would also be possible to recognise the more 'Frankenstate-like' interactions Scheppele (2013) identifies; proposals that in itself do not ring any alarm bells but, when taken together, could very well threaten democracy.

The second variant of the detection problem focuses on whether militant democracy and its 'democratic vs. anti-democratic' framework is still geared towards the *right* threat; i.e. is the correct antenna being used when the current threat to democracy primarily comes from *anti-liberal* parties? By taking a closer look at the Hungarian Fidesz party and the Dutch PVV, it was concluded that, at least, the rise of purely 'anti-liberal but still democratic' parties should be doubted – therefore, militant democracy's 'democratic vs. anti-democratic parties' framework remains relevant on factual grounds. But even *if* such exclusively anti-liberal parties would exist, it was argued that this would not need to change militant democracy's focus on anti-democratic parties, since the question of anti-liberal and anti-democratic parties is, seen from the political-philosophical perspective of defending democracy, ultimately the *same* question. That question is: at what moment is it justified for a democracy to intervene by using its strongest means of defence, the party ban? Is this when a party proposes anti-liberal plans, or when a party threatens democracy itself? Democracy as self-correction, while fully acknowledging the need to also protect the 'liberal' in 'liberal democracy', only sees the latter category of threats as justifying a party ban.

Notes

1. This chapter is a substantially reworked version of 'Democratie als zelfcorrectie: nadere aantekeningen bij de weerbare democratie', in Afshin Ellian, Gelijn Molier and Bastiaan Rijpkema (eds), *De strijd om de democratie: essays over democratische zelfverdediging*, Amsterdam: Boom (2018). Translation by Sarah Strous; reworked by the author. All English quotations from Dutch sources are translations. The

author thanks Anthoula Malkopoulou and Alexander Kirshner, editors of this volume, for their insightful comments, as well as the participants in the 'Should the People Rule? Conceptualizing Democratic Institutions' workshop for the fruitful discussion at the ECPR Joint Sessions 2018 in Nicosia, Cyprus, where an earlier version of this chapter was presented.

2. References in the present chapter are to the 2015 Dutch edition; an English edition is published as Bastiaan Rijpkema, *Militant Democracy: The Limits of Democratic Tolerance*, London/New York: Routledge 2018.

3. The term 'democracy as self-correction' was introduced in Cliteur and Rijpkema (2012) to describe Van den Bergh's concept of militant democracy.

4. Rijpkema (2015: 147–205); the following discussion is based on this.

5. An electoral threshold of five per cent does not affect the essence of the principle of political competition (although an electoral threshold of, for instance, twenty per cent higher evidently does), just as a proposal to hold elections every five years instead of four years does not affect the essence of the principle of evaluation (while an interval of, say, twenty years clearly does). We can (and must) provide the courts with as much clarity as possible (in the form of the concrete principles of democracy as self-correction), but in the end it is up to the judge – who should be able to make these types of distinctions. See Rijpkema (2015: 164–165).

6. An approach for which the court was also criticised because too much attention was said to be paid to the utterances of individual party members, see Bale (2014: 198). ECtHR 13 February 2003, 41340/98, 41342/98 and 41344/98, Refah Partisi v. Turkey.

7. BVerfG 17 January 2017, 2 BvB 1/13 (NPD II).

8. The idea of the 'double lesson of Weimar' emerged in a fruitful conversation with political scientist and Dutch *Vrij Nederland* reporter Thijs Broer, see Broer (2017).

9. ECtHR 23 June 2016, no. 20261/12, Baka v. Hungary.

10. According to the Hungarian author György Konrád, quoted in Rupnik (2012: 134).

11. For a defence of 'checklists' against a number of critiques, see Beetham (1999: 157–162). Beetham does not address the problem of 'interaction effects' that Scheppele warns of (see after this); he does, however, address the question (among others) of how to assess 'unique' characteristics of political systems within generalised criteria.

12. BVerfG 23 October 1952, E 2, 1 (SRP).

13. See, in the EU-context, Müller (2013b: 23): 'A simple check-list, as so often used in the EU accession process ("Do the judiciary's offices have computers? Check."), will not do. Somebody needs to see and understand the whole picture. On the other hand, judgments cannot be – and certainly cannot be seen as – partisan.'

14. Of course, it is important to realise that parties are often inclined to slightly alter the system to their advantage, but a distinction can be made between small shifts in emphasis and a whole complex of changes that, as in the Hungarian

case, puts the opposition at a serious disadvantage. See on this point: Mickey, Levitsky and Way (2017: 20–22, especially p. 21).

15. The German Constitutional Court *did* emerge from this political minefield fairly unscathed (see Kommers 1997: 237–238, 2006: 111–128, and *contra* Greenberg 2014: 206–208, 210); as argued above, however, this is not to the credit of the German constitutional legislator.

16. Full quotations can be found in Rijpkema 2018. A small note on terminology beforehand: it is common to largely equate the term *liberal democracy* with a '*democracy* combined with a *rechtsstaat*' (the German and Dutch term), or a *democracy under the rule of law* (see the translator's note in the English translation of AIV 2017: 9, and Cliteur and Ellian (2016: 53–54).

17. The deteriorations of the position of the Hungarian Constitutional Court were mentioned above; with regard to Turkey, President Erdoğan fired 107 judges and prosecutors in May 2017, bringing the count to 4,238 fired judges and prosecutors. See Verschuren (2017).

18. For the inability of Dutch citizens of Moroccan descent to discard their Moroccan citizenship (of which Wilders is clearly aware, being pressed on this point by the interviewers), see on the Dutch government's website: https://www.rijksoverheid.nl/onderwerpen/nederlandse-nationaliteit/dubbele-nationaliteit

19. The idea of positioning democracy as self-correction within the other defence mechanisms of liberal democracy emerged in responding to questions at debates, particularly at the Dutch ProDemos: House for Democracy and the Rule of Law, about the 'minimalistic' character of democracy as self-correction (see also above, §2).

20. This contextualisation of militant democracy within three lines of defence of liberal democracy is a modification of Van der Woude (2009), in which the idea of consequential lines of defence is used to give an overview of the existing defensive mechanisms for liberal democracy in Dutch law, for more on this see Van der Woude (2009: 10); regarding further differences see Rijpkema (2018: note 51 to p. 41).

21. Jessurun D'Oliveira (2017: 26–27) seems to come close to this type of view; see also ten Napel (2016: 9).

TEN

Militant Constitutionalism

András Sajó

Democratic republics liable to perish from a misuse of their power, and not by impotence.

> Alexis de Tocqueville (1835), *Democracy in America*,
> Volume I, Chapter 15–Part II

Democracy is one of the gravest threats to democracy. Democratic means can be used to obtain power (control over the state) which can be used to destroy democracy. To block enemies of democracy taking power via democratic procedures, militant democracies preventively restrict certain rights, limiting the freedom of parties and movements. Militant democracy therefore concentrates power to counter 'evil'. The risks of this strategy are well known. Militant democracy rests on the assumption that the enemies of democracy can be identified *ex ante* – i.e. before these actors grab the political power. Such identification was relatively easy in the 1920s and 1930s and it is not impossible even today.

Yet the principal contemporary threat to democracy is different. Populist parties menace democracy by perpetuating the power of a democratically elected ruler. They rely on manipulated and shallow forms of democracy. The result is illiberal, a despotism *within* democracy.

This chapter is written at a time when the world moves towards illiberalism at growing speed. For many citizens, politicians and scholars this is a welcome development. For too many others, it is only a passing difficulty and therefore of limited interest. This is not the place to discuss how grave the situation is: the chapter takes that for granted and tries to identify points of resistance in institutions, recognising the limits on institutional power. Are the logic and techniques of militant democracy applicable here? The question is made more troubling given the ambivalence of militant democracy. Are there additional elements of constitutionalism that could be mobilised to protect constitutional democracy? Are they compatible with liberal constitutionalism? Will adherents of constitutionalism make themselves powerless vis-à-vis populism because of their 'genetic' commitment to neutrality?

In principle, constitutions contain self-preservation mechanisms (e.g. entrenched procedures for amendment or requirements for co-decision among the branches of power). In this chapter, I answer the following question: to what extent can constitutional self-defence be developed as a militant preventive system (*militant constitutionalism*). Constitutional self-preservation measures were designed to contain the exercise of existing power and provide insurance for temporary losers of elections who remain in the longer-term political game, making both losses and wins impermanent (Dixon and Ginsburg 2017). Once populists grab power, the issue is how much resistance can be provided by mechanisms of constitutional self-defence institutions. This question rarely informs constitutional design. Democratic constitutions assume that those who win a free and fair election can be trusted, that they will act for the people and respect the existing constitution; constitutional and other amendments are permissible and legitimate because these will not be turned against the constitution.

Is the existing edifice of protections for the constitution and constitutionalism impotent vis-à-vis populist takeovers? One obvious possibility is that the law is of limited power. But there are important theoretical considerations too, limiting the applicability of these measures. Restrictive anti-populist efforts face serious objections from the very constitutional principles these measures are supposed to protect. Moreover, the implementation of such measures may not be feasible, not only because of the short-term interests of politicians and institutional inertia but simply because of a lack of public social support for such action.

Constitutional democracy means limited government. In this form of government, despotism is avoided by the separation of powers, democratic decision making, democratic accountability through free and fair elections, a vigorous and free civil society, fundamental rights and the restriction of state power through the rule of law. It is a system of limitations that sustains itself by the very institutions of power limitation. Many of these institutions are preventive per se but do not restrict specific rights. But there is an element of abstract militancy here too: these institutions are protected by measures which restrict the right of the government to change the constitutional system in an illiberal direction. The problem, or perhaps tragedy, of liberal democracy is that it can produce (re)elected autocracy within the existing constitutional frame.

This chapter will first discuss the damage to democracy stemming from illiberal democracy in particular from the illiberalism of a Caesaristic personal rule (§1). The chapter distinguishes two forms of preventive constitutionalism which can counter the current populist trend in politics and government (§2). In the third section I will argue that constitutional self-defence was a foundational and constitutive idea of modern legal constitutionalism. This self-defence, like constitutionalism itself, was specifically directed against the popular abuse of power, and not just all forms of despotism. However, the institutions of self-defence are not systematically built up and are full of loopholes in most (perhaps all) constitutional democracies and the chapter provides a list of the main shortcomings (§3). This is followed by a discussion of the technical possibilities of improving preventive constitutionalism (§4). Admitting that the victory of populism and illiberalism is above all a problem of mentality and not of the law, the chapter discusses the possibilities and legitimacy of a militant intervention in the formation of the populist mindset (§5).

The Damage to Democracy Stemming from Illiberal Democracy[1]

Illiberal democratic movements such as populist and nationalist authoritarian parties pose comparable but not identical problems to those of anti-democratic movements. Populist parties are not avowed enemies of democracy; on the contrary they claim to be its only genuine friends. They represent the people, therefore what they do *is* democratic. Once democratically ushered into power such parties will enable the genuine expression of people's will in democratic forms. The populist seeks cover behind an empirically demonstrable will of a right-minded people, and this democratic trait remains with the populist leader even when he turns autocratic. Once populist-nativist forces obtain control over the government and gradually the state, they tend to perpetuate their power through multi-party regular elections and plebiscite. The formal principle of a narrowly understood electoral democracy is upheld, but the liberal constitutionalist component is curtailed to the extent necessary to maintain political power and for its extension over society.

From a theoretical perspective populist democracy offers an extremely shallow concept of democracy but one that is difficult to reject in ordinary politics: it walks like a duck . . . .[2] As Alessandro Ferrara has aptly pointed out from a Rawlsian perspective: the democracy of populism is based on an '*indigenous unreasonability* arising within native constituencies' (Ferrara

2018: 466). But, at least for Tocqueville, this imperfect system counts as democracy, even admitting that this is a highly problematic government with seriously negative consequences (Tocqueville 2002: chapter XV: 'Unlimited power of majority, and its consequences, Part II'). The hope of modern constitutional democracy was that the shortcomings identified by Tocqueville, the tyranny of the majority can be eliminated. If not, it is still democracy.

The common-sense perspective of shallow democracy is centred on regular elections. It is satisfactory for the average voter who is not particularly concerned about politics and has the opportunity to go out and vent her dissatisfaction by voting against what she found disappointing.

What is wrong with the government emerging from populist democracy? After all, the partisans of populism stand for democracy and once in power they continue to operate the institutions of democratic decision making with gusto, maintaining a direct contact of a sort with *their* people. How could democracy turn into its own enemy in such hands?

In the emerging illiberal democracies, the increasingly personal rule relies on the constant support coming from the people. But what is emerging is a plebiscitarian personal rule of minuscule de Gaulles. We are confronted with Caesarism, the currently prevalent form of populist governance. Ceasarism is a form of government aptly described by Max Weber. Weber emphasised the plebiscitarian aspects of this rule (Weber 1918, 1968).[3] The Caesaristic leader 'responds to his electorate's psychic, physical, economic, ethical, religious, or political needs; he knows no supervisory or appeals body, no technical jurisdiction' (Weber 1968: 1451; see further Casper 2017, emphasising the charismatic nature of the Caesar).

In European illiberal democracies the popular confirmation of the views of the ruler are crucial for his legitimacy. The ruler recognises the wishes and fears of his people and the people recognises itself in the ruler's views. Consequently, the views of the people (the relevant majority) have to be regularly checked and manipulated. The leader presents his policies (including personal power-enhancing measures) as simply reflecting the commonsense judgements of ordinary nationals. Hence the importance of the referendum and plebiscite. These are highly praised in democratic theory as direct democracy but are intimately associated with populism. Indeed, the legitimacy and popularity of referendum on the basis of popular initiative originated, among others, from its use by populists in Western US states in the late nineteenth century. (Of course, there are other pathways leading to referendum, like the local tradition in Switzerland, or the Caesaristic use of plebiscite beginning with Napoleon I and his nephew.) Beginning with President Jackson, the populist leader at the helm of state affairs – be he/she the president, prime minister or a respected person in the back seat with files on all players – claims to represent *all* the people, or at least the people that deserves that name, the better and therefore only part of the Nation.

Caesarism has its fans. Max Weber had no major difficulty with this form of democracy. However, in this permissive qualification he relied on a rather naïve constitutionalist assumption about Caesaristic rule which was based on an ideal type of English parliamentarism:[4]

> Vis-à-vis the factually caesarist representative of the masses [Parliament] safe-guards in England 1) the continuity and 2) the supervision of his power position, 3) the preservation of civil rights, 4) a suitable political proving ground of the politicians wooing the confidence of the masses, and 5) the peaceful elimination of the caesarist dictator once he had lost the trust of the masses. (Weber 1968: 1452)

In the history of Western illiberal democracies of populist origin these safeguards are deliberately disregarded and set aside. Moreover, contrary to Weber's assumption, the contemporary Caesarist leader is most often charismatic only in the sense of being able to generate enthusiasm, even if one that is rooted in hatred and resentment and is not committed to a specific mandate and mission. Most of the safeguards mentioned above are missing here, being eliminated earlier in the democratic stage or destroyed by the populist in power. Hence the incompatibility with constitutionalism as liberal order and hence the need to confront it, presumably in a militant (*Wehrhaft*, defensive) manner.

Given the potentially irreversible consequences of illiberal democracy on constitutionalism and democracy it is morally imperative to consider to what extent the arsenal of militant democracy or other rights-restricting and democracy-limiting preventive measures shall be applicable to counter the current trend. But moral necessity is not legitimacy. Is populist illiberalism with regular elections really an illegitimate form of government by democratic standards?[5] If so, are preventive measures similar to those of militant democracy applicable here? Which measures are we talking about? Assuming that there are preventive restrictive measures (existing in the arsenal of militant democracy or elsewhere in the armoury of constitutionalism) one should also enquire into the social and political readiness of their utilisation. And what are the criteria of the application where populist movements are prima facie fully lawful by democratic standards and laws enacted by previous non-populist governments? If the ordinary restrictive measures of militant democracy are not applicable, is at least the *logic* of militant democracy relevant here? This question forces one to consider the democratic legitimacy of populism.

Populism promises to protect the genuine people, the common men and women on the street against the traitors called elite and threats coming from aliens (liberals, migrants, etc.). If legitimacy is a matter of increased public following, and where the applicable legitimacy is based on relative majoritarianism, populism cannot be held illegitimate, even less so illegal.[6] Hence, the objections to populist rule are not irresistible, in particular among those large masses that consider majoritarianism non-problematic. Contrary to the 1930s, contemporary Western autocrats do not deny the appropriateness of democracy. (After all it is electoral democracy that keeps the regime in power.) An illiberal regime is not a totalitarian dictatorship and in many illiberal democracies people are endorsing a power that is *not* engaging in brutal repression but enables 'only' a form of life that is alien for a minority but allows this minority to live the life-form of the majority (or even their own as long as this is not troubling for the majority). Populism and the illiberal democracy that it brings in may result in the perpetuation of (fundamentally different) illiberal regimes, but the alleged 'perpetuation' relies on the repeated democratic reinforcement of the government in power. In the case of the enemies of democracy in the 1930s (and their followers to this day), the statements and acts of these movements were clearly anti-democratic, and once in power their rejection of democracy was undeniable. The criticism (moral objection) to illiberal democracy is different: what the ruler offers is a shallow form or formal democracy. This electoral democracy is without rational, discursive decision making. Further, it treats its opponents and potential opponents and the constitutional institutions that provide safeguards to these minorities as enemies. The liberal constitution promises a co-existence, or living together to all, under terms that do not force the individual, even if a member of a minority, to make a unilateral fundamental sacrifice for the majority's preferences. In contrast, illiberal democracies gradually tend to impose specific forms of life on society and concentrate power which increases social control. Such control makes democratic choices illusory. At the end of a rather short road there is electoral autocracy.

Populist (illiberal) democracy resembles the authoritarian regimes of the 1930s in a crucial aspect: here too the alleged source or subject of power is an undifferentiated people (although in the case of Nazi rule the Führer was the unmediated expression of the will of the German Nation and Volk). In front of such undifferentiated people militant constitutionalism has to rely on what the militant democracy tried to do: apply measures to prevent people reverting politically to a single, allegedly homogeneous, 'natural' entity. Once again, the nature of populism and resulting illiberal democracy differs from anti-democratic extremist movements and resulting barbarian authoritarianism. Therefore, while militancy in the prevention of the populist rule is a necessity, the constitution-protective reactions must be different.

Two Forms of Preventive Constitutionalism

There are important similarities between the techniques of abuse of democracy of the 1930s and contemporary populist tinkering with democracy. However, the extremists of the 1930s and the populists today stand for different values. But populist government in Europe results typically in autocratic, authoritarian or other freedom-restricting hybrid regimes, even if the degree of autocracy in Russia and Turkey clearly differs from what is emerging in member states of the EU. But after all, during the interwar period, authoritarianism in many European countries did not rely on brutal oppression.[7] It was common to 'suspend' democracy, often in an attempt to fight extremists, which meant that democracy as a principle was not rejected.[8]

Legal, political and social thought is inclined to squeeze problems into existing frames and apply existing solutions. It is, therefore 'natural' (to a point) to conclude that the preventive logic and instruments of militant democracy might be relevant to fight populists.

The logic of militant democracy suggests two kinds of defensive mechanisms. The first is a toolkit of rights restrictions limiting the possibility that putative enemies of democracy will gain power through elections.[9] The second consists of measures that would limit the possibilities of abuse of government power, especially abuses aimed at perpetuating the government. The first toolkit of militant democracy is well known. The restrictions are typically directed against identifiable 'enemies' of democracy (party ban, restrictions of propaganda, including restrictions on forms of organisation such as a ban on uniforms, incitement, etc.) The argument against fascists, Soviet communists or religious fundamentalists is that they will destroy democracy once in power; this cannot be applied to populists (even if such assumption seems to be correct) as they stand for democracy and the constitution. Indeed, populists can turn a country into an illiberal or authoritarian one without changing the constitution. Nevertheless, there are elements in ordinary constitutional orders which can have a militant application (see below).

Preventing attacks on liberal institutions after populists gain power is harder to conceptualise: the populists lawfully control the state apparatus; their legislative majority constitutionally enacts the laws which may result in autocracy. However, the constitution may contain institutional mechanisms to prevent its undoing by democratically and constitutionally legitimated means. Constitutional safeguards include enhanced constitutional protection of the separation of powers, mandatory regular elections, the constitutional protection of electoral fairness, the right to resistance, term limits, etc. I will come back to these measures in the discussion of constitutional self-defence.

As to the preventive restrictions that serve militant constitutionalism, many measures exist today that help sustain democracy. Some of these are partly militant (i.e. directed against identified enemies) and some are neutral, democracy-enhancing measures. Neutral rules limit all groups from unfairly seizing power. But populists do not come to power unfairly, at least the first time. Most often, the populist victory relies on emotional electoral messages, messages conveying nativist and xenophobic content.

Self-Defence is Part of the Constitutional Tradition

One kind of constitutional self-defence concerns the preservation of the state against external and internal enemies, including the protection of territorial integrity. Familiar means to achieve this end include: proper rules of emergency, authorisation to prevent criminal conspiracies and terrorist attacks, and so on. This is the 'constitution is not a suicide pact' aspect of constitutional self-preservation.[10] But my focus here is different: it is the defence from majoritarianism of fundamental constitutional values like equal liberty and democratic rule. Defences against the excesses of democracy is an inherent feature of liberal constitutions.

Once in power, illiberal populist forces seek to consolidate and perpetuate Caesaristic personal rule. It is at this stage that militant self-defence and the self-preservation of constitutionalism can have an effect. And those efforts will be treated as elitist and illegitimate obstacles to the people's power.

Constitutional self-defence was a foundational and constitutive idea of modern legal constitutionalism. And this form of self-defence, like constitutionalism itself, was specifically directed against the popular abuse of power. Constitutional institutions were not just instruments of government. They were intended to prevent despotism, and in particular a specific form of despotism, namely that of the people. However, the institutions of self-defence are not systematically built up and are full of loopholes in most (perhaps all) constitutional democracies and this chapter provides a list of the main shortcomings.

The foundational documents of constitutionalism were deeply concerned with the consequences of popular power.[11] The founders accepted that the people were the only source of power. But they maintained reservations about the people. The *locus classicus* is Federalist 10. Separation of powers, regular elections, federalism and the Bill of Rights were thought to provide constraints on people's formal power. In what follows I offer an incomplete list of the standard arrangement of liberal constitutions with some of its weak points:

Amendment

In theory, procedural requirements can make regime perpetuation and illiberal or anti-democratic rule extremely difficult. In practice, supermajorities, referenda or constituent assemblies can be used to undermine these protections and achieve illiberal change. For instance, legislative majorities large enough to amend the constitution can be reached with the vote of a bare majority (or even less). And a governing populist majority, in control of the media and administrative resources, can produce favourable results with referenda. Staggered systems like the one in the US (with qualified majority of the states) and the Norwegian-Dutch system promise more resilience. The Norwegian and Dutch Constitutions create a two-stage process for amendments – one parliament proposes and a newly elected second parliament must pass the amendment with a supermajority. This allows greater time for public reflection (compared to a referendum), it reduces the outgoing government's power to influence an amendment's adoption and it keeps a single, popular vote from consuming the constitution.

Unamendable provisions are the strongest mechanism of self-protection possessed by constitutions.[12] Of course, unamendability cannot protect against an unconstitutional coup d'état. But undemocratic coup-like actions (e.g. an unconstitutional dissolution of parliament by constitutional amendment) can be prevented this way, or at least will force aspiring autocrats to rely on the military.

According to the Venice Commission: 'An overview in comparative constitutional law shows that most Constitutions do not provide for unamendable provisions, and these are not required by international standards. Moreover, nearly all unamendable provisions are substantive, and therefore not related to the procedure for the revision of the Constitution' (Venice Commission 2012). However, according to Yaniv Roznai (2015: 24), out of the world constitutions which were enacted between 1989 and 2013 more than half included unamendable provisions.

Judicially protected unamendable constitutional 'cores' are consistent with the militant defence of the constitution. But the practical impact remains questionable: what is the force of these measures once a populist government has altered the composition of the supreme court? The changes that are needed for the concentration and perpetuation of power are sel-dom captured by entrenched provisions. Illiberal takeovers can be carried out at the sub-constitutional level.

Institutions Guarding the Constitution

The constitution requires bodies which can stand against abuse. The need for such protection was a logical necessity from the very first days of mod-ern constitutionalism. *Marbury* v. *Madison* concluded that the judiciary shall be the protector of the constitution out of a logical necessity. While judicial guardianship of the constitution is the prevalent model today, other consti-tutional actors can participate in constitutional protection (e.g. the King as neutral power according to Benjamin Constant, the *Reichspresident* accord-ing to Carl Schmitt, or Simon Bolivar according to Simon Bolivar).

Term Limits

Regimes which started as charismatic electoral democracies tend to perpetu-ate themselves as permanent autocracies. Permanent rule is the result of continued electoral success. The strongest constitutional protections against this possibility are term limits. But these provisions are often amended by referendum.[13,14]

Electoral Systems

With respect to electoral systems, constitutions typically outline limited principles of fairness. Filling out electoral system design is left to ordinary legislation (Raabe 2014). Matters related to electoral financing and access to resources are also left to ordinary legislation (in some countries to leg-islation with qualified majority) with limited and reluctant constitutional oversight.[15] The constitutional review of electoral laws is primarily based on individual voting rights' protection. Structural distortions (e.g. malap-portionment) are also poorly supervised.[16] This is not surprising: in the his-tory of democracy incumbents tend to make use of the broad constitutional possibilities of electoral manipulation to their advantage, and incumbent advantages are tolerated even in stable democracies.

Constitutional review is fundamentally deferential when it comes to distortions in electoral systems providing a boost to small majorities. Con-sider recent judgments of the Italian Constitutional Court. In Sentenza 1/2014 and again in Sentenza 35/2017 it struck down the Italian electoral system, finding that there was an insufficient relation between the seats allocated and the votes cast and that the design of voter lists kept citizens from expressing their preferences. But in Sentenza 35/2017 it recognised a constitutional interest in stable government, accepting a 15 per cent bonus for a party that obtains 40 per cent of the vote. The election of a parliament elected under an unconstitutional election rule was upheld.[17]

Even electoral systems specifically designed to counter majoritarian tyranny seem to fail. For instance, the US Constitution allows popular minorities to come to power. Presidents can be elected without gaining a majority of the popular vote and Senate majorities often represent a minority of the electorate. But once in office, the party in power rarely acts as if it lacks a majority.

Elections are indispensable for democracy (as representative government). But they do not guarantee a democracy based in rational discourse nor one respectful of fundamental rights. According to the populist understanding of democracy the electorate produces government simply by choosing the leaders. With the progress of the Caesaristic rule this is reduced to accepting a leader. In principle the electorate also has the right to evict the ruler by withdrawing this acceptance (Schumpeter 1976: 272). Contemporary autocrats in the making institutionalise a system where such a withdrawal is practically impossible.

Against Direct Democracy

Given the plebiscitary nature of populist political power, direct democracy plays an important role in the legitimation of populists rulers and even their exercise of power. Classic constitutions limited popular participation. The US Constitution is illustrative.

Other countries are more open to direct democracy. Italy's constitution allows referenda for a limited range of subjects. Referenda can be called by popular initiatives, but they can only strike down existing legislation. The constitutionally prohibited subject matters are exactly those which would be the obvious targets of any illiberal populist movement: ratification of international treaties, pardon and amnesty, tax and budget, provisions of the constitution (Article 75). The Constitutional Court has added additional prohibited topics to protect the constitutional order.

Hungary, a country that is considered the paradigmatic example of European illiberalism, has similar provisions. The Fundamental Law does not allow referenda to dissolve parliament which is a legitimate protective measure of the constitutional order. Yet the rule denies the last popular defence against legislative populism when a majority systematically legislates against the spirit of constitutionalism.

Multi-Layered Constitution

The Caesaristic ruler acts as if he were the sovereign. This is what makes him potentially totalitarian or at least autocratic. But the possibilities for autocracy are limited where elements of sovereignty were transferred to international organisations. Consequently, in many areas, decision making is made by international bodies and networks. Such multi-level constitutionalism limits any majority's power to enact constitutional change. For illiberal EU member states, the EU could be the barrier to illiberalism. Even where there is no formal transfer of sovereignty, international dependency is a de facto limit of national sovereignty. Understandably, autocrats aim to regain such transferred or de facto powers. Of course, he will act in the name of the inalienable right to sovereignty of the people that was thrown away by cosmopolitan elites. But the economic and geopolitical interdependencies, and legitimacy considerations stemming from international law and international relations, make such return to sovereignty difficult and costly. Multi-layered constitutionalism restrains, to a considerable degree, countries that are dependent financially of the Union.

Improving Preventive Constitutionalism

The mixed experience with the existing constitutional self-protecting measures and in particular their use in the prevention of illiberal democracy indicates that these technical solutions are suboptimal. Notwithstanding the readiness at the time of the foundation of constitutionalism to make constitutions resilient, most constitutions show little concern about threats to liberalism. The prevailing preference for constitutional neutrality reflects a trust in all democratic political parties and all elected governments. It is assumed that they all respect constitutional procedures. As long as this is the prevailing mindset militant considerations hardly fit into contemporary constitutional thought. Here lies the inherent weakness of contemporary constitutionalism.

How might that weakness be met? Not even the best design can provide adequate protection against the abuse of democracy. But there are legitimate and even efficient countermeasures to populist illiberalism. This is comforting and an inspiration to concerned citizens: the victory of populism is not fate. Moreover, a clear design serves as a standard of constitutionalism: it helps identify unjust acts even amidst the uncertainty created by the emergence of autocracy. And it can serve as a standard even when they fail to keep populists from coming to power.

Here, I briefly list some possible, defensive institutional mechanisms together with the most common objections, which stem either from democratic theory or efficiency considerations.

1. Super-entrenching and making unamendable the elements of the constitution which are crucial for liberal democracy.
2. Super-entrenching mechanisms to ensure that constitutional courts can be effective guardians of the constitution. As far as possible, the court should be depoliticised and autonomous. They can have long-term non-renewable mandates, they should be fixed to avoid court-packing and terms could be staggered. Ideally, candidates would be selected by non-political permanent bodies, including the judicial council. Judicial policy should be set by the courts and individuals should be aware of their right to a neutral judge (see the German and Italian Constitutions on the right to the 'natural judge').
3. Independent agencies should be led by non-partisan leadership, appointed by processes driven by political consensus. The autocratic potential of presidential systems increases when presidents appoint agency heads and power is centralised. Of course, similar powers are held by Caesaristic prime ministers. But in parliamentary systems, the legitimacy comes from actual democratic endorsement in the loyal parliament and the importance of constitutional justification is lessened. At the same time, civil servants should be protected institutionally to protect against mass dismissal as a strategy of regime change. Strong conflict of interest rules shall apply to public functionaries and elected representatives (including family members) with automatic sanctions.

   The rule of law should be enhanced in the administration of justice, among others by diminishing the influence of the state administration. For example, prosecutors shall not be subordinated to a politically controlled hierarchy that cannot be instructed to initiate or drop investigations and press charges.
4. The personal rule of the Caesaristic ruler is in constant need of a formal popular recognition or endorsement, hence the crucial role of the electoral system. The cornerstones of a fair political process can also be entrenched. I understand 'electoral system' very broadly, including rules on how parties and procedures are funded and how candidates access the media.
   4(a). Proportional representation may make a difference. This system is likely to curtail the chances of populists where more than two parties are competing, forcing the parties to join coalitions.[18] Coalitions diminish the possibilities of an unchecked populist majority. Of course, the price is fragmentation. Coalitions bring constant negotiations and frictions, making daily government more difficult. The possibility of instability has pushed some countries towards

electoral majoritarianism and giving premiums to the election winner. When a supermajority is generated by bonuses, but the popular vote is below a supermajority, the governing parties should not be allowed to amend the constitution.

4(b). Referenda called by the government itself should be limited and high thresholds for quorums might be entrenched. By contrast popular initiatives can be facilitated.

5. With respect to parties and representatives, constitutions might protect enhanced powers for parliamentary opposition (e.g. facilitate minority committees of enquiry with strong powers). Parliamentary immunity certainly deserves enhanced protection, contrary to the populist theory of constitutionalism which considers this another elite privilege. Parliamentary procedures such as guaranteed question time, rules forcing reasonable debate (duty to debate, no expedited legislation) and the right of the parliamentary minority to carry out effective enquiries might also be entrenched. The same logic applies to term limits, applicable both to members of legislative bodies and executive positions.

6. Of course, the abuse of emergency powers is a threat to constitutionalism. The standard answer to this threat is to create strict criteria for using such powers and to ensure that they lapse automatically.

7. Militantly defending the constitution requires national and international courts to carefully consider the context of attempts to curtail liberal constitutionalism. This would require the reconsideration of the legal problems, such as the violation of the rule of law or human rights, in the context of the stability of the constitutionalist liberal order. Constitutionally sensitive cases would be given priority and where necessary interim measures (injunctions) would be deployed to prevent irreversible damage to constitutional democracy. The import of a contextual approach is illustrated by the mass dismissal of Hungarian judges. Hungary reduced the age of mandatory retirement for Hungarian judges, leading to vacancies. The EU Court of Justice treated the matter as one of age discrimination. It did not see it as a fundamental attack on the rule of law. As a result, key positions in the Hungarian judiciary were successfully vacated without significant cost (Uitz 2015; Pech and Scheppele 2017).[19] The European Court of Human Rights has a similar attitude but weighed the possibility of irreversible damage to democratic institutions in 2017 when it enjoined a transfer of the only opposition media outlet in Georgia. A militant approach to interpretation would apply, for example, to districting cases, considering whether malapportionment carries fatal consequences to constitutionalism. Such an approach is consistent with the traditional canon of interpretation, requiring that all the circumstances of the case be taken into consideration. However, courts are traditionally deferential to the political branches and respect the outcome of the political process. They continue to eschew this broader role, embracing a purely procedural

understanding of democracy. But a militant (apparently more activist) interpretation of the constitution is not contrary to the constitution and constitutionalism. After all, a constitutional court is called to uphold the constitution, and the manipulation of the democratic process may sunder that constitution.

The Problem of the Mindset

The communicative sphere remains essential to the rise of populism. If electoral confirmation is crucial for the exercise and extension of Caesaristic rule in illiberal democracies, the first duty of the ruler is to generate popular support at least among a considerable number of the electorate. This 'considerable number' can be expanded into a majority through the use of 'administrative' and increasingly institutional tools. But the key component remains influence over minds. To win elections, authoritarian and illiberal political forces must have a place in the mindset of the electorate. Preventing dangerous emotionalism and the consolidation of anti-liberal, authoritarian and substantively anti-democratic attitudes is a major task for those who would like to protect constitutional democracy.

The electoral success of populism (like that of fascism) is grounded in emotionalism.[20] The programme or promise is often based on mobilising fear, hatred (against minorities, foreigners and alien global and foreign powers) and resentment. One of the keys to the success of populism is that it legitimises it as just and appropriate expressions of resentment and rage. Populists rely on misinformation ('fake news') and more importantly on the one-sided representation of select factoids. What is particularly troubling is the reliance on dehumanisation (removal of outgroups from the treatment applicable to humans) in the populist movements: contrary to the basic humanistic assumptions of the post-1945 world nativism is reinforced with the denial of the humanity of people (in particular migrants) who are considered different and threatening.[21]

This problem is worsened by predictable media dynamics. Following their commercial interests, media organisations generate news that arouses emotions and serves populist interests. They do so whether they are under the influence of the media owners who support populists, or simply because sensation sells. As to social media, there is no mechanism of fact-checking and it can reinforce both negative emotions and stereotypes.

What can be the contribution of speech regulation here? Mere displays of emotions cannot be prohibited under the prevailing understanding of liberal constitutionalism. Beyond openly racist incitement instances, which are rare, there is little factual ground to ban even an extremist party like the Hungarian Jobbik Party or the German AfD which is less radical (both parties are the largest opposition party in their respective parliament), not to mention 'mainstream' populists. The right to display political and social outrage is protected equally for all and hence neither populist outrage and contempt nor the populists as such can be singled out just because they rely regularly on hate.

Critically, populist rhetoric does not fall into the net of hate speech. While law, especially in Europe, may accept that certain forms of hate speech are prohibited, the expression of hate per se – especially when it is not targeting specific vulnerable groups and without incitement to violence – seldom falls into the legally proscribed. The target differs somewhat: the attack is directed against conspiring elites and criminal or culturally sub-versive migrants. These target groups are hard to identify, and the language that is used does not fall in normal cases into hate speech as generally understood. Proposing exclusionary measures to would-be migrants or illegal entrants even on stereotypical grounds and with obvious hatred does not count as discriminatory in law, as migrants are different from citizens and (contrary to asylum seekers) are without the right to entry. An extension of the concept of hate speech in a militant fashion (for example the prohibition of factual misrepresentation capable of dehumanisation) would be extremely broad and impossible to implement.[22]

Are there militant alternatives to speech restrictions? Loewenstein was very sceptical: 'Democracy is utterly incapable of meeting an emotional attack by an emotional counter-attack. Constitutional government, by its very nature, can appeal only to reason; it never could successfully mobilize emotionalism; even its emotional ingredients are only a prelude to reason' (Loewenstein 1937a: 428). Defensive constitutionalism may rely on less objectionable pos-sibilities like restrictions on media ownership concentration, fairness require-ments in private media and stricter campaign spending rules. (The non-legal aspect, namely strong journalistic ethics, is also of help and it could be fos-tered by state action.) Further, the rational quality of the public discourse can be enhanced. This is strategically preventive but not excessively restrictive: it is not based on rights restrictions but on governmental support of civilised communication. Depoliticised public broadcasting with sufficient financial means can also foster rational political debate.

Of course, these structural measures are of little relevance once the populists control the government. The ruler will control the media, starting with public broadcasting and including to some extent social media (with a paid army of bloggers, etc.) At this point the earlier regulation is turned on its head: hate speech rules might be applied against independent voices and public broadcasting will become factories of fake news, fear and hate.

In consequence the authoritarian regime can rely on its vigilant supporters to silence criticism in areas where it has not yet taken over control.

Conclusion: Is It Too Late?

Constitutions contain mechanisms of self-protection but the robustness of a constitutional democracy depends on the formative and prevailing political concerns (sovereignty, fear of totalitarian rule, fear of disintegration, desire to maintain national identity or national rule, independence, national glory, etc.). Before they take power it is difficult to determine whether populists (and illiberal, asocial, authoritarian, anti-modern social feelings and relations) are a serious threat justifying militant restrictions. Generally, we can only be sure of the peril after the transformative event has occurred.

Preventive constitutionalism *can* be justified within liberal constitutional theory as self-preservation. But the justification for militantly restricting populists remains very problematic – in part, because of the difficulty of identifying the anti-constitutional element in a democratic populist movement. Of course, the constitution may trigger certain pre-existing protective measures even after the populists come to power. And those measures will necessarily conflict with the popular will. This is also why autonomous institutions (like courts, the central bank, etc.) and strong constitutional courts are vilified in radical democratic theory. And why they are the first to fall victim in the populist takeovers.

Notwithstanding the well-known normative objections to entrenching constitutionalism and the practice of militant constitutionalism, I believe they have a place in the struggle to sustain electoral democracy. But whatever is written into laws is of secondary relevance where there is no one to stand up for the constitution. The institutions of militant constitutionalism may work against populism in conditions of social inertia but not where populists systematically mobilise hatred and disparagement against the institutions; where democracy is understood simply as regular voting and where constitutional freedoms are not cherished, democracy will fail. A democracy cannot be sustained in the absence of (reasonable) democrats. And it cannot be sustained when people believe that they are still good democrats even as they work to undermine it.

Notes

1. There is considerable debate concerning the term because for many people a democracy cannot be illiberal. The term is used here because this is how the leaders of such regimes describe the system.

2. One can say with some reservation that populist rule satisfies Dahl's (1971) textbook definition of democracy (universal suffrage, universal eligibility for public office, free elections, and freedom of expression and association and public policies that are responsive to the voters' preferences). But all elements are qualified: speech is free as long as it does not reach larger chunks of the electorate; there is response to preferences but these preferences are first manipulated by the ruler.

3. For Weber on Caesarism and Casearism's historical development see Baehr (2008); here I follow Casper (2007).

4. In Weber's opinion presidential as well as parliamentary regimes can be Caesaristic. In this approach Lloyd George counted as a plebiscitary leader.

5. Other sources of legitimacy include spiritual salvation, welfare, national glory, justice, general happiness. It may well be that these regimes will find their legitimacy outside democracy. For example, in Russia national grandeur plays a role but at the moment electoral democracy is the frame most illiberal democracies use.

6. Relative majoritarianism means here that the majority that is claimed by a victorious populist is only a minority of the electorate and an even smaller minority of the citizenry which is turned into legislative or constituent majorities thanks to specific electoral rules. Moreover, this is often a majority in the making: the populists (and this is not their privilege) refer to trends in public opinion polls to claim that what they insist upon is the real will of the people. Such references are becoming self-fulfilling prophecies in the cascades generated by distorted media, and because of the desire to adhere to the majority. The conformism of resentment helps populists.

7. Admiral Horthy was a life-time governor of Hungary from 1920. Regular parliamentary elections were held with an electoral system that regularly brought in pro-government majorities.

8. In the interwar period in Europe permanent suspension occurred in the relative majority of the countries (Capoccia 2005). The suspension of democracy that was characteristic in Europe in the interwar period did not make a country internationally unacceptable. Of course, the standards of international acceptability were very different at that time.

9. Such rules may go beyond public law. For example, strict anti-trust law can be implemented to prevent economic concentrations which would favour similar political concentration. The Celler-Kefauver anti-trust amendment (1950) considered concentration as resulting in totalitarianism (Crane 2018). Concentration in the broadcasting industry represents comparable problems today.

10. Attributed to President Lincoln, when he justified the disregard of the habeas corpus provisions of the Constitution. See further *Terminiello* v. *City of Chicago* 337 U.S. 1 (1949).

11. The containment of the people which was suddenly recognised as sovereign was a crucial concern of the French Revolution too. The constitutional documents of 1789–1791 replaced people with Nation and used all sorts of tricks and theories to limit people's voting rights.

12. In addition, some supreme courts (e.g. India – basic structure doctrine) subscribe to the doctrine of unamendable provisions that are essential or structural components of the constitution even in the absence of specific provisions.

13. In Nicaragua, the Supreme Court held that the term limit itself is an unconstitutional idea as it restricts people's right. Of course, in this popular democratic logic all the restrictions on the popular vote are unconstitutional. Available at <https://www.reuters.com/article/oukwd-uk-nicaragua-ortega-idAFTRE59J1182009102> (last accessed 15 July 2018). Decision 504 of 2009, 19 October 2009.

14. There were state-level ballot initiatives and referenda in some US states about congressional term limits and Republican populists tabled a term limit proposal in 1994 in Congress. Comparable rules regarding term limits for parliamentarians are rare (see the Philippines and approximately fifteen US states; Ecuador reinstated the two-term limit to members of the National Assembly in 2018 and the French government submitted a similar draft amendment in 2018). Such restrictions run into serious objections of democratic and constitutional theory.

15. The German Constitutional Court found that the 5 per cent threshold in the German electoral system is not an unconstitutional distortion of electoral representation and the European Court of Human Rights found a 10 per cent threshold in Turkey compatible with the right of the free expression of the opinion of the people in the choice of legislation.

16. Of course, malapportionment can be reviewed relying on the principle of equal voting rights. The Hungarian Constitutional Court under the Fidesz government (Fidesz has been the government party since 2010) found that the disparities between the size of voting districts are unconstitutional. Parliament dutifully carried out a redistricting which has created electoral districts of reasonably equal size. However, the boundaries of the districts were drawn in a way that resulted in additional seats to the incumbent government guaranteeing constituent supermajority.

17. Courts seem powerless in the face of popularly endorsed unconstitutionality: the amendment by referendum of the French Constitution which was held to be unconstitutional was held valid in 1961 in France.

18. A consequential application of proportional representation would require the abolition of electoral districting which is a major source of abuse. Interestingly, such districts exist in Germany, notwithstanding the proportional representation system, the justification being that this brings the representatives closer to the people. On balance, in the logic of militant constitutionalism the prevention of populism shall prevail against this democracy-enhancing consideration.

19. The EU Commission has adopted a more aggressive position in the case of the Polish Supreme Court (but not with respect to the Polish Constitutional Tribunal) and brought the case to the Court of Justice of the European Union (CJEU) in terms of the violation of the rule of law. The CJEU promptly applied

an interim measure and the Polish government has acquiesced and restored the status quo ante.

20. In his classic study Loewenstein considered the authoritarian state as rooted in emotionalism. See Loewenstein (1937a: 418).

21. Migrants have been represented in increasingly negative terms over the last fifteen years, i.e. before the 2015 refugee wave, in the media (Esses, Medianu and Lawson 2013). On the psychology of dehumanisation see Haslam et al. 2008.

22. The closest to a militant (short-term) mind-manipulation prohibition is to be found in the 2018 French legislation on misinformation in electoral periods, a measure that must wait for the test of its application.

ELEVEN

Militant Democracy as an Inherent Democratic Quality

Svetlana Tyulkina

Introduction

Democracy is a precarious thing and it is also 'the very thing that can bring democracy to its own knees' (Chou 2012: 67). Democracy, even today, has an unfortunate capacity to come undone, to risk its own safety, to take its own life, all while doing what it was intended to do (Chou 2013: 24). To a great extent this is to the fact that democracy is an inherently liberal and accommodating system of governance premised on a plurality of political ideas and opinions. These characteristics can facilitate the activities of groups and individuals who want to harm or overturn democracy by abusing or misusing democratic institutions and procedures such as free elections, freedom of speech and freedom of association. Militant democracy is a concept which explains how democracy can protect its structures from such attempts and remain internally coherent.

Over the past few decades militant democracy has emerged as an important way of understanding constitutional systems around the world. Generally speaking, militant democratic states protect their continued existence as democracies by pre-emptively restricting the exercise of civil and political freedoms. Initially, militant democracies focused on electoral integrity, adopting measures such as the prohibition of allegedly undemocratic political parties. However, in recent years the practice of militant democracy has expanded to include policies aimed at addressing, for example, the threats of religious fundamentalism and global terrorism. The rise of political populist movements in various parts of the world reinstated the debate about the importance and relevance of militant democracy.

The practice of militant democracy allows us to understand constitutional systems and evaluate and explore their practical operation, particularly in relation to the actions of the state directed at self-defence from internal threats. It is especially useful where it provides a rationale for constitutional concepts and approaches that might otherwise be considered outside the liberal conception of democracy. Taking into account the importance of the idea of militant democracy, and its wide use in constitutional scholarship (Fox and Nolte 1995; Harvey 2004; Sajó 2004; Issacharoff 2007; Macklem 2012), the concept's application should be investigated in respect to the recent rise of populist political movements.

This chapter focuses on the constitutional dimension of militant democracy and its growth in contemporary constitutional theory and practice. First, it examines the treatment of militant democracy in constitutional theory, including major criticisms of this notion and attempts to provide justifications for its application. Second, the chapter briefly examines the contemporary interpretation and application of this concept in constitutional practice by domestic and international courts. The chapter is based on the assumption that all democracies are militant to some extent and possess a capacity to protect themselves from various threats, including those posed by the rise of populist political parties. This chapter also investigates the capacity of international institutions, such as the Council of Europe and the EU, to apply militant measures. Therefore, those institutions could play a more prominent role in protecting the democratic structures of their member states and addressing the rise of populist political movements.

Militant Democracy and Constitutional Theory

As stated above, democracy has an unfortunate capacity to come undone, to risk its own safety, to take its own life, all while doing what it was intended to do. Militant democracy is a concept which explains how democracy can protect its structures from such attempts and remain internally coherent. Today, militant democracy is primarily understood as the fight against radical movements, especially radical political parties and their activities (Sajó 2006: 2262). In that form, it is usually agreed that militant democracy was first explicitly constitutionalised in Germany: the 'cradle' of militant democracy.[1] The Basic Law of 1949 introduced militant democracy and gave the German political system a new form, including the mechanism to protect its founding principles against the potential enemies of the state. The central element of Germany's militant democracy is Article 21 of the Basic Law, which established the procedure to ban unconstitutional political parties.

Later, the concept of militant democracy was widely utilised to curb the activities of communist political parties. More recently, the

11 September 2001 terrorist attacks and the anti-terrorism policies and legislation that followed returned issues of militant democracy to the forefront of constitutional and political discourse. Many Western democracies regarded themselves as implicated in an undeclared war between extremist Islam and Western liberal democratic values (Avineri 2004: 2). Interest was also boosted by the world's heightened awareness of the threats posed by religious fundamentalism. Democracies world-wide had to accept that the electoral arena was not merely 'a forum for the recording of preferences, but a powerful situs for the mobilisa-tion of political forces' (Issacharoff 2007: 1410). So, the possibility was raised that militant democracy could be used in a much wider sense, to protect democracy not only from undemocratic political parties but also from other emerging threats. Therefore, militant democracy is by no means a concept that is 'withering away', but it can be an important tool for protecting democracy.

Militant democracy itself has been a topic of debate even before Loewen-stein's conception of militant democracy was put into practice in post-war constitutions in Europe. More frequently, militant policies are implemented in response to certain events and developments in the constitutional legisla-tion and jurisprudence of various states (for more details, see Tyulkina 2015a: 16–21). This, obviously, demonstrates that militant democracy is not an iso-lated, old-fashioned abstract idea from post-war Europe. Militant democracy has close ties with various ideas about how to deal with intolerant political actors and citizens, and with the essence of constitutional democracy. This justifies the conclusion that militant democracy has a prominent place in democratic and constitutional theory and therefore deserves ongoing, thor-ough investigation.

One of the reoccurring topics discussed by various constitutional theo-rists is whether militant democracy is compatible with the very nature of democracy and how to justify the use of militant democracy mea-sures (Pfersmann 2004: 51–52). Legitimate concerns can be raised about whether democracies engage in self-contradiction by limiting fundamen-tal rights and liberties in order to secure the very existence of those rights. And legitimate questions can be asked about whether democracy can behave in a militant way while remaining true to itself. While the concept of militant democracy might be attractive to those concerned with the protection of democracy generally, it nevertheless requires careful con-sideration. The potential pitfalls of militant democracy are easily identifi-able in both the realm of constitutional jurisprudence and theory; and the idea of democracies taking a militant stance towards their perceived adversaries has been vehemently criticised since the concept first emerged in the 1920s (Thiel 2009a: 417), including by Loewenstein himself. He acknowledges that 'democracy stands for fundamental rights, for fair play for all opinions, for free speech, assembly, press' (Loewenstein 1937a: 430–431) and agrees that it might be a difficult task for any democracy to curtail these freedoms 'without destroying the very basis of its existence and justification'. Applying this caution to modern democracies, one interpretation is that militant measures require extensive explanation and justification from governments in jurisdictions with strong democratic traditions and an effective system of fundamental rights protection. Having said that, this chapter defends the view that militant democracy is a justified and inherent quality of the democratic state.

Loewenstein, who coined the term 'militant democracy' and was perfectly aware of the available critiques of his solution, suggests a simple – at least in theory – justification. He has a firm belief in liberalism as a spiritual movement which has survived various hardships but nevertheless managed to conquer the world in the second half of the nineteenth century. He contends that democracy has proven to be an immortal idea. In light of these considerations, Loewenstein's solution is relatively straightforward: once fundamental rights are institutionalised and taken seriously, their temporary suspension in the name of democratic self-preservation is justified (Loewenstein 1937a: 432). He continues that 'if democracy believes in the superiority of its absolute values', it must meet the demands of reality and make every effort to rescue it, 'even at the risk and cost of violating fundamental rights' (Loewenstein 1937a: 432). According to Loewenstein, the ultimate end of a liberal government is human dignity and freedom, and governments can and should take preventive legal measures, sometimes even aggressive ones, to ensure progress towards that end.

Another view is that an intolerant reaction from democracies is justified by the mere presence of intolerant actors. Thus, John Locke notes that 'the state's tolerance cannot be extended to those who (in the name of religion) are not willing to be tolerant [of] others' (Locke 1963, as quoted in Sajó [2002: 79]). Karl Popper claims that 'unlimited tolerance must lead to the disappearance of tolerance' (Popper 1950: 546). These views suggest that intolerance can be invoked (temporarily) for the sake of preserving tolerance. John Rawls concludes that intolerant groups do not have any entitlement to complain if they are not tolerated by the majority, because a 'person's right to complain is limited to violations of principles he acknowledges himself' (Fox and Nolte 1995: 18). Although Rawls centres his legal philosophy on his knowledge and experience of American constitutionalism, and strongly believes in the natural strength of free institutions and the inherent stability of a just constitution, he agrees that limits on freedom of the intolerant can be legitimate and justified where a constitutional system seems to be incapable of withstanding the forthcoming crises (Rawls 1971: 219).

Other justifications of militant democracy attempt to address the so-called paradox of majority. This paradox can be found in early works of the well-known advocate for states governed by emergency rule, Carl Schmitt. He claimed that constitutional theory and practice should praise the so-called 'unalterable core' of the constitution. His book *Legality and Legitimacy* explained the problem of democratic states regarding their adherence to the robust regime of proceduralism: in the absence of particular substantive norms, democracy becomes defenceless against organised political forces such as communism or national socialism (Schmitt 2004). Schmitt argues in favour of certain substantive principles in democratic constitutions which cannot be overlooked or abolished, even when prescribed procedures are fully followed (Fox and Nolte 1995: 19). The idea of the unalterable core may serve as an ideal basis by which to legitimise democracy's self-protective measures. Thus, the Schmittian justification of the militant character of democracy primarily aims to prevent the paradox of majority rule becoming reality by ensuring that the foundations of the constitutional order can be suspended through a prescribed procedure.

Sajó develops this argument further and observes that democracy based on majority rule could lead to the deformation of democracy and the establishment of regimes that dissolve it. In the light of this observation he claims that the state's most natural characteristic is self-defence, and that militant democracy can be justified with this characteristic in mind (Sajó 2004: 213). The instinct of democratic self-preservation is inherent to the nature of democracy, which is otherwise nonsensical and susceptible to the threat of overthrow from within. Moreover, democracies are often less troubled by this rationale where specific historical experience has empirically justified its logic. Those democracies have the experience of precautionary activity (Sajó 2004: 215). In other words, a democratic constitution should not be a suicide pact and should incorporate guarantees of its self-preservation to prevent the suspension and alteration of the basic democratic features of current constitutional structures.

There are two final points relevant to the debate on justifying militant democracy. The first observation is that currently there are no realistic alternatives to militant democracy to rescue a democracy when its existence is endangered.[2] The idea that democracy should refrain from providing legal regulations and measures of a militant character and rely on the self-regulative powers of the electoral and political processes is rather idealistic, especially for transitional or fragile democracies. The second observation is that the necessity to have certain self-preservation measures in democratic constitutions is dictated by the tragic events of the past. While it is unlikely that something like communism or fascism will re-emerge, and while the existence of democracy and declarations of rights are currently not at any risk of being transformed into a 'suicide pact', the last couple of decades have demonstrated that democracy – albeit accepted worldwide as the only structure of the state – is not yet completely secured from ideological and physical attacks from within and without. As Loewenstein states at the end of his essay 'to neglect the experience of democracies deceased would be tantamount to surrender for democracies living' (Loewenstein 1937b: 658). Therefore, keeping in mind the tragedies of the past, and in the absence of any realistic alternatives, militant democracy appears to be a justified concept so long as it is 'capable of excluding conceptually and institutionally the abuse of opportunities for restricting rights' (Sajó 2004: 211).

Constitutional Militancy: Contemporary Democracies

The constitutional practice of contemporary democracies reveals that it is hard to find a modern constitution completely lacking militant provisions, even where there is no precise reference to the militant character of a state. Often, it can be inferred from the text of constitutional provisions and pre-ambles.[3] In this respect Pfersmann, for example, claims that democracies are always more or less militant, as the legal structure of militant democracy is on 'a scale of degree with other forms of democracy' (Pfersmann 2004: 53). Sajó develops this argument further by claiming that the state's most natural characteristic is self-defence (Sajó 2004: 213), and if we are to accept these statements then it is only logical to assume there are at least traces of militant democracy in the constitutional framework of most contemporary democracies.

The militancy of a particular constitutional system cannot ordinarily be determined by the text of its national constitution alone. Examples exist of states whose constitutions are silent about militant democracy, yet those polities have nonetheless adopted militant policies via ordinary legislation, as occurred in Spain. The Spanish Constitution of 1978 does not reserve any militant powers for state institutions, nor does it refer to militant measures; however, such features were added in 2002 when the Law on Political Parties was adopted. That law introduced a procedure to ban political parties from politics for certain proscribed activities.[4] Also, some states may attempt to hide or mask their endorsement of the concept of militant democracy, as the idea is often seen as contrary to the very idea of a liberal democracy, and can seem too aggressive to be employed in a true democracy (the Spanish example supports this argument well). The question of the ideal 'domicile' of militant democracy is a challenging one. Pfersmann, for example, admits that once militant elements are introduced through ordinary legislation, the relationship between that legislation and constitutional principles might become problematic (Pfersmann 2004: 63). The only way to overcome this difficulty, according to Pfersmann, is to entrench the measures into the constitution directly. While at a superficial level this option might seem a plausible way to solve potential contradictions, it becomes less realistic when taking into account the complexity and length of constitutional amendment processes, let alone the inherent rigidity of some constitutions. It therefore seems unreasonable to reject the possibility of enacting militant democracy measures through the regular legislative process. The question of the 'domicile of militancy' is arguably incapable of being answered in general terms, and the appropriate method will depend on the particular legal system (Thiel 2009a: 416).

Another aspect of constitutional militancy is the arsenal of militant measures. Loewenstein himself made a contribution to this debate concerning which practices can amount to militant democracy (Loewenstein 1937b: 644). Loewenstein's 'systematic account of anti-fascist legislation in Europe' (Loewenstein 1937b: 638) offers fourteen groups of legislative measures employed to fight fascism and other dangerous movements (Tyulkina 2015a: 55). However, eighty years later, his list of militant measures might be seen to extend beyond the traditional understanding of militant democracy. For example, many measures listed by Loewenstein have since migrated to the domain of criminal law. They are not considered controversial or illiberal by the majority of contemporary liberal democracies. These measures include the prohibition on wearing firearms and the formation of paramilitary armies. Loewenstein's list aims to capture all potential legal provisions directed against any kind of extremist behaviour, including open calls to violence, rebellion, high treason and the formation of armies. However, the practice of militant democracy is more complex than a simple set of measures to deal with all forms of violence and dangerous behaviour directed against the state's structures and its population. Loewenstein's vision of militant democracy is 'naturally . . . dated and rooted in a historical situation completely different from the present' (Thiel 2009a: 401n10). But unlike his justification for a militant stance, the contemporary experience of entrenching militant democracy measures into constitutions and applying them in practice is a far cry from what Loewenstein envisaged.

Germany became the first country in which militant democracy was overtly elevated as a constitutional principle. This was achieved via the German Basic Law of 1949, a response to the criminality of the Nazi regime. Shortly after its establishment, militant democracy became a preventive technique against a new enemy: communism. The next phase in the development of militant democracy as a constitutionally recognised legal structure was the collapse of communist regimes on the European continent. Many young democracies in Central and Eastern Europe followed the German example and introduced various elements of militant democracy in their new constitutions. These mostly allowed restrictions to be imposed on political parties. But constitutional theory and practice can accommodate new realities of social and political life in the domestic and international legal space. 'Every generation [has] its own disease' (Thiel 2009a: 379) and each is fully applicable to the 'life' of democracy. The ideals of constitutional patriotism and democratic romanticism were given up some time ago as viable ways to rescue democracy by ridding 'societies of unjust and oppressive forms of political rule' (Thiel 2009a: 382) (fascist and communist movements). In their absence, it is only logical to equip democracies with the means to stand up against the 'enemies' of new generations. Loewenstein's slogan 'fire is fought with fire' remains apt. However, the fight is no longer limited to the banning of political parties, and the enemies of democracy are no longer just those with communist and fascist agendas.

Militant democracy and its logic might be applied and justified in a much wider range of cases than has traditionally been contemplated, especially in the light of events that have recently dominated constitutional debate, including the rise of populist movements. Constitutional practice of the last decade demonstrates that the scope of application of militant policies now extends beyond the mere prohibition of political parties. For example, today militant practices are employed in response to global terrorism, fundamentalist and coercive religions, and other threats.[5] The jurisprudence of the European Court of Human Rights (ECHR) provides examples of cases involving freedom of religion which could be better rationalised and understood through the prism of militant democracy.[6] The Court's jurisprudence involving, for example, the analysis of Islam and Sharia, is substantially different from traditional religious association cases (Uitz 2007: 177). Moreover, state responses to the threat of terrorism are also being reviewed through the lens of militant democracy, and this concept seems to have great relevance in the so-called war on terror (Roach 2004: 171–208; Sajó 2004).

The translation of militant measures into the anti-terrorism context is clearly symptomatic of the extension of militant democracy generally to a broader sphere of participation in the public discourse. In other words, militant democracy is no longer directed simply to the question of which political parties can compete for elections, but rather who can participate in political discourse in a general sense. If democracy is now concerned with general risk aversion, then new challenges to its structures might be addressed by militant democracy. The depth of theory surrounding militant democracy means that locating our responses within this context provides us with a rich knowledge base and diverse tools with which to respond to emerging crises of legitimacy. These considerations do not help clarify the list of possible militant measures, but they do widen our understanding of the state practices that can be used to protect democracies from their various enemies.

To sum up, today militant states are not a rarity. The list of countries where militant policies are employed is a rather long one.[7] The list of acceptable militant measures has narrowed since Loewenstein's time, yet the scope of application of militant democracy has expanded in the past decade or so. Indeed, it is hard to find a modern constitutional system completely devoid of any sign of militant democracy. The practice no longer carries a negative connotation. Self-defence is the state's most natural characteristic and democracies should make their potential enemies aware that there are legal means at the state's disposal to counteract any efforts to harm to democracy from within.

National constitutions, legislation and jurisprudence are keys to defining the meaning of militant democracy and its place in modern polities; public international law has a prominent role in the constitutional development of modern regimes, especially in the domain of human rights and in the context of a commitment to major democratic principles such as the rule of law, separation of powers, and others. In this respect, it seems legitimate to ask whether public international law is favourable to militant approaches, and if the militant character of a democracy might be a positive obligation imposed on democratic states due to their participation in various international treaties? This query can be taken further. It can be argued that public international law allows various regional and global international organisations to follow a militant course, protecting the democratic foundations and integrity of national institutions as well as guarding the democratic structures of their member states. The rest of this chapter examines this issue further.

Militant Democracy and Public International Law

Militant Democracy: An Obligation Imposed by Public International Law?

This question has been raised and discussed often in recent legal scholarship, but these debates often overlap with debates on the right to democratic governance (or political participation), and even more with the general notion of a 'democratic society'. This is due to the fact that participatory rights are considered to be a critical tool for empowering citizens. Furthermore, the freedom to form and join associations, including political parties, belongs to a list of rights and freedoms usually designated as fundamental to democracy.[8] Among scholars of international law there is a vast amount of scholarly interest in the right to participate and whether popular participation is essential to fully legitimate and responsible governments. Of course, militant measures might be construed as, or indeed amount to, limitations on the right to participate. That is why public international law, especially in its engagement with the right to democratic governance, might be helpful in answering the above question.

One of the most comprehensive accounts of the state of international law on the question of militant democracy was given by Fox and Nolte (1995: 38–59, 59–68). They discuss, at length, whether contemporary international law favours a substantive or procedural view of democracy, and whether democracies have obligations to the international community to maintain democratic government. As to the first query, the authors claim that international law favours a substantive view of democracy, but at the same time it does not entirely reject the procedural view (Fox and Nolte 1995: 38). There are a few examples from international treaties that can be cited in support of the argument that a substantive stance of democracy is more readily welcomed than a purely procedural one. Thus, Article 22(2) of the *International Covenant on Civil and Political Rights* (ICCPR) offers an example of restricting fundamental rights if it is 'necessary in democratic society'. Further, the authors refer to similar limitation clauses elsewhere, and endorse Oscar Garibaldi's conclusion that the notion of 'democracy' used by the ICCPR contemplates a traditional Western society in which the panoply of rights established by the human rights instruments is respected in theory and in practice (Fox and Nolte 1995: 39).

Additional support for this argument can be found in various international treaties such as the EU's admission criteria (also known as the 'Copenhagen Criteria')[9] and the Council of Europe's membership requirements.[10] Further, Fox and Nolte seek to more thoroughly answer the question of whether contemporary international law favours a substantive or procedural view of democracy by evaluating the practice of dissolving political parties and groups combined with the 'abuse clause' provided in Article 5(1) of the ICCPR. Their conclusion is that public international law allows for actions against anti-democratic parties and states can undertake these actions pre-emptively by enacting self-protection legislation (Fox and Nolte: 1995: 59). Therefore, it can at least be said that militant measures do not contravene international human rights standards, and it might even be concluded that a substantive view of democracy is supported to some extent by public international law. This finding is by no means surprising, but it can be counted as an additional argument for the far more vexed debate on the justification of militant democracy. Clearly, it adds to the legitimacy of the practice if it is consistent with general rules and principles endorsed in international law.

Fox and Nolte also tried to determine whether the international community can dictate to a nation the kind of constitution and social contract they should adopt, including whether national constitutions must have elements of self-preservation. The common and reasonable position is that citizens of each state should decide themselves whether they want to live in a democracy regulated by a constitutional 'suicide pact'. However, some provisions in international human rights treaties indicate that certain legal provisions are not allowed even if they are approved by the political majority (such as torture or slavery).

Following this line of argument, Fox and Nolte use as an example the international duty to hold genuine periodic elections.[11] They interpret this as the obligation of states to protect their democratic systems from unelected rulers. This argument might be developed further to the extent that states are obliged to protect their democracies in general from internal overthrow, an obligation that does not only apply to elections. However, even if we establish that a duty to preserve democratic rule exists under public international law, it does not automatically follow that states can be required to enact preventive measures. Provisions requiring states to adopt legislative and other measures to give effect to enumerated rights offer little guidance here, as they typically describe state obligations at a very general level. In the end, Fox and Nolte arrive at the conclusion that while the international community may define a permissible range of responses to authoritarian movements, it should not dictate a choice among them (Fox and Nolte 1995: 69).

I, however, have found that public international law has a more prominent role in promoting and protecting democracy in individual states than outlined above. For example, O'Connell refers to the case of the prohibition of the Batasuna Party (O'Connell 2010: 3) decided by the ECHR in 2009.[12] He argues that the Court's judgment in that case envisages a positive obligation to ban certain parties (O'Connell 2010: 277). The Strasbourg Court approbated governmental actions to outlaw the Batasuna Party, due to the existence of evidence that this party supported the use of political violence. However, as O'Connell argues, the Court 'also went on to indicate that such a conclusion was in accordance with the state's positive obligations' (O'Connell 2010: 278). He warns, however, that paragraph 82 of the judgment should not be read as an explicit declaration of a positive obligation to ban the party (as the Court most likely included that paragraph of the judgment to tacitly bolster the legitimacy of the national authority's actions, while not including that reasoning as part of the ratio decidendi), but it 'leaves open the possibility to argue that the state may have a duty to ban certain political parties' (O'Connell 2010: 278) This argument can be advanced and supported further by the logic that emerges from Article 4 of the *Convention on the Elimination of all Form of Racial Discrimination*, which requires states to proscribe racist organisations. It can be legitimately expected that this requirement be extended to, for example, political parties driven by a racist political agenda (Brems 2006: 131).

Scholars seem to be cautious and sceptical in declaring that militant democracy can be rightly perceived as positively obligatory under public international law. However, there are some signs of moving towards the development of such an obligation, at least in certain cases and in certain international institutions. Furthermore, I have argued that public international law not only supports a substantive view of democracy but also allows various regional and global international organisations to exercise militant measures to protect democratic structures in their member states. The positive orientation of international law towards militant democracy is especially relevant today because of the growing popularity and success of various populist movements across the globe.

Militant Democracy, Political Populism and the Role of International Institutions

Various international treaties reference the ideas and practices of militant democracy. Institutions created by those treaties have the legal capacity to guard and protect democracy in their member states. For example, the EU imposes a duty on its member states to take democracy-protecting measures, with a failure to do so resulting in sanctions. Article 2 of the Treaty of Lisbon states:

the Union is founded on the values of respect for human dignity, freedom, democracy, equality, the rule of law and respect for human rights, including the rights of persons belonging to minorities. These values are common to the Member States in a society in which pluralism, non-discrimination, tolerance, justice, solidarity and equality between women and men prevail.[13]

When these principles are breached, a member state might have some of its rights suspended. This is provided for in Article 7, an article that outlines a two-phased procedure the EU can invoke against a member state.[14] For many years, this so-called 'nuclear option' (Witte and Birnbaum 2018) was considered an exceptional measure and Article 7 was assumed to have been neutralised. This became obvious after the European Commission triggered the article for the first time against Poland in late 2017. By that time, the political environment in Hungary and Poland had deteriorated to the extent that both governments vowed to protect each other in case the EU moved to use its 'emergency option'. Why and how did the EU find itself in a situation in which it was unable to act, even in the presence of the Article 7 mechanism? This is a challenging question to answer in constitutional terms (see Olsen, Chapter 8 this volume). However, despite practical barriers to its use, the importance and meaning of Article 7 should not be underestimated. The very possibility of sanctions provides a firm ground for the claim that the EU can, indirectly, oblige its member states to react and provide defensive legal mechanisms to assist in the preservation of democracy. Politicians and constitutional lawyers should now investigate how this capacity might be translated into practice. The EU should be able to exercise its capacity to employ militant democracy measures as per its foundational legal rules.

To lend additional support to the above claim, one might turn to the provisions of the European Convention on Human Rights and the jurisprudence of the ECHR on various matters related to the activities of political parties. The Court's jurisprudence on the dissolution of political parties clearly indicates that militant democracy is an explicit feature of European law (Macklem 2006: 11). Various provisions of the Convention hint at the presence of a militant spirit, in particular the so-called limitation clauses allowing the imposition of restrictions on the exercise of rights listed in the Convention[15] and the 'abuse clause' in Article 17. The Court defined the function of Article 17 in terms very similar to Loewenstein's argument in support of militant democracy: 'protecting the rights enshrined in the Convention by safeguarding the free functioning of democratic institutions'.[16] One of the main objectives of the abuse clause was defined by the Court as 'to prevent totalitarian or extremist groups from justifying their activities by referring to the Convention'[17] and the Court has closely connected this objective with the notion of self-protective democracy (Harris et al. 2009: 649). Under this interpretation, provisions of the Convention may not be invoked by individuals or groups 'to weaken or destroy the ideals and values of a democratic society' (Harris et al. 2009: 649). In other words, the Convention grants the Court (and hence the Council of Europe) the capacity to apply a militant logic in its decision making and guard democracy in the member states by denying protection to those who attack democracy, its principles and institutions. The Court relied on Article 17 in its early jurisprudence to strike down various appeals of political parties with fascist and communist agendas that were challenging decisions of national authorities to ban them (for details see Harvey 2004: 407). However, the Court changed its tone in more recent cases and left almost no room to invoke the Article 17 'abuse clause' in relation to cases involving the prohibition of political parties (for more details see Tyulkina 2015a: 96–100). The Court made it clear it was not ready anymore to accept abuse clause claims with ease because democracy is a system based on a plurality of political views and ideas. Article 17 cannot be read as a tool to silence political dissent and opposition but targets only very exceptional cases of abuse of rights.

However, this ECHR case law may still support preventive action taken by democratic states in order to prevent harm to the established order. But this possibility is rather limited. ECHR jurisprudence and Venice Commission recommendations[18] helped shape the common European approach to the issue of how a democracy should respond to attempts to threaten its existence: that is, by opening a free marketplace of ideas which is capable of neutralising extremist and allegedly dangerous ideologies. However, states are only allowed to utilise militant measures in extreme situations. This was the main message Council of Europe institutions signalled to the member states – political parties should be banned only in exceptional circumstances and only where political parties openly call for violence or aim to overthrow the existing constitutional order (Tyulkina 2015a: 95–104). As a result, Central and Eastern Europe post-communist states demonstrated a strong hesitance to ban political parties. In 2014, an important study provided statistics on party dissolution cases in Europe and referred to twenty-two party bans in twelve European states (Bourne 2011: 6). Leaving aside pre-1989 party dissolution cases and cases from Turkey after 1989, by 2014 there have only been eight parties banned in post-communist Europe (Bourne 2011: 6). While political parties have also been refused registration in a number of cases, most often these refusals have stemmed from non-compliance with purely formal requirements. So, militant measures were applied by post-communist democracies only sparingly. This trend was welcomed by some commentators. It was understood as a sign of the lack of influence of extremist parties and associations in the region (Tyulkina 2015a: 92).

A few years later, one might claim that militant measures have been underutilised – if the frequency of party dissolution is measured against the number of extremist political movements. It is true that militant provisions are present in national constitutions and legislative acts. And they have important symbolic meaning. They send a message to potential targets, directing and encouraging them to adjust their agendas and programmes to comply with the rules of the game (that is, the democratic principles of political participation and state governance). However, considering the growing support for populist political parties, leaders and governments with sometimes openly anti-democratic agendas, we need to ask ourselves if the Council of Europe, the ECHR and the EU have done enough to stop or at least slow down the rise of such political movements in post-communist European states and more 'aged' democracies in the region.

It appears that, in the case of the ECHR, hesitance to rely on Article 17 and militant measures sent the wrong message to populist political move-ments and their leaders. Instead, the ECHR emphasised the importance of political parties in a democratic setting. It is true that political parties bring together voters and those who exercise power, they voice the views of the society at large and help to make laws that respond to the needs, expecta-tions and requests of the people. This is the very essence of representative aka party democracy. However, ECHR jurisprudence, the Council of Europe and the EU's reaction to political developments in Poland, Hungary and other countries indicate an 'over-trust' in political parties and their good intentions in promoting the ideas of representative governance. Political parties in the region adopted and adjusted their electoral campaigns and political agendas to a common European approach: they act as if parties are safe from dissolution as long as they do not openly advocate violence or an overthrow of the existing constitutional order. At the moment, we can observe in various European democracies how democracy can gradually be harmed and diminished via a peaceful process of legislation-making. It is frustrating to think that European authorities, which have capacity and obligations to defend and protect democracy in the region, did not react more promptly and did not adjust their views on the destructive potential of populist political parties early enough.

Given the success of populist movements, it is important to remind our-selves of one of Loewenstein's arguments in support of militant democracy. Loewenstein treated fascism as an effective legal and political technique (but not an ideology). According to Loewenstein, fascism had no proper intellectual content. Fascists employed 'emotional mobilization' as opposed to reason (Sajó 2012: 562). They sought to intimidate all 'others' – individuals and their groups who did not endorse the movement or the regime (Sajó 2012: 562). Emotions provided the social and political cohesion necessary for the assumption of power through a legal and formally democratic electoral process. As a result, Loewenstein's vision of militant democracy was tailored to the events of the interwar period in Germany. However, Loewenstein's ideas should not be read narrowly. Paradoxically, emotionalism is inherent in democracy and individual rights tend to spur emotionalism. But democracy, especially in the form of representative government, was designed as a non-emotional arrangement. Emotional politics is not a strategy exclusive to fascism. Today, there are many examples of political movements which are rely on emotionalism (Sajó 2012: 562). Therefore, militant democracy, as understood by Loewenstein, should be 'perceived as a set of measures directed against radical emotionalism, a technique that may be relevant in all situations and jurisdictions where emotionalism takes over the political processes' (Sajó 2012: 562; for a critique, see Malkopoulou and Norman, Chapter 5 this volume). In the past few years various democracies experienced exactly this phenomenon – emotionalism, frustrations and disappointment allow populist leaders to mobilise new voters, granting the former access to power and decision making. The similarity between Loewenstein's emotional politics and current populist movements is a painful reminder that democracy is a fragile construction; yet it has a built-in mechanism to guard its own safety. It is about time to remind democracies about their 'right to self-defence' and emphasise the role of public international law and various international organisations in the business of protecting democracy, its values and institutions against those who rely on the benefits of democracy to harm or destroy it. Much has been done; still more remains to be done (Loewenstein 1937b: 656).

Conclusion

Militant democracy is a concept which explains how democracy can protect its structures from attempts to harm or overturn it by abusing or misusing democratic institutions and procedures such as free elections, freedom of speech and freedom of association. It is, however, important to acknowledge that militant democracy is not the only option. It is not a universal panacea that can be applied uniformly to any factual circumstances. There is also a variety of more liberal alternatives which can be adopted instead. These may – in some circumstances – be preferable. However, this chapter has argued that militant democracy is a needed and justified feature of any constitutional system. The state's most natural characteristic is self-defence, and militant democracy can be justified with this characteristic in mind. The instinct of democratic self-preservation is inherent to the nature of democracy, which is otherwise nonsensical and susceptible to the threat of overthrow from within. That is why democratic constitutions worldwide incorporate guarantees of their self-preservation to prevent the suspension and alteration of the basic democratic features of current constitutional structures. These days, it is hard to find a constitutional system lacking elements of constitutional militancy, be it expressly stated in the constitution or implied from constitutional practice.

Recent political developments around the globe demonstrate the strong capacity of populist political movements to mobilise voters, gain their support and access power. Those politicians have acted quickly to turn their electoral promises into legislation and actions. The question is whether constitutional law scholars and practitioners can add anything to the debate on this troubling issue. This chapter has argued that militant democracy is a notion which deserves a place in this debate as it can offer valuable theoretical and practical tools to explain how and why democracy should protect itself from those who abuse its values to harm or destroy it.

The chapter also assessed the role of public international law and international organisations, in particular the EU and the Council of Europe. There are strong signs that public international law not only favours a substantive view of democracy but also establishes a positive obligation for states to preserve and guard democracy and its institutions. Furthermore, public international law allows international organisations to exercise militant measures in relation to member states. Both the EU and the Council of Europe have expressed this in clear legal terms. But their activities indicate that both institutions are hesitant to 'discipline' their member states.

As a matter of fact, democracies are not immune from new types of threats. There is a compelling need to develop a more consistent and legitimate approach to militant democracy. Democracies and the international community cannot be over-optimistic about the future of self-rule. We cannot afford to ignore the fact that populist political movements are gaining support in various parts of the world. In Loewenstein's words,

[s]alvation of the absolute values of democracy is not to be expected from abdication in favour of emotionalism, utilized for wanton or selfish purposes by self-appointed leaders, but by deliberate transformation of obsolete forms and rigid concepts into the new instrumentalities of 'disciplined,' or even – let us not shy from the word – 'authoritarian,' democracy. (Loewenstein 1937b: 657)

It is detrimental for democracy's survival to neglect the experiences of deceased democracies; therefore, constitutional theory and practice should be on guard to protect democracy from the unfortunate mistake of giving its deadly enemies the means by which they may destroy it. Militant democracy is an inherent feature of any constitutional system (domestic or international) based on plural political ideas and opinions. This is the very reason the EU and the Council of Europe should reassess their approach on party prohibition and other militant measures. Militant democracy should not become 'business as usual'. But it should not be treated as irrelevant or as illiberal and dangerous. Rather, militant democracy should be considered as an inherent quality of any democratic state.

Notes

1. For a summary of German Basic Law provisions on militant democracy see Pfersmann (2004: 52); Thiel (2009b: 109–146).
2. For further debate on this see Chapter 5 of this book, Anthoula Malkopoulou and Ludvig Norman, 'Three Models of Democratic Self-Defence'.
3. For example, Article 89 of the French Constitution.
4. Ley 54/1978 de Partidos Politicos/Law 54/1978 on Political Parties.
5. For further details see Tyulkina (2015a: 45–46).
6. See for example, *Kalifatstaat v. Germany* (2000) (Application no. 3828/04); *Refah Partisi (the Welfare Party) and Others* v. *Turkey* (2001) (Applications nos 41340/98, 413428, 41343/98 and 41344/98); *Leyla Sahin* v. *Turkey* (2004) (Application no. 44774/98); *Dogru* v. *France* (2008) (Application no. 7058/05).
7. For more on the case of Australia see Tyulkina (2015b: 517).
8. See for more details see Marks (1996: 209) and ten Napel (2009: 473–478).
9. European Council in Copenhagen, 21–22 June 1993, *Conclusion of the Presidency*, Article 7(A) (iii).
10. Statute of the Council of Europe adopted on 5 May 1949, Articles 3, 4, 7 and 8.
11. Article 25(b) of the ICCPR or Article 3 of the Protocol 1 to the European Convention on Human Rights.
12. *Herri Batasuna* v. *Spain* (2009) (Applications nos 25803/04, 25817/04).
13. The Treaty of Lisbon amending the Treaty on European Union and the Treaty establishing the European Community, signed at Lisbon, 13 December 2007.
14. Article 7(2) and (3) as amended by the Treaty of Lisbon amending the Treaty on European Union and the Treaty establishing the European Community, signed at Lisbon, 13 December 2007.
15. See for example Articles 10(2) and 11(2).

16. *KPD* v. *FRG* (1957) (Application no. 250/57). Decision of the Former European Commission of Human Rights (1957).
17. *Zdanoka* v. *Latvia* (2006) (Application no. 58278/00).
18. The European Commission for Democracy through Law (Venice Commission), *Guidelines on Prohibition of Political Parties and Analogous Measures.* Adopted by the Venice Commission at the 41st Plenary session (Venice, 10–11 December 1999).

REFERENCES

Achen, C. and Bartels, L. 2016. *Democracy for Realists: Why Elections do not Produce Responsive Government*. Princeton, NJ: Princeton University Press.

Ackerman, B. and Fishkin, J. 2004. *Deliberation Day*. New Haven, CT: Yale University Press.

AIV ([Dutch] Advisory Council on International Affairs), The Hague. 2017. *De wil van het volk? Erosie van de democratische rechtsstaat in Europa* [The will of the people? Erosion of democracy under the rule of law in Europe] (No. 104). https://aiv-advice.nl/download/efa5b666-1301-45ef-8702-360939cb4b6a.pdf [https://perma.cc/4V6R-EV5T]

Ágh, A. 2016. 'The decline of democracy in East-Central Europe: Hungary as the worst-case scenario'. *Problems of Post-Communism* 63 (5–6): 277–287.

Akkerman, T. and Rooduijn, M. 2015. 'Pariahs or partners? Inclusion and exclusion of radical right parties and the effects on their policy positions'. *Political Studies* 63 (5): 1140–1157.

Akkerman, T., de Lange, S. and Rooduijn, M. (eds). 2016. *Radical Right-Wing Populist Parties in Western Europe: Into the Mainstream?* London: Routledge.

Albertazzi, D. and Mueller, S. 2013. 'Populism and liberal democracy: populists in government in Austria, Italy, Poland and Switzerland'. *Government and Opposition* 48 (3): 343–371.

Almond, G. 1990. *A Discipline Divided. Schools and Sects in Political Science*. London: Sage.

Anderson, E. S. 1999. 'What is the point of equality?' *Ethics* 109 (2): 287–337.

Armony, A. and Schamis, A. 2005. 'Babel in democratization studies'. *Journal of Democracy* 16 (4): 113–128.

Arvan, M. 2010. 'People do not have a duty to avoid voting badly: reply to Brennan'. *Journal of Ethics and Social Philosophy* 5 (1): 1–6.

Austen-Smith, D. and Banks, J. 2000. *Positive Political Theory I: Collective Preference*. Ann Arbor, MI: University of Michigan Press.

Avineri, S. 2004. 'Introduction'. In A. Sajó (ed.), *Militant Democracy*. Utrecht: Eleven International, 1–14.

Bachrach, P. 1967. *The Theory of Democratic Elitism: A Critique*. Boston, MA: Little Brown.

Backes, U. 1998. *Schutz des Staates: Von der Autokratie zur streitbaren Demokratie*. Wiesbaden: Springer.

Baehr, P. 2008. *Caesarism, Charisma and Fate*. Piscataway, NJ: Transaction Publishers.

Bahry, D., Boaz, C. and Gordon, S. 1997. 'Tolerance, transition, and support for civil liberties in Russia'. *Comparative Political Studies* 30 (4): 484–510.

Bale, T. 2007. 'Are bans on political parties bound to turn out badly? A comparative investigation of three "intolerant" democracies: Turkey, Spain, and Belgium'. *Comparative European Politics* 5 (2): 141–157.

Bale, T. 2014. 'Will it all end in tears? What really happens when democracies use law to ban political parties'. In I. Biezen and H. M. ten Napel (eds), *Regulating Political Parties: European Democracies in Comparative Perspective*. Leiden: Leiden University Press, 195–224.

Ball, T. 1976. 'From paradigms to research programs: towards a post-Kuhnian political science'. *American Journal of Political Science* 20 (1): 151–177.

Bárd, P., Carrera, S., Guild, E. and Kochenov, D. 2016. *An EU Mechanism on Democracy, the Rule of Law and Fundamental Rights*. Brussels: Centre for European Policy Studies. https://www.ceps.eu/publications/eu-mechanism-democracy-rule-law-and-fundamental-rights [https://perma.cc/6KB6-KP56] (accessed 14 June 2018).

Barnett, A. and Carty, P. 2008. *The Athenian Option. Radical Reform for the House of Lords*. Exeter: Imprint Academic.

Barnum, D. 1982. 'Decision making in a constitutional democracy: policy formation in the Skokie free speech controversy'. *The Journal of Politics* 44 (2): 480–508.

Barnum, D. and Sullivan, J. 1989. 'Attitudinal tolerance and political freedom in Britain'. *British Journal of Political Science* 19 (1): 136–146.

Barnum, D. and Sullivan, J. 1990. 'The elusive foundations of political freedom in Britain and the United States'. *Journal of Politics* 52 (3): 719–739.

Barsøe, A. D. 2018. 'A new democratic deficit of the European Union: how the EU should protect liberal democracy and the democratic and self-governing status of member states' citizens'. MA thesis. Aarhus: Department of Political Science, Aarhus University.

Batory, A. 2016. 'Populists in government? Hungary's "system of national cooperation"'. *Democratization* 23 (2): 263–282.

Bedau, H. A. and Kelly, E. 2017. 'Punishment'. In E. N. Zalta (ed.), *The Stanford Encyclopedia of Philosophy*. Winter 2017 edition. https://plato.stanford.edu/archives/win2017/entries/punishment/ [https://perma.cc/BDB2-BAUD]

Beetham, D. 1999. *Democracy and Human Rights*. Cambridge: Polity Press, 157–162.

Belinfante, A. D. and De Reede, J. L. 2015. *Beginselen van het Nederlandse Staatsrecht* (bewerkt door L. Dragstra e.a.). Deventer: Kluwer.

Berlin, I. 2002 [1969]. 'Two concepts of liberty'. In H. Hardy (ed.), *Liberty*. Oxford: Oxford University Press, 166–217.

Bernstein, E. 1993 [1899]. *The Preconditions of Socialism*. Cambridge: Cambridge University Press.

Besselink, L. 2017. 'The bite, the bark and the howl: Article 7 and the rule of law initiatives'. In A. Jakáb and D. Kochenov (eds), *The Enforcement of EU Law against the Member States: Methods against Defiance*. Oxford: Oxford University Press, 128–144.

Blauberger, M. and Kelemen, R. D. 2017. 'Can courts rescue national democracy? Judicial safeguards against democratic backsliding in the EU'. *Journal of European Public Policy* 24 (3): 321–336.

Böckenförde, E. W. 1991. *Staat, Verfassung,Demokratie. Studien zur Verfassungstheorie und zum Verfassungsrecht*. Frankfurt: Suhrkamp.

Bohman, J. 2010. *Democracy Across Borders: From Dêmos to Dêmoi*. Cambridge, MA: The MIT Press.

Bourne, A. 2011. 'Democratisation and the illegalisation of political parties in Europe'. *Working Paper Series on the Legal Regulation of Political Parties*, No. 7, 1–26. http://www.partylaw.leidenuniv.nl/uploads/wp0711.pdf [https://perma.cc/8F9W-XGV9] (last assessed 15 June 2018).

Bourne, A. 2012. 'The proscription of parties and the problem with militant democracy'. *The Journal of Comparative Law* 7 (1): 196–213.

Bourne, A. 2018. 'Militant democracy and the banning of political parties in democratic states: why some do and some don't'. In A. Ellian and B. Rijpkema (eds), *Militant Democracy: Political Science, Law and Philosophy*. Cham: Springer, 23–46.

Brems, E. 2006 'Freedom of political association and the question of party closures'. In W. Sadurski (ed.), *Political Rights Under Stress in the 21st Century Europe*. Oxford: Oxford University Press, 120–195.

Brennan, G. and Lomasky, L. 1997. *Democracy and Decision: The Pure Theory of Electoral Preference*. New York: Cambridge University Press.

Brennan, G. and Pettit, P. 1990. 'Unveiling the vote'. *British Journal of Political Science* 20 (3): 311–333.

Brennan, J. 2009. 'Polluting the polls: when citizens should not vote'. *Australasian Journal of Philosophy* 87 (4): 535–549.

Brennan, J. 2011. *The Ethics of Voting*. Princeton, NJ: Princeton University Press.

Brennan, J. 2017. *Against Democracy*. Princeton, NJ: Princeton University Press.

Brettschneider, C. L. 2007. *Democratic Rights: The Substance of Self-Government*. Princeton, NJ: Princeton University Press.

Brettschneider, C. L. 2010. 'When the state speaks, what should it say?' *Perspectives on Politics* 8 (4): 1–39.

Brettschneider, C. L. 2012. *When the State Speaks, What Should it Say? How Democracies Can Protect Expression and Promote Equality*. Princeton, NJ: Princeton University Press.

Brighouse, H. 1998. 'Civic education and liberal legitimacy'. *Ethics* 108 (4): 719–745.

Brighouse, H. and Fleurbaey, M. 2010. 'Democracy and proportionality'. *Journal of Political Philosophy* 18 (2): 137–155.

Broer, T. 2017. 'Langs de fascistische meetlat'. *Vrij Nederland*. https://www.vn.nl/langs-de-fascistische-meetlat/

Buchstein, H. and Hein, M. 2009. 'Randomizing Europe: the lottery as a decision-making procedure for policy creation in the EU'. *Critical Policy Studies* 3 (1): 29–57.

Bugaric, B. and Ginsburg, T. 2016. 'The assault on postcommunist courts'. *Journal of Democracy* 27 (3): 69–82.

Burke, E. 1999 [1774]. 'Speech to the electors of Bristol'. In E. Burke (ed.), *Select Works of Edmund Burke*. New Imprint of the Payne Edition, Vol. 4. Indianapolis, IN: Liberty Fund, 12–17.

Burnheim, J. 2006. *Is Democracy Possible?* 2nd edn. Sydney: Sydney University Press.

Callenbach, E. and Phillips, M. 2008. 'A citizen legislature'. In E. Callenbach, M. Phillips and K. Sutherland (eds), *A Citizen Legislature/A People's Parliament*. Exeter: Imprint Academic.

Camus, J. and Lebourg, N. 2017. *Far-Right Politics in Europe [Les droites extrêmes en Europe]*. Trans. J. M. Todd. Cambridge, MA: Harvard University Press.

Caney, S. 2009. 'Cosmopolitanism and justice'. In T. Christiano and J. Christman (eds), *Contemporary Debates in Political Philosophy*. Oxford: Blackwell Publishing, 387–407.

Capoccia, G. 2002. 'Anti-system parties: a conceptual reassessment'. *Journal of Theoretical Politics* 14 (1): 9–35.

Capoccia, G. 2005. *Defending Democracy: Reactions to Extremism in Interwar Europe*. Baltimore, MD: Johns Hopkins University Press.

Capoccia, G. 2013. 'Militant democracy: the institutional bases of democratic self-preservation'. *Annual Review of Law and Social Science* 9: 207–226.

Capoccia, G. 2016. 'When do institutions bite? Historical institutionalism and the politics of institutional change'. *Comparative Political Studies* 49 (8): 1095–1127.

Capoccia, G. 2018a. Bounding Democracy. Policy Responses to the Extreme Right in Western Europe 1945–2015. Book manuscript, University of Oxford.

Capoccia, G. 2018b. Between Stools: Militant Democracy and Comparative Politics. Manuscript, University of Oxford.

Capoccia, G. 2018c. Restrictions of Political Freedoms in Democratic States: Conceptualization and Measurement. Manuscript, University of Oxford.

Capoccia, G. and Ziblatt, D. 2010. 'The historical turn in democratization studies: a new research agenda for Europe and beyond'. *Comparative Political Studies* 43 (8–9): 931–968.

Caramani, D. 2017. 'Will vs. reason: the populist and technocratic forms of political representation and their critique to party government'. *American Political Science Review* 111 (1): 54–67.

Casper, G. 2007. 'Caesarism in democratic politics: reflections on Max Weber'. https://ssrn.com/abstract=1032647 (accessed 15 July 2018).

Casper, G. 2017. 'Moving towards an American Caesar'. https://medium.com/ freeman-spogli-institute-for-international-studies/moving-toward-an-american-caesar-e241c32a7696 [https://perma.cc/CDH2-32FB] (accessed 15 July 2018).

Chou, M. 2012. 'Addressing democide and its implications for politics'. *Political Reflection Magazine* 11: 67–70.

Chou, M. 2013. *Theorising Democide: Why and How Democracies Fail*. Basingstoke: Palgrave Pivot.

Cliteur, P. and Ellian, A. 2016. *Legaliteit en legitimiteit: de grondslagen van het recht*. Leiden: Leiden University Press.

Cliteur, P and Rijpkema, B. 2012. 'The foundations of militant democracy'. In A. Ellian and G. Molier (eds), *The State of Exception and Militant Democracy in a Time of Terror*. Dordrecht: Republic of Letters Publishing, 227–272.

Closa, C. 2016. 'Reinforcing EU monitoring of the rule of law: normative arguments, institutional proposals and the procedural limitations'. In C. Closa and D. Kochenov (eds), *Reinforcing Rule of Law Oversight in the European Union*. Cambridge: Cambridge University Press, 15–35.

Cohen, J. 1989. 'Deliberation and democratic legitimacy'. In a. Hamlin and P. Pettit (eds), *The Good Polity: A Normative Analysis of the State*. Oxford: Basil Blackwell, 17–34.

Cohen, J. 1994. 'Pluralism and proceduralism'. *Chicago-Kent Law Review* 69 (3): 589–618.

Cohen, J. 2003. 'For a democratic society'. In S. Freeman (ed.), *The Cambridge Companion to Rawls*. New York: Cambridge University Press, 86–138.

Council of the EU. 2014. 'Press release of the 3362nd Council Meeting, General Affairs'. 16936/14. 16 December 2014. https://www.consilium.europa.eu/ media/24763/146348.pdf [https://perma.cc/XPH9-MGFS]

Crane, D. A. 2018. 'Antitrust and democracy: a case study from German fascism'. University of Michigan Public Law Research Paper No. 18-009. https://ssrn.com/ abstract=3164467 (accessed 15 July 2018).

Crouch, C. 2004. *Post-Democracy*. Cambridge: Polity Press.

Dahl, R. 1961. *Who Governs?* New Haven, CT: Yale University Press.

Dahl, R. 1971. *Polyarchy: Participation and Opposition*. New Haven, CT: Yale University Press.

Dahl, R. 1989. *Democracy and its Critics*. New Haven, CT: Yale University Press.

Dahl, R. A. 2003. *How Democratic is the American Constitution?* New Haven, CT: Yale University Press.

Darwall, S. L. 1977. 'Two kinds of respect'. *Ethics* 88: 36–49.

Davidson, C. and Grofman, B. (eds). 1994. *Quiet Revolution in the South: The Impact of the Voting Rights Act, 1965–1990*. Princeton, NJ: Princeton University Press.

De Koning, P. 2016. '"Patriottische lente" in Milaan'. *NRC Handelsblad*. 30 January 2016. https://www.nrc.nl/nieuws/2016/01/30/patriottische-lente-in-milaan-1581420-a210117 [https://perma.cc/X8PX-79YZ]

de Lange, S. L. and Akkerman, T. 2012. 'Populist parties in Belgium: a case of hegemonic liberal democracy?' In C. Mudde and C. Rovira Kaltwasser (eds), *Populism in Europe and the Americas. Threat or Corrective for Democracy?* Cambridge: Cambridge University Press, 27–46.

Delannoi, G., Dowlen, O and Stone, P. 2013. 'The lottery as a democratic institution'. *Studies in Public Policy* 28. Dublin: The Policy Institute, Trinity College Dublin. https://www.tcd.ie/policy-institute/assets/pdf/Lottery_Report_Oct12.pdf [https://perma.cc/7JRL-3UU4]

Deutscher Bundestag. 2012. https://www.bundestag.de/blob/421028/1cd8348557 7f7f85544885f80a790f34/wd-3-170-12-pdf-data.pdf

Dixon, R. and Ginsburg, T. 2017. 'The forms and limits of constitutions as political insurance'. *International Journal of Constitutional Law* 15 (4): 988–1012.

Downs, A. 1957. *An Economic Theory of Democracy.* New York: HarperCollins.

Duch, R. and Gibson, J. 1992. '"Putting up with" fascists in Western Europe: a comparative, cross-level analysis of political tolerance'. *Western Political Quarterly* 45 (1): 237–273.

Dunn, J. 2005. *Setting the People Free: The Story of Democracy.* London: Atlantic Books.

Dyzenhaus, D. 2000. 'Hermann Heller'. In A. Jacobson and B. Schlink (eds), *Weimar: A Jurisprudence in Crisis.* Berkeley: University of California Press, 249–256.

Dzehtsiarou, K. 2017. *Prisoner Voting and Power Struggle: a Never-Ending Story? VerfBlog.* 30 October 2017. https://verfassungsblog.de/prisoner-voting-and-power-struggle-a-never-ending-story/ [https://dx.doi.org/10.17176/20171030-225743]

Eckberg, D. and Hill, L. 1979. 'The paradigm concept and sociology: a critical review'. *American Sociological Review* 44: 925–937.

Ellian, A., Molier, G. and Rijpkema, B. 2017. 'Weerbare democratie en het probleem van timing: de zaak tegen de NPD'. *Nederlands Juristenblad* 24: 1650–1660.

Elster, J. 1989. *Solomonic Judgments.* New York: Cambridge University Press.

Elster, J. 1998. 'Deliberation and constitution making'. In J. Elster (ed.), *Deliberative Democracy.* Cambridge: Cambridge University Press, 97–122.

Elster, J. 2018. The resistible rise of Louis Bonaparte'. In C. R. Sunstein (ed.), *Can It Happen Here? Authoritarianism in America.* New York: Dey Street Books, 277–312.

Espejo, P. O. 2011. *The Time of Popular Sovereignty: Process and the Democratic State.* Pennsylvania, PA: Pennsylvania State University Press.

Esses, V. M., Medianu, S. and Lawson, A. S. 2013. 'Uncertainty, threat, and the role of the media in promoting the dehumanization of immigrants and refugees'. *Journal of Social Issues* 69 (3): 518–536.

European Commission. 2014. 'A new EU Framework to strengthen the rule of law. COM (2014)158 final. 3 November 2014. https://eur-lex.europa.eu/legal-content/EN/TXT/PDF/?uri=CELEX:52014DC0158&from=EN [https://perma.cc/77Y3-LALF]

Farr, J. 1995. 'Remembering the revolution: behaviouralism in political science'. In J. Farr, J. Dryzek and S. Leonard (eds), *Political Science in History. Research Programs and Political Traditions.* Cambridge: Cambridge University Press, 198–224.

Farrell, D. 2013. 'Deliberative democracy Irish style: Ireland's Constitutional Convention of 2013'. *Inroads* 34: 110–117.

Fennema, M. 2016. *Geert Wilders: tovenaarsleerling.* Amsterdam: Prometheus.

Fennema, M. and Maussen, M. 2000. 'Dealing with extremists in public discussion: Front National and 'Republican Front' in France'. *Journal of Political Philosophy* 8 (3): 379–400.

Ferrara, A. 2018. 'Can political liberalism help us rescue "the people" from populism?' *Philosophy and Social Criticism* 44 (4): 463–477.

Fishkin, J. S. 1993. *Democracy and Deliberation: New Directions for Democratic Reform.* New Haven, CT: Yale University Press.

Fishkin, J. S. 1995. *The Voice of the People: Public Opinion and Democracy.* New Haven, CT: Yale University Press.

Fishkin, J. S. 2011. *When the People Speak: Deliberative Democracy and Public Consultation.* New Haven, CT: Yale University Press.

Flüman, G. 2015. *Streitbare Demokratie in Deutschland und den Vereinigten Staaten. Der staatliche Umgang mit nichtgewalttätigem politischem Extremismus im Vergleich.* Weisbaden: VS Verlag.

Follesdal, A. and Hix, S. 2006. 'Why there is a democratic deficit in the EU: a response to Majone and Moravcsik. *JCMS: Journal of Common Market Studies* 44 (3): 533–562.

Forsdyke, S. 2005. *Exile, Ostracism, and Democracy: The Politics of Expulsion in Ancient Greece.* Princeton, NJ: Princeton University Press.

Fox, G. H. and Nolte, G. 1995. 'Intolerant democracies'. *Harvard International Law Journal* 36 (1): 1–70.

Frankenberg, G. 2004. 'The learning sovereign'. In A. Sajó (ed.), *Militant Democracy.* Utrecht: Eleven International Publishing, 113–132.

Freeden, M. 1996. *Ideologies and Political Theory: A Conceptual Approach.* Oxford: Clarendon.

Freeden, M. 2003. *Ideology. A Very Short Introduction.* New York: Oxford University Press.

Freedom House. 2017. 'Freedom in the world 2017'. https://freedomhouse.org/report/freedom-world/freedom-world-2017 [https://perma.cc/JRU6-DJBT]

Fung, A. 2003. 'Recipes for public spheres: eight institutional design choices and their consequences'. *Journal of Political Philosophy* 11 (3): 338–367.

Garry, J., Stevenson, C. and Stone, P. 2015. 'Imagined contact and deliberating across deep divides: how random citizens can make binding decisions'. Paper presented at the Annual Meeting of the International Society of Political Psychology.

Geling, G. J. 'We moeten niet antidemocratische, maar illiberale partijen vrezen'. *Knack.* 31 October 2016. https://www.knack.be/nieuws/wereld/we-moeten-niet-antidemocratische-maar-illiberale-partijen-vrezen/article-opinion-771105.html [https://perma.cc/HV8L-CGUJ]

Gibson, J. 1987. 'Homosexuals and the Ku Klux Klan: a contextual analysis of political tolerance'. *Western Political Quarterly* 40 (3): 427–448.

Gibson, J. 1988. 'Political intolerance and political repression during the McCarthy Red scare'. *American Political Science Review* 82 (2): 511–529.

Gibson, J. 1989. 'The policy consequences of political intolerance: political repression during the Vietnam War era'. *Journal of Politics* 51 (1): 13–35.

Gibson, J. 1992a. 'Alternative measures of political tolerance: must tolerance be "least-liked"?' *American Journal of Political Science* 36 (2): 560–577.

Gibson, J. 1992b. 'The Political consequences of intolerance: cultural conformity and political freedom'. *American Political Science Review* 86 (2): 338–356.

Gibson, J. 1996. 'The paradoxes of political tolerance in processes of democratisation'. *Politikon* 23 (2): 5–21.

Gibson, J. 2002. 'Becoming tolerant? Short-term changes in Russian political culture'. *British Journal of Political Science* 32 (April): 309–334.

Gibson, J. 2006. 'Enigmas of intolerance: fifty years after Stouffers communism, conformity, and civil liberties'. *Perspectives on Politics* 4 (1): 21–34.

Gibson, J. 2011. 'Political intolerance in the context of democratic theory'. In R. Goodin (ed.), *The Oxford Handbook of Political Science*. Oxford: Oxford University Press, 409–427.

Gibson, J. 2013. 'Measuring political tolerance and general support for pro-civil liberties policies'. *Public Opinion Quarterly* 77 (1): 45–68.

Gibson, J. and Bingham, R. 1982. 'On the conceptualization and measurement of political tolerance'. *American Political Science Review* 76 (3): 603–620.

Gibson, J. and Bingham, R. 1984. 'Skokie, Nazis, and the elitist theory of democracy'. *The Western Political Quarterly* 37 (1): 32–47.

Gibson, J. and Bingham, R. 1985. *Civil Liberties and Nazis: The Skokie Free-Speech Controversy*. New York: Praeger.

Gibson, J. and Duch, R. 1991. 'Elitist theory and political tolerance in Western Europe'. *Political Behavior* 13 (3): 191–212.

Gibson, J. and Duch, R. 1993. 'Political intolerance in the USSR: the distribution and etiology of mass opinion'. *Comparative Political Studies* 26 (3): 286.

Gibson, J. and Gouws, A. 2001. 'Making tolerance judgments: the effects of context, local and national'. *Journal of Politics* 63 (4): 1067–1090.

Goldstein, R. 1978. *Political Repression in Modern America: From 1870 to the Present*. Boston, MA: Schennckmann.

Goodin, R. E. 2007. 'Enfranchising all affected interests, and its alternatives'. *Philosophy and Public Affairs* 35 (1): 40–68.

Goodin, R. E. and Dryzek, J. S. 2006. 'Deliberative impacts: the macro-political uptake of mini-publics'. *Politics and Society* 34 (2): 219–244.

Greenberg, U. 2014. *The Weimar Century: German Émigrés and the Intellectual Foundations of the Cold War*. Princeton, NJ: Princeton University Press.

Greskovits, B. 2015. 'The hollowing and backsliding of democracy in East Central Europe'. *Global Policy* 6 (1): 28–35.

Griffith, E., Plamenatz, J. and Pennock R. 1956. 'Cultural prerequisites to a successfully functioning democracy: a symposium'. *American Political Science Review* 50 (1): 101–137.

Guerrero, A. 2014. 'Against elections: the lottocratic alternative'. *Philosophy and Public Affairs* 42 (2): 135–178.

Habermas, J. 1985. 'Civil disobedience: litmus test for the democratic constitutional state'. *Berkeley Journal of Sociology* 30: 95–116.

Habermas, J. 1992. *Faktizität und Geltung: Beiträge zur Diskurstheorie des Rechts und des Demokratischen Rechtstaates*. Revised edn. Frankfurt: Suhrkamp.

Habermas, J. 1996. *Die Einbeziehung des Anderen: Studien zur Politischen Theorie*. Frankfurt: Suhrkamp.

Hall, P. and Taylor, R. 1996. 'Political science and the three new institutionalisms'. *Political Studies* 44: 936–957.

Harris, D., O'Boyle, M., Bates, E. and Buckley, C. 2009. *Law of the European Convention on Human Rights*. Oxford: Oxford University Press.

Harvey, P. 2004. 'Militant democracy and the European Convention on Human Rights'. *European Law Review* 29: 407–420.

Haslam, N., et al. 2008. 'Attributing and denying humanness to others'. *European Review of Social Psychology* 19 (1): 55–85.

Hawkins, K. A. 2016. 'Chavismo, liberal democracy, and radical democracy'. *Annual Review of Political Science* 19: 311–329.

Hawkins, K. A. and Rovira Kaltwasser, C. 2017a. 'The ideational approach to populism'. *Latin American Research Review* 52 (4): 513–528.

Hawkins, K. A. and Rovira Kaltwasser, C. 2017b. 'What the (ideational) study of populism can teach us, and what it can't'. *Swiss Political Science Review* 23 (4): 526–542.

Hayek, F. A. 1944. *The Road to Serfdom*. Chicago: University of Chicago Press.

Heller, A. 2017. 'Commentary on "The rise of illiberalism in Europe: a discussion of Peter Krasztev and Jon Van Til's *The Hungarian Patient: Social Opposition to an Illiberal Democracy*"'. *Perspectives on Politics* 15 (2): 542–544.

Heller, H. 2000 [1928]. 'Political democracy and social homogeneity'. In A. Jacobson and B. Schlink (eds), *Weimar: A Jurisprudence in Crisis*. Berkeley: University of California Press, 256–279.

Heller, H. 2007 [1929]. *Europa und der Faschismus*. Ed. E. Von Krosigk. Saarbrucken: VDM Verlag.

Heller, H. 2015 [1933]. 'Authoritarian liberalism?' *European Law Journal* 21 (3): 295–301.

Hermens, F. A. 1941. *Democracy or Anarchy? A Study of Proportional Representation*. South Bend, IN: University of Notre Dame Press.

Honig, B. 2001. 'Dead rights, live futures: a reply to Habermas's "Constitutional democracy"'. *Political Theory* 29 (6): 792–805.

Invernizzi Accetti, C. and Zuckerman, I. 2017. 'What's wrong with militant democracy?' *Political Studies* 65 (1S): 182–199.

Isaacs, T. 2014. 'Collective responsibility and collective obligation'. *Midwest Studies in Philosophy* XXXVIII: 40–57.

Issacharoff, S. 2007. 'Fragile democracies'. *Harvard Law Review* 120 (6): 1405–1467.

Issacharoff, S. 2015. *Fragile Democracies: Contested Power in the Era of Constitutional Courts*. New York: Cambridge University Press.

Jabloner, C. 1998. 'Kelsen and his circle: the Viennese years'. *European Journal of International Law* 9 (2): 368–385.

Jackman, R. 1972. 'Political elites, mass publics, and support for democratic principles'. *Journal of Politics* 34 (3): 753–773.

Jackson, B. 2013. 'Social democracy'. In M. Freeden, M. Stears, M. and L. T. Sargeant (eds), *The Oxford Handbook of Political Ideologies*. Oxford: Oxford University Press, 348–363.

Jakab, A. 2016. 'The EU Charter of Fundamental Rights as the most promising way of enforcing the rule of law against EU member states'. In C. Closa and D. Kochenov (eds), *Reinforcing Rule of Law Oversight in the European Union*. Cambridge: Cambridge University Press, 187–205.

Jenne, E. K. and Mudde, C. 2012. 'Can outsiders help? Hungary's illiberal turn'. *Journal of Democracy* 23 (3): 147–155.

Jessurun D'Oliveira, H. U. 2017. 'De grenzen van de tolerantie (review of: Weerbare democratie: de grenzen van democratische tolerantie)'. *De Republikein* 13 (1): 22–29.

Johst, D. 2016. *Begrenzung des Rechtsgehorsams: Die Debatte um Widerstand und Widerstandsrecht in Westdeutschland 1945–1968*. Tübingen: Mohr Siebeck.

Jonker, J. and de Winther, W. 2018. 'Hardvochtig? Het gaat om overleven'. *De Telegraaf.* 7 April 2018. https://www.telegraaf.nl/nieuws/1884196/wilders-hardvochtig-het-gaat-om-overleven [https://perma.cc/525R-4RZU].

Jovanovic, M. 2016. 'How to justify "militant democracy": meta-ethics and the game-like character of democracy'. *Philosophy and Social Criticism* 42 (8): 745–762.

Kelsen, H. 1948. 'Absolutism and relativism in philosophy and politics'. *American Political Science Review* 42 (5): 906–914.

Kelsen, H. 1955. 'Foundations of democracy'. *Ethics* 66 (1, Part 2): 1–101.

Kelsen, H. 1967. *Demokratie und Sozialismus: Ausgewählte Aufsätze*. Vienna: Wiener Volksbuchhandlung.

Kelsen, H. 2006 [1932]. *Verteidigung der Demokratie: Abhandlungen zur Demokratietheorie*. Tübingen: Mohr Siebeck.

Kelsen, H. 2013 [1929]. *The Essence and Value of Democracy*. Plymouth: Rowman & Littlefield.

Key, V. O. 1961. *Public Opinion and American Democracy*. New York: Knopf.

Kieft, E. 2017. *Het Verboden Boek: Mein Kampf en de aantrekkingskracht van het nazisme*. Amsterdam/Antwerpen: Atlas Contact.

Kirchhof, P. and Kommers, D. (eds). 1993. *Germany and its Basic Law*. Baden-Baden: Nomos.

Kirshner, A. S. 2010. 'Proceduralism and popular threats to democracy'. *Journal of Political Philosophy* 18 (4): 405–424.

Kirshner, A. S. 2014. *A Theory of Militant Democracy. The Ethics of Combatting Political Extremism*. New Haven, CT: Yale University Press.

Kochenov, D. and Pech, L. 2015. 'Monitoring and enforcement of the rule of law in the EU: rhetoric and reality'. *European Constitutional Law Review* 11 (3): 512–540.

Kolodny, N. 2014. 'Rule over none II: social equality and the justification of democracy'. *Philosophy & Public Affairs* 42 (4): 287–336.

Kommers, D. P. 1997. *The Constitutional Jurisprudence of the Federal Republic of Germany*. 2nd edn, revised and expanded. Durham, NC and London: Duke University Press.

Kommers, D. P. 2006. 'The Federal Constitutional Court: guardian of German democracy'. *The Annals of the American Academy of Political and Social Science* 603: 111–128.

Kornai, J. 2015. 'Hungary's U-turn: retreating from democracy'. *Journal of Democracy* 26 (3): 34–48.

Krastev, I. 2007. 'The strange death of the liberal consensus'. *Journal of Democracy* 18 (4): 56–63.

Laclau, E. 2005. *On Populist Reason*. London: Verso.

Laclau, E. and Mouffe, C. 1985. *Hegemony and Socialist Strategy: Towards a Radical Democratic Politics*. London: Verso.

Landemore, H. 2012. *Democratic Reason: Politics, Collective Intelligence, and the Rule of the Many*. Princeton, NJ: Princeton University Press.

Leib, E. 2004. *Deliberative Democracy in America: A Proposal for a Popular Branch of Government*. University Park, PA: Pennsylvania State University Press.

Lenowitz, J. A. 2015. 'Book review: *A Theory of Militant Democracy: The Ethics of Combatting Political Extremism*'. *The Journal of Politics* 77 (4): e1–e2.

Lerner, M. 1938. *It Is Later Than You Think: The Need for a Militant Democracy*. New York: Viking Books.

Levitsky, S. and Way, L. 2010. *Electoral Authoritarianism*. Cambridge University Press.

Levitsky, S. and Ziblatt, D. 2018. *How Democracies Die*. New York: Penguin Random House.

Lievens, M. 2010. 'Carl Schmitt's two concepts of humanity'. *Philosophy and Social Criticism* 36 (8): 917–934.

Linz, J. and Stepan, A. 1996. *Problems of Democratic Transition and Consolidation: Southern Europe, South America, and Post-Communist Europe*. Baltimore, MD: Johns Hopkins University Press.

Lipset, S. M. 1959. 'Some social requisites of democracy: economic development and political legitimacy'. *American Political Science Review* 53 (1): 69–105.

Locke, J. 1963 [1689]. *A Letter Concerning Toleration: Latin and English Texts*. Ed. Mario Montuori. The Hague: Martinus Nijhoff.

Loewenstein, K. 1937a. 'Militant democracy and fundamental rights, I'. *American Political Science Review* 31 (3): 417–432.

Loewenstein, K. 1937b. 'Militant democracy and fundamental rights, II'. *American Political Science Review* 31 (4): 638–658.

López-Guerra, C. 2005. 'Should expatriates vote?' *Journal of Political Philosophy* 13 (2): 216–234.

López-Guerra, C. 2010. 'The enfranchisement lottery'. *Politics, Philosophy & Economics* 10 (2): 211–233.

López-Guerra, C. 2014. *Democracy and Disenfranchisement: The Morality of Electoral Exclusions*. New York: Oxford University Press.

López-Guerra, C. 2017. 'Book review: *A Theory of Militant Democracy: The Ethics of Combating Political Extremism*, by Alexander Kirshner'. *Political Theory* 45 (3): 419–423.

Lublin, D. 2007. *The Republican South: Democratization and Partisan Change.* Princeton, NJ: Princeton University Press.

Lupia, A. and McCubbins, M. 1998. *The Democratic Dilemma: Can Citizens Learn What They Need to Know?* New York: Cambridge University Press.

McCloskey, H. 1964. 'Consensus and ideology in American politics'. *American Political Science Review* 58 (2): 361–382.

McCloskey, H. and Brill, A. 1983. *The Dimensions of Tolerance. What Americans Believe About Civil Liberties.* New York: Russell Sage.

Macklem, P. 2006. 'Militant democracy and the paradox of self-determination'. *International Journal of Constitutional Law* 4 (3): 488–516.

Macklem, P. 2012. 'Guarding the perimeter: militant democracy and religious freedom in Europe'. *Constellations* 19 (4): 575–590.

Macklin, A. and Bauböck, R. (eds). 2015. *The Return of Banishment.* EUI Working Paper RSCAS 2015/14. http://cadmus.eui.eu/bitstream/handle/1814/34617/RSCAS_2015_14.pdf [https://perma.cc/5ES8-WWXR]

Mainwaring, S. 2012. 'From representative democracy to participatory competitive authoritarianism: Hugo Chávez and Venezuelan politics'. *Perspectives on Politics* 10 (4): 955–967.

Mainwaring, S. and Pérez-Liñán, A. 2013. *Democracies and Dictatorships in Latin America. Emergence, Survival, and Fall.* New York: Cambridge University Press.

Mair, P. 2013. *Ruling the Void: The Hollowing-Out of Western Democracy.* London: Verso.

Malik, M. 2008. 'Engaging with extremists'. *International Relations* 22 (1): 85–104.

Malkopoulou, A. 2016. 'De-presentation rights as a response to extremism'. *Critical Review of Social and Political Philosophy* 19 (3): 301–319.

Malkopoulou, A. 2017. 'Ostracism and democratic self-defence in Athens'. *Constellations* 24 (4): 623–636.

Malkopoulou, A. and Norman, L. 2018. 'Three models of democratic self-defence: militant democracy and its alternatives'. *Political Studies* 66 (2): 442–458.

Manin, B. 1997. *The Principles of Representative Government.* New York: Cambridge University Press.

Mannheim, K. 1943. *Diagnoses of Our Time: Wartime Essays of a Sociologist.* London: Routledge.

Marks, S. 1996. 'The European Convention on Human Rights and its "democratic society"'. *The British Yearbook of International Law* 66 (1): 209–223.

Marquart-Pyatt, S. and Paxton, P. 2007. 'In principle and in practice: learning political tolerance in Eastern and Western Europe'. *Political Behavior* 29 (1): 89–113.

May, K. 1952. 'A set of independent necessary and sufficient conditions for simple majority decision'. *Econometrica* 20 (4): 680–684.

Meijers, M. J. 2016. 'Democratische Wilders'. *Trouw.* 24 October 2016.

Menéndez, A. J. 2015. 'Herman Heller NOW'. *European Law Journal* 21 (3): 285–294.

Mickey, R., Levitsky, S. and Way, L. A. 2017. 'Is America still safe for democracy? Why the United States is in danger of backsliding'. *Foreign Affairs* 96 (3): 20–29.

Mill, J. S. 2008 [1861]. 'Considerations on representative government'. In J. Gray (ed.), *On Liberty and Other Essays*. New York: Oxford University Press, 203–467.

Miller, D. 2007. *National Responsibility and Global Justice*. Oxford: Oxford University Press.

Miller, D. 2012. 'Are human rights conditional?' *Centre for the Study of Social Justice Working Paper Series SJ020*. University of Oxford. September 2012. https://www.politics.ox.ac.uk/materials/centres/social-justice/working-papers/SJ020_Miller_Are%20Human%20Rights%20Conditional%20final%20draft.pdf [https://perma.cc/6H9X-7MW9]

Minkenberg, M. 2006. 'Repression and reaction: militant democracy and the radical right in Germany and France'. *Patterns of Prejudice* 40 (1): 25–44.

Molier, G. 2016. 'Het verbod van een politieke partij: een anomalie in een democratie?' *Nederlands Juristenblad* 34: 2438–2446.

Molier, G. and Rijpkema, B. 2017. 'Naar een afzonderlijke wettelijke bepaling inzake het partijverbod'. *Nederlands Juristenblad*: 662–664.

Molier, G. and Rijpkema, B. 2018. 'Germany's new militant democracy regime: National Democratic Party II and the German Federal Constitutional Court's 'potentiality' criterion for party bans: Bundesverfassungsgericht, Judgment of 17 January 2017, 2 BvB 1/13, National Democratic Party II'. *European Constitutional Law Review* 14 (2): 394–409.

Möllers, H. 2010. Extremisten vor dem Bundesverfassungsgerich. In *Jahrbuch für Extremismus- und Terrorismusforschung* 2009/10.

Mommsen, H. 1996. *The Rise and Fall of Weimar Democracy*. Chapel Hill, NC: University of North Carolina Press.

Moravcsik, A. 2004. 'Is there a "democratic deficit" in world politics? A framework for analysis'. *Government and Opposition* 39 (2): 336–363.

Morris, C. W. 1991. 'Punishment and loss of moral standing'. *Canadian Journal of Philosophy* 21 (1): 53–79.

Mouffe, C. 2000. *The Democratic Paradox*. London: Verso.

Mouffe, C. 2005a. *On the Political*. London: Routledge.

Mouffe, C. 2005b. 'The "end of politics" and the challenge of right-wing populism'. In F. Panizza (ed.), *Populism and the Mirror of Democracy*. London: Verso, 50–71.

Mouffe, C. 2013. *Agonistics: Thinking the World Politically*. London: Verso.

Mudde, C. 2004a. 'The populist zeitgeist'. *Government and Opposition* 39 (4): 541–563.

Mudde, C. 2004b. 'Conclusion: defending democracy and the extreme right'. In R. Eatwell and C. Mudde (eds), *Western Democracies and the New Extreme Right Challenge*. London: Routledge, 191–212.

Mudde, C. 2015. 'A discussion of Alexander S. Kirschner's *A Theory of Militant Democracy: The Ethics of Combatting Political Extremism*'. *Perspectives on Politics* 13 (3): 789–791.

Mudde, C. 2016. 'Europe's populist surge: a long time in the making'. *Foreign Affairs* 95 (6): 25–30.

Mudde, C. and Rovira Kaltwasser, C. 2012. 'Populism: corrective *and* threat to democracy'. In C. Mudde, and C. Rovira Kaltwasser (eds), *Populism in Europe and the Americas. Threat or Corrective for Democracy?* Cambridge: Cambridge University Press, 205–222.

Mudde, C. and Rovira Kaltwasser, C. (eds). 2012. *Populism in Europe and the Americas: Threat or Corrective for Democracy?* Cambridge: Cambridge University Press.

Mudde, C. and Rovira Kaltwasser, C. 2013. 'Exclusionary vs. inclusionary populism: comparing contemporary Europe and Latin America'. *Government and Opposition* 48 (2): 147–174.

Mudde, C. and Rovira Kaltwasser, C. 2017. *Populism. A Very Short Introduction.* New York: Oxford University Press.

Mudde, C. and Rovira Kaltwasser, C. 2018. 'Studying populism in comparative perspective: reflections on the contemporary and future research agenda'. *Comparative Political Studies* 51 (13): 1667–1693.

Müller, J.-W. 2011a. 'Militant democracy'. In M. Rosenfeld and A. Sajó (eds), *The Oxford Handbook of Comparative Constitutional Law.* Oxford: Oxford University Press, 1253–1269.

Müller, J.-W. 2011b. *Contesting Democracy.* New Haven, CT: Yale University Press.

Müller, J.-W. 2012a. 'A "practical dilemma which philosophy alone cannot resolve?" Rethinking militant democracy: an introduction'. *Constellations* 19 (4): 536–539.

Müller, J.-W. 2012b. 'Beyond Militant Democracy?' *New Left Review* 73 (January–February): 39–47.

Müller, J.-W. 2012c. 'Militant democracy', in A. Sajó and M. Rosenfeld (eds), *Oxford Handbook of Comparative Constitutional Law.* Oxford: Oxford University Press, 1253–1269.

Müller, J.-W. 2013a. 'Defending democracy within the EU'. *Journal of Democracy* 24 (2): 138–149.

Müller, J.-W. 2013b. *Safeguarding Democracy Inside the EU.* Washington, DC: Transatlantic Academy.

Müller, J.-W. 2015. 'Should the EU protect democracy and the rule of law inside member states?' *European Law Journal* 21 (2): 141–160.

Müller, J.-W. 2016a. 'Protecting popular self-government from the people? New normative perspectives on militant democracy'. *Annual Review of Political Science* 19: 249–265.

Müller, J.-W. 2016b. *What is Populism?* University Park, PA: University of Pennsylvania Press.

Müller, J.-W. 2017a. 'A democracy commission of one's own, or what it would take for the EU to safeguard liberal democracy in its member states'. In A. Jakáb and D. Kochenov (eds), *The Enforcement of EU Law against the Member States: Methods against Defiance.* Oxford: Oxford University Press, 234–251.

Müller, J.-W. 2017b. 'Commentary on "The rise of illiberalism in Europe: a discussion of Peter Krasztev and Jon Van Til's *The Hungarian Patient: Social Opposition to an Illiberal Democracy*"'. *Perspectives on Politics* 15 (2): 549–550.

Niesen, P. 2002. 'Anti-extremism, negative republicanism, civic society: three paradigms for banning political parties'. *German Law Journal* 3 (7): 1–46.

Niesen, P. 2004. 'Anti-extremism, negative republicanism, civic society: three paradigms for banning political parties'. In P. Zumbansen and R. A. Miller (eds), *Annual of German and European Law. Volume I (2003)*. Oxford: Berghahn, 81–112.

Niesen, P. 2012. 'Banning the former ruling party'. *Constellations* 19 (4): 540–561.

Norman, L. 2017. 'Defending the European political order: visions of politics in the response to the radical right'. *European Journal of Social Theory* 20 (4): 531–549.

Nunn, C., Crockett, H. and Williams, A. 1978. *Tolerance for Nonconformity*. San Francisco, CA: Jossey-Bass.

Ochoa Espejo, P. 2011. *The Time of Popular Sovereignty*. University Park, PA: Pennsylvania State University Press.

O'Connell, R. 2010. 'Realising political equality: the European Court of Human Rights and positive obligations in a democracy'. *Northern Ireland Legal Quarterly* 61 (3): 263–279.

O'Donnell, G. 1973. *Modernization and Bureaucratic-Authoritarianism: Studies in South American Politics*. Berkeley, CA: University of California Press.

Olsen, T. V. and Rostbøll, C. F. 2017. 'Why withdrawal from the European Union is undemocratic'. *International Theory* 9 (3): 436–465.

Orbán, V. 2014. 'Speech at the 25th Bálványos Summer Free University and Student Camp'. 26 July 2014. http://www.kormany.hu/en/the-prime-minister/the-prime-minister-s-speeches/prime-minister-viktor-orban-s-speech-at-the-25th-balvanyos-summer-free-university-and-student-camp [https://perma.cc/K29B-UBK2]

Pappas, T. 2014. 'Populist democracies: post-authoritarian Greece and post-communist Hungary'. *Government and Opposition* 49 (1): 1–23.

Pech, L. and Scheppele, K. L. 2017. 'Illiberalism within: rule of law backsliding in the EU'. *Cambridge Yearbook of European Legal Studies* 19: 3–47.

Pedahzur, A. 2004. 'The defending democracy and the extreme right: a comparative analysis'. In R. Eatwell and C. Mudde (eds), *Democracy and the New Extreme Right Challenge*. London: Routledge, 108–133.

Peffley, M. and Rohrschneider, R. 2003. 'Democratization and political tolerance in seventeen countries: a multi-level model of democratic learning'. *Political Research Quarterly* 56 (3): 243–257.

Peters, B. 1993. *Die Integration moderner Gesellschaften*. Frankfurt am Main: Suhrkamp.

Petersen, M., Slothuus, R., Stubager, R. and Togeby, L. 2011. 'Freedom for all? The strength and limits of political tolerance'. *British Journal of Political Science* 41 (3): 581–597.

Pettit, P. 1997. *Republicanism: A Theory of Freedom and Government*. Oxford: Oxford University Press.

Pettit, P. 2012. *On the People's Terms*. Cambridge: Cambridge University Press.

Pfersmann, O. 2004. 'Shaping militant democracy: legal limits to democratic stability'. In A. Sajó (ed.), *Militant Democracy*. Utrecht: Eleven International Publishing, 47–68.

Pierson, P. 2006. 'Public policies as institutions'. In I. Shapiro, S. Skowronek and D. Galvin (eds), *Rethinking Political Institutions*. New York: New York University Press, 114–134.

Plattner, M. 2010. 'Populism, pluralism, and liberal democracy'. *Journal of Democracy* 21 (1): 81–92.

Popper, K. 1950. *The Open Society and its Enemies*. Princeton, NJ: Princeton University Press.

Posner, E. A. 2005. 'Political trials in domestic and international law'. *Duke Law Journal* 55: 75–152.

Prothro, J. and Grigg, C. 1960. 'Fundamental principles of democracy: bases of agreement and disagreement'. *Journal of Politics* 22 (1): 276–294.

Przeworski, A. 1991. *Democracy and the Market*. New York: Cambridge University Press.

Przeworski, A. 1999. 'Minimalist conception of democracy: a defense'. In I. Shapiro and C. Hacker-Cordón (eds), *Democracy's Value*. Cambridge: Cambridge University Press, 23–55.

Quong, J. 2004. 'The rights of unreasonable citizens'. *Journal of Political Philosophy* 12 (3): 314–335.

Raabe, J. 2014. 'Principles of representation throughout the world: constitutional provisions and electoral systems'. *International Political Science Review* 36 (5): 578–592.

Rawls, J. 1971. *A Theory of Justice*. Cambridge, MA: Harvard University Press.

Raz, J. 1979. *The Authority of Law*. New York: Oxford University Press.

Rehfeld, A. 2005. *The Concept of Constituency: Political Representation, Democratic Legitimacy, and Institutional Design*. New York: Cambridge University Press.

Rigoll, D. 2017. 'Streit um die Streitbare Demokratie: Ein Rückblick auf die Anfangsjahrzehnte der Bundesrepublik'. *Aus Politik und Zeitgeschichte* 67: 40–45.

Rijpkema, B. 2015. *Weerbare democratie: de grenzen van democratische tolerantie*. Amsterdam: Nieuw Amsterdam Uitgevers. (English edition: Rijpkema, B. 2018. *Militant Democracy: The Limits of Democratic Tolerance*. London: Routledge.)

Rijpkema, B. 2018. 'Democratie als zelfcorrectie: nadere aantekeningen bij de weerbare democratie'. In A. Elian, G. Molier and B. Rijpkema (eds), *De strijd om de democratie: essays over democratische zelfverdediging*. Amsterdam: Boom.

Riker, W. H. 1982. *Liberalism Against Populism: A Confrontation Between The Theory of Democracy and The Theory of Social Choice*. Prospect Heights, IL: Waveland Press.

Rivers, J. 2018. 'Counter-extremism, fundamental values and the betrayal of liberal democratic constitutionalism'. *German Law Journal* 19 (2): 267–299.

Roach, K. 2004. 'Anti-terrorism and militant democracy: some western and eastern responses'. In A. Sajó (ed.), *Militant Democracy*. Utrecht: Eleven International, 171–208.

Roberts, K. M. 2017. 'Populism and political parties'. In C. Rovira Kaltwasser, et al. (eds), *The Oxford Handbook of Populism*. Oxford: Oxford University Press, 287–304.

Rogin, M. 1967. *The Intellectuals and McCarthy*. Boston, MA: The MIT Press.

Rosenblum, N. L. 2007. 'Banning parties: religious and ethnic partisanship in multicultural democracies'. *Law and Ethics of Human Rights* 1 (1): 17–75.

Rosenblum, N. L. 2008. *On the Side of the Angels: An Appreciation of Parties and Partisanship*. Princeton, NJ: Princeton University Press.

Ross, A. 1952. *Why Democracy?* Cambridge, MA: Harvard University Press.

Rovira Kaltwasser, C. 2012. 'The ambivalence of populism: threat and corrective for democracy'. *Democratization* 19 (2): 184–208.

Rovira Kaltwasser, C. 2013. 'Populism vs. constitutionalism? Comparative perspectives on contemporary Western Europe, Latin America, and the United States'. Policy Brief. The Foundation for Law, Justice and Society. https://www.fljs.org/files/publications/Kaltwasser.pdf

Rovira Kaltwasser, C. 2014. 'The responses of populism to Dahl's democratic dilemmas'. *Political Studies* 62 (3): 470–487.

Rovira Kaltwasser, C. 2017. 'Populism and the question of how to deal with it'. In C. Rovira Kaltwasser, et al. (eds), *The Oxford Handbook of Populism*. Oxford: Oxford University Press, 90–507.

Roznai, Y. 2015. 'Towards a theory of unamendability'. New York University School of Law, Public Law Research Paper No. 15-12. https://ssrn.com/abstract=2569292 [http://dx.doi.org/10.2139/ssrn.2569292] (accessed 15 July 2018).

Rummens, S. 2006. 'Debate: the co-originality of private and public autonomy in deliberative democracy'. *Journal of Political Philosophy* 14 (4): 469–481.

Rummens, S. 2009. 'Democracy as a non-hegemonic struggle: disambiguating Chantal Mouffe's agonistic model of politics'. *Constellations* 16 (3): 377–391.

Rummens, S. and Abts, K. 2010. 'Defending democracy: the concentric containment of political extremism'. *Political Studies* 58 (4): 649–665.

Rupnik, J. 2012. 'How things went wrong'. *Journal of Democracy* 23 (3): 132–137.

Sajó, A. 2002. 'The self-protecting constitutional state'. 12 *Eastern European Constitutional Review*: 79.

Sajó, A. (ed.). 2004. *Militant Democracy*. Utrecht: Eleven International Publishing.

Sajó, A. 2004. 'Militant democracy and transition towards democracy'. In A. Sajó (ed.), *Militant Democracy*. Utrecht: Eleven International Publishing, 209–230.

Sajó, A. 2006. 'From militant democracy to the preventive state?' *Cardozo Law Review* 27 (5): 2255–2294.

Sajó, A. 2012. 'Militant democracy and emotional politics'. *Constellations* 19 (4): 562–574.

Sanders, L. 1997. 'Against deliberation'. *Political Theory* 25 (3): 347–376.

Scanlon, T. 2000. *The Importance of What We Care About*. Cambridge, MA: Belknap Press.

Schäfer, M. 2002. 'Memory in the construction of constitutions'. *Ratio Juris* 15 (4): 403–417.

Scheinin, M. 2016. 'The potential of the EU Charter of Fundamental Rights for the development of the rule of law indicators'. In C. Closa and D. Kochenov (eds), *Reinforcing Rule of Law Oversight in the European Union*. Cambridge: Cambridge University Press, 172–188.

Scheppele, K. L. 2013. 'The rule of law and the Frankenstate: why governance checklists do not work'. *Governance: an International Journal of Policy, Administration, and Institutions* 26 (4): 559–562.

Scheppele, K. L. 2016. 'Enforcing the basic principles of EU law through systemic infringement actions'. In C. Closa and D. Kochenov (eds), *Reinforcing Rule of Law Oversight in the European Union*. Cambridge: Cambridge University Press, 105–132.

Schmitt, C. 1996 [1932]. *The Concept of the Political*. Chicago, IL: University of Chicago Press.

Schmitt, C. 2004 [1932]. *Legality and Legitimacy*. Trans. J. Seitzer. Durham, NC: Duke University Press.

Schmitt, C. 2005 [1922]. *Political Theology: Four Chapters on the Concept of Sovereignty*. Chicago, IL: University of Chicago Press.

Schmitt, C. 2008 [1928]. *Constitutional Theory*. Durham, NC: Duke University Press.

Schneider, C. J. 1957. 'Political parties and the German Basic Law of 1949'. *Western Political Quarterly* 10 (3): 527–540.

Schnelle, E. M. 2014. *Freiheitsmissbrauch und Grundrechtsverwirkung: Versuch einer Neubestimmung von Artikel 18 GG*. Berlin: Duncker and Humblot.

Schumpeter, J. 1976. *Capitalism, Socialism and Democracy*. London: Routledge.

Schumpeter, J. 2003 [1942]. *Capitalism, Socialism, Democracy*. London: Routledge.

Schupmann, B. A. 2017. *Carl Schmitt's State and Constitutional Theory: A Critical Analysis*. Oxford: Oxford University Press.

Schwartzberg, M. 2007. *Democracy and Legal Change*. New York: Cambridge University Press.

Schwartzberg, M. 2013. *Counting the Many: The Origins and Limits of Supermajority Rule*. New York: Cambridge University Press.

Sedelmeier, U. 2017. 'Political safeguards against democratic backsliding in the EU: the limits of material sanctions and the scope of social pressure'. *Journal of European Public Policy*, 24 (3): 337–351.

Sen, A. 1983. *Poverty and Famines: An Essay on Entitlement and Deprivation*. New York: Oxford University Press.

Simonin, A. 2008. *Le déshonneur dans la République: une histoire de l'indignité, 1791–1958*. Paris: Grasset

Skinner, Q. 1998. *Liberty Before Liberalism*. Cambridge: Cambridge University Press.

Smiley, M. 2017. 'Collective responsibility'. In E. N. Zalta (ed.), *The Stanford Encyclopedia of Philosophy*. Summer 2017 edition. https://plato.stanford.edu/archives/sum2017/entries/collective-responsibility/ [https://perma.cc/ST6Q-EDMQ]

Smith, W. 2011. 'Civil disobedience and the public sphere'. *Journal of Political Philosophy* 19 (2): 145–166.

Snel, J. D. 2016. 'Intolerante democratie, weerbare rechtsstaat?' *De Nederlandse Boekengids*.

Sniderman, P., Fletcher, J., Russell, P. and Tetlock, P. 1989a. 'Political culture and the problem of double standards: mass and elite attitudes toward language rights in the Canadian Charter of Rights and Freedoms'. *Canadian Journal of Political Science* 22 (2): 259–284.

Sniderman, P., Tetlock, P., Glaser, J., Green, D. and Hout, M. 1989b. 'Principled tolerance and the American mass public'. *British Journal of Political Science* 19 (1): 25–45.

Sottiaux, S. and Rummens, S. 2012. 'Concentric democracy: resolving the incoherence in the European Court of Human Rights' case law on freedom of expression and freedom of association'. *International Journal of Constitutional Law* 10 (1): 106–126.

Stilz, A. 2016. 'The value of self-determination'. In D. Sobel, P. Vallentyne and S. Wall (eds), *Oxford Studies in Political Philosophy*. Volume 2. Oxford: Oxford University Press, 98–127.

Stone, P. 2011. *The Luck of the Draw: The Role of Lotteries in Decision Making*. New York: Oxford University Press.

Stone, P. 2016. 'Sortition, voting, and democratic equality'. *Critical Review of International Social and Political Philosophy (CRISPP)* 19 (3): 339–356.

Stouffer, S. 1955. *Communism, Conformity, and Civil Liberties: A Cross-section of the Nation Speaks its Mind*. Garden City, NY: Doubleday.

Streeck, W. 2014. *Buying Time: The Delayed Crisis of Democratic Capitalism*. London: Verso Books.

Sullivan, J., Piereson, J. and Marcus, G. 1979. 'An alternative conceptualization of political tolerance: illusory increases 1950s–1970s'. *American Political Science Review* 73 (3): 781–794.

Sullivan, J., Piereson, J. and Marcus, G. 1982. *Political Tolerance and American Democracy*. Chicago, IL: University of Chicago Press.

Sullivan, J., Marcus, G., Feldman, S. and Piereson, J. 1981. 'The sources of political tolerance: a multivariate analysis'. *American Political Science Review* 75 (1): 92–106.

Sullivan, J., Shamir, M., Walsh, P. and Roberts, N. 1985. *Political Tolerance in Context: Support for Unpopular Minorities in Israel, New Zealand, and the United States*. Boulder, CO: Westview.

Surowiecki, J. 2005. *The Wisdom of Crowds*. New York: Anchor Books.

Sutherland, K. 2008. 'A people's parliament'. In E. Callenbach, M. Phillips and K. Sutherland (eds), *A Citizen Legislature/A People's Parliament*. Exeter: Imprint Academic.

Svolik, M. 2012. *The Politics of Authoritarian Rule*. New York: Cambridge University Press.

Taggart, P. 2000. *Populism*. Buckingham: Open University Press.

Te Slaa, R. 2017. *Wat is fascisme? Oorsprong en ideologie*. Amsterdam: Boom.

ten Napel, H.-M. 2009. 'The European Court of Human Rights and political rights: the need for more guidance'. *European Constitutional Law Review* 5 (3): 473–478.

ten Napel, H.-M. 2016. 'Wat heeft voorrang: de meerderheid of de rechtsstaat?' *Christelijk Weekblad* 64 (3): 8–9.

The Economist Intelligence Unit. 2016. 'Democracy Index 2016'. http://www.eiu.com/topic/democracy-index

Thiel, M. (ed.). 2009a. *The 'Militant Democracy' Principle in Modern Democracies*. Farnham: Ashgate.

Thiel, M. (ed.). 2009b. 'Germany'. In M. Thiel (ed.), *The 'Militant Democracy' Principle in Modern Democracies*. Farnham: Ashgate, 109–146.

Thompson, D. F. 2015. *John Stuart Mill and Representative Government*. Princeton, NJ: Princeton University Press.

Tilly, C. 2007. *Democracy*. New York: Cambridge University Press.

Tocqueville, A. de. 2002. *Democracy in America*. Chicago, IL: University of Chicago Press.

Toggenburg, G. N. and Grimheden, J. 2016. 'The rule of law and the role of fundamental rights: seven practical pointers'. In C. Closa and D. Kochenov (eds), *Reinforcing Rule of Law Oversight in the European Union*. Cambridge: Cambridge University Press, 147–171.

Tóth, C. 2014. 'Full text of Viktor Orbán's speech at Băile Tuşnad (Tusnádfürdő) of 26 July 2014'. [Translation from Hungarian.] *The Budapest Beacon*. 29 July 2014. https://budapestbeacon.com/full-text-of-viktor-orbans-speech-at-baile-tusnad-tusnadfurdo-of-26-july-2014/ [https://perma.cc/DTY3-S4YY]

Tribe, L. 2000. *American Constitutional Law*. Mineola, NY: Foundation Press.

Tribe, L. and Matz, J. 2018. *To End a Presidency*. New York: Basic Books.

Tyulkina, S. 2015a. *Militant Democracy: Undemocratic Political Parties and Beyond*. Abingdon, UK and New York: Routledge.

Tyulkina, S. 2015b. 'Militant democracy: an alien concept for Australian constitutional law?' *Adelaide Law Review* 36 (2): 517–539.

Uitz, R. 2007. *Freedom of Religion in European Constitutional and International Case-Law*. Council of Europe Publishing.

Uitz, R. 2015. 'Can you tell when an illiberal democracy is in the making? An appeal to comparative constitutional scholarship from Hungary'. *International Journal of Constitutional Law* 13 (1): 279–300.

Urbinati, N. and Invernizzi Accetti, C. 2013. 'Editors' Introduction'. In H. Kelsen (ed.), *The Essence and Value of Democracy*. Plymouth: Rowman & Littlefield, 1–24.

Van den Bergh, G. 2014 [1936]. *Wat te doen met antidemocratische partijen? De oratie van George van den Bergh uit 1936*. (With an introduction by B. Rijpkema.) Amsterdam: Elsevier Boeken.

Van der Woude, W. 2009. *Democratische waarborgen*. Deventer: Kluwer.

van Spanje, J. 2010. 'Parties beyond the pale: why some political parties are ostracized by their competitors while others are not'. *Comparative European Politics* 8 (3): 354–383.

van Spanje, J. and van der Brug, W. 2007. 'The party as pariah: the exclusion of anti-immigration parties and its effect on their ideological positions'. *West European Politics* 30 (5): 1022–1040.

van Spanje, J. and van der Brug, W. 2009. 'Being intolerant of the intolerant. The exclusion of Western European anti-immigration parties and its consequences for party choice'. *Acta Politica* 44 (4): 353–384.

Venice Commission (European Commission for Democracy through Law). 1999. *Guidelines on Prohibition of Political Parties and Analogous Measures*. Adopted by the Venice Commission at the 41st Plenary Session. 10–11 December.

Venice Commission (European Commission for Democracy through Law). 2002. Code of Practice in Electoral Matters: Guidelines and Explanatory Report. http://www.venice.coe.int/webforms/documents/default.aspx?pdffile=CDL-AD(2002)023rev-e [https://perma.cc/U3ZY-SE2V]

Venice Commission (European Commission for Democracy through Law). 2009. Opinion on the Legal and Constitutional Provisions Relevant to the Prohibition of Political Parties in Turkey. http://www.venice.coe.int/webforms/documents/default.aspx?pdffile=CDL-AD(2009)006-e [https://perma.cc/NC2N-GKLD]

Venice Commission (European Commission for Democracy through Law). 2011. Opinion on the New Constitution of Hungary. 87th Plenary Session. https://www.venice.coe.int/webforms/documents/default.aspx?pdffile=CDL-AD(2011)016-e [https://perma.cc/TL24-RHR6]

Venice Commission (European Commission for Democracy through Law). 2012. Opinion on the Revision of the Constitution of Belgium. CDL-AD(2012)01. 91st Plenary Session. http://www.venice.coe.int/webforms/documents/default.aspx?pdffile=CDL-AD(2012)010-e [https://perma.cc/UH7P-83CY] (accessed 15 July 2018).

Verschuren, E. 2017. 'Turkije ontslaat honderd rechters en aanklagers'. *NRC Handelsblad* (online). 5 May.

Viehoff, D. 2014. 'Democratic equality and political authority'. *Philosophy & Public Affairs* 42 (4): 337–375.

Von Bogdandy, A., Antpöhler, C. and Ioannidis, M. 2017. 'Protecting EU values: reverse solange and the rule of law framework'. In A. Jakáb and D. Kochenov (eds), *The Enforcement of EU Law against the Member States: Methods against Defiance*. Oxford: Oxford University Press, 218–233.

Wagemans A. and Talib, M. 2016. 'Stemmen? Eerst examen doen'. *Trouw*. 9 August 2016.

Wagrandl, U. 2018. 'Transnational militant democracy'. *Global Constitutionalism* 7 (2): 143–172.

Waldron, J. 1981. 'A right to do wrong'. *Ethics* 92 (1): 21–39.

Waldron, J. 1989. 'Rights in conflict'. *Ethics* 99 (3): 503–519.

Waldron, J. 1993. 'A right to do wrong'. In *Liberal Rights*. New York: Cambridge University Press, 63–87.

Waldron, J. 2003. 'Security and liberty: the image of balance'. *Journal of Political Philosophy* 11 (2): 191–210.

Waldron, J. 2006. 'The core of the case against judicial review'. *Yale Law Journal* 115 (6): 1346–1406.

Weber, M. 1918. *Parliament und Regierung im neugeordneten Deutschland*. München-Leipzig: Duncker & Humblot.

Weber, M. 1968. *Economy and Society*. Ed. R. Guenther and C. Wittich. Berkeley, CA: University of California Press.

Weil, P. 2017. 'Denaturalization and denationalization in comparison (France, the United Kingdom, the United States)'. *Philosophy & Social Criticism* 43 (4–5): 417–429.

Weiler, J. H. H. 1999. *The Constitution of Europe*. Cambridge: Cambridge University Press.

Weiler, J. H. H. 2016. 'Epilogue: living in a glass house: Europe, democracy and the rule of law'. In C. Closa and D. Kochenov (eds), *Reinforcing Rule of Law Oversight in the European Union*. Cambridge: Cambridge University Press, 313–326.

Whitman, J. 2000. 'Enforcing civility and respect: three societies'. *The Yale Law Journal* 109 (6): 1279–1398.

Whittington, K. 2017. 'Possibly impeachable offenses'. *Niskanen Center*. 2 August 2017. https://niskanencenter.org/blog/possibly-impeachable-offenses/ [https://perma.cc/R8ZU-QL3D]

Whittington, K. 2018. 'Should Congress treat impeachable offenses cumulatively?' *Lawfare*. 29 August 2018. https://www.lawfareblog.com/should-congress-treat-impeachable-offenses-cumulatively [https://perma.cc/X6GY-ANMW]

Witte, G. and Birnbaum, M. 'In Eastern Europe, the E.U. faces a rebellion more threatening than Brexit'. *The Washington Post*. 5 April 2018. https://wapo.st/2GxD7lH [https://perma.cc/S42E-EWZL] (last accessed 4 July 2018).

Wittenberg, J. 2017. 'Commentary on 'The rise of illiberalism in Europe: a discussion of Peter Krasztev and Jon Van Til's *The Hungarian Patient: Social Opposition to an Illiberal Democracy*''. *Perspectives on Politics* 15 (2): 553–554.

Wolf, R. 1993. 'Hermann Heller'. *Kritische Justiz* 24 (4): 500–507.

World Justice Project. 2016. World Justice Project Rule of Law Index 2016. https://worldjusticeproject.org/our-work/publications/rule-law-index-reports/wjp-rule-law-index%C2%AE-2016-report [https://perma.cc/7EWG-CSVE]

Wróbel, A. 2018. 'Hungary rejects "blackmail" through EU funds'. *POLITICO*. 3 May 2018. https://www.politico.eu/article/hungary-rejects-blackmail-through-eu-funds/ [https://perma.cc/P6SR-7KZV] (accessed 14 June 2018).

Zakaras, A. 2010. 'Lot and democratic representation: a modest proposal'. *Constellations* 17 (3): 455–471.

INDEX

Abts, Koen, 19, 122
agonistic adversaries, 115–17
antagonism, political, 112–13
antagonistic enemies, 115–17
Argentina, 81–2
authoritarianism
  anti-democratic actions in post-
    authoritarian democracies, 141
  competitive authoritarianism, 176
  control of adversaries, 77
  in Europe, 193
  need for in state of emergency
    situations, 126
  parallels with populist democracy,
    192–3
  rise of through democratic procedures,
    74, 75–6, 77, 79, 88
autophagy, 44

Bárd et al. (2016), 159
behaviouralism, 136, 138
Bergh, George van den, 169, 170, 177
Brennan, Geoffrey, 46
Brettschneider, C.L., 152–3, 156, 164
British National Party (BNP), 38

Caesarism, 190–1, 194, 197, 198, 201
Capoccia, G., 95, 100
Chávez, Hugo, 74, 79
citizen juries, 40
citizens
  citizen equality under the electoral
    process, 39–40
  instrumental interests of, 58–9

intrinsic interests of, 59–60
partial exclusion of from democratic
  government, 150–1
uncitizen-like conduct, 22
citizenship
  democratic equality, 40–1, 43
  denationalisation debates, 22–3
  principle of democracy's public
    reason, 153
  principle of democratic inclusion, 153
civil disobedience, 15–16, 17–18,
  27–30, 32
communism, 104, 135, 214
conflict
  agonistic pluralism, 115–16
  hegemonic struggle, 116
  moralisation of politics argument,
    123–5
  non-hegemonic struggle, 116–17
  within social democracy, 103, 105–7
constitutional self-defence
  court-backed constitutional
    restraints, 156
  defensive institutional mechanisms,
    198–201, 211
  electoral systems, 196–7
  freedom of speech and populist
    rhetoric, 201–3
  limitations on direct democracy, 197
  multi-layered constitutionalism, 198
  against populist takeover, 188, 193–5
  protection of constitutions, 196
  term limits, 196
  unamendable provisions, 195–6

EU representative:
Easy Access System Europe
Mustamäe tee 50, 10621 Tallinn, Estonia
Gpsr.requests@easproject.com

www.ingramcontent.com/pod-product-compliance
Lightning Source LLC
Chambersburg PA
CBHW051958270326
41929CB00015B/2701